PILAF, *POZOLE,*
AMERICAN WOMEN AND ETHNIC FOOD
AND PAD THAI

PILAF, *POZOLE,*

AMERICAN WOMEN AND ETHNIC FOOD

AND PAD THAI

EDITED BY

Sherrie A. Inness

UNIVERSITY OF MASSACHUSETTS PRESS   AMHERST

Copyright © 2001 by University of Massachusetts Press
All rights reserved
Printed in the United States of America

LC 00-048882
ISBN 1-55849-285-2 (library cloth), 1-55849-286-0 (paper)

Designed by Sally Nichols
Set in Bembo by Graphic Composition, Inc.
Printed and bound by Sheridan Books, Inc.

Library of Congress Cataloging-in-Publication Data
Pilaf, pozole, and pad thai : American women and ethnic food / edited by
Sherrie A. Inness.
p. cm.
Includes bibliographical references and index.
ISBN 1-55849-285-2 (library cloth : alk. paper) — ISBN 1-55849-286-0
(pbk. : alk. paper)
1. Food habits—United States. 2. Ethnic food industry—United States.
3. Women—United States—Social life and customs. 4. United States—
Social life and customs.   I. Inness, Sherrie A.

GT2853.U5 P55 2001
394.1'2'08900973—dc21
00-048882

British Library Cataloguing in Publication data are available.

For a pair of wonderful friends—Ruth Ebelke Inness and Di Maddison

Nothing but heaven itself is better than a friend who is really a friend.
—Plautus, *Bacchides*

CONTENTS

ACKNOWLEDGMENTS

I want to thank all the contributors to this anthology. I enjoyed working with each of them tremendously, as they know. I also appreciate the efforts of the people who read various chapters included in this collection, including Lowell Inness and Stephanie Levine. Faye Parker Flavin deserves special thanks for reading every chapter in the volume. I always appreciate her rigorous and thoughtful criticism, and my work benefits tremendously from her insights. She is someone I treasure.

I would also like to thank a network of food scholars whose work has inspired this book, including Amy Bentley, Anne L. Bower, Carole Counihan, Barbara Haber, Harvey A. Levenstein, Lucy M. Long, Laura Shapiro, Penny Van Esterik, and Doris Witt. Warren Belasco, Janet Theophano, and Jane Dusselier deserve special appreciation because of all the help they have generously offered me. They are models of what food scholars should be. I also appreciate the help given to me by everyone at the University of Massachusetts Press, especially Bruce Wilcox and Carol Betsch, and by Marsha Kunin, our copy editor.

I save my last words of appreciation for some important friends and family members, including Julie Hucke, Julie Inness, Lowell Inness, Stephanie Levine, Michele Lloyd, Heather Schell, Lisa Somer, Wendy W. Walters, Liz Wilson, and my colleagues at Miami University. Finally, this book is dedicated in loving memory of a pair of dear friends, my mother, Ruth Ebelke Inness (1920–1998), and her friend Di Maddison.

PILAF, *POZOLE,*

AMERICAN WOMEN AND ETHNIC FOOD

AND PAD THAI

Eating Ethnic
Sherrie A. Inness

As a young girl in northern California, I accompanied my mother to numerous small neighborhood food stores. Although we also patronized large
grocery chain stores, my mother liked to purchase special food items at
more intimate shops. I can remember going to separate places for fish, fruit,
cheese, sausage, spices, and breads. We went to a German deli, where the
women workers always handed out cookies to me and my twin sister, Julie,
to order cold cuts—pastrami, corned beef, thuringer, summer sausage, liv-
erwurst, smoked turkey, roast beef, dry salami, ham—and a huge chunk of
pale yellow butter; each item was wrapped up with white butcher paper,
then unwrapped like so many Christmas presents when we arrived home. I
remember the magic of unwrapping those packages, revealing the neatly
cut and stacked meats. We visited another store, even though to do so required a twenty-minute drive to the neighboring town, especially to purchase its famous sausage. I still recall those plump white sausages, so large
that one long curl filled my mother's iron frying pan. She cut the sausage
into serving-sized pieces, split them lengthwise, and grilled their sides in
butter until they were brown, crispy, delectable—ready to be speared out
of the pan onto our plates, where they would be served with vinegary sauerkraut and thickly cut soft rye bread. There were never leftovers. At other
times, she bought liver sausage, which she would squeeze out of its casing,
frying the crumbled mixture until it turned a golden brown. The hot

sausage was heaped on rounds of crunchy French bread, the soft meat contrasting perfectly with the firm bread.

But these sausages from my childhood, no matter how memorable, paled in comparison, my mother always used to say, to the sausages that her father, a German Lutheran minister, carried back to North Scituate, Rhode Island, from his visits to Worcester, Massachusetts. Mom went into rhapsodies about the sausages her father brought home for his wife, Rose, to cook, along with great loaves of pumpernickel bread. Throughout her life, my mother searched for similar sausages, but, despite countless visits to German delis and sausage makers, mom's "perfect" sausage remained elusive. This is true for many of us—we can never re-create the foods of our childhoods. Like childhood itself, they remain forever just outside of our grasp.

Although my mother craved the sausage she remembered from her German American childhood, she was not conservative or lacking in adventure as an eater, solely pursuing the comforting, familiar foods of her distant youth. She liked trying unfamiliar food, and we enjoyed visiting new restaurants and hole-in-the-wall eateries. I remember trying falafel and stuffed grape leaves in the early 1970s when Mom and I visited a new Greek sandwich shop—a single room, redolent of a delicious mixture of olive oil, cumin, pepper, and other more mysterious spices. The place was so small that you had to take your cardboard container of six stuffed grape leaves or a wrapped-up falafel sandwich out to the curbside and eat it there in the hot California sun. But our favorite place to eat was Cho's, a Chinese restaurant where my mother and I inevitably ordered the same item: pot-stickers, one of half a dozen items on the short menu. We squeezed around one of the two small tables that filled most of the room and polished off the best pot-stickers I have ever consumed. With their crispy, crunchy golden bottoms, the hot dumplings were filled to bursting with ginger, minced pork, bean sprouts, and scallions. They were dipped in a chili dipping sauce that I still strive (and fail) to match. Sometimes, if we were ravenous, we would also buy a steamed bun or two filled with red barbecued pork for fifty cents; they were so large that two would fill the steamer basket in which they were delivered. Despite the appeal of the buns, pot-stickers remained our standard order at Cho's. I cannot number the times I went there, either biking from school for a snack or driving over with my mother and sister. I have searched high and low for similar pot-stickers, but they have eluded me; even the ones I make at home lack the flavor of those dumplings from my childhood. Like my mother, I seem fated never to recapture the foods from my youth.

Meals at my home included specialties from a broad range of ethnicities, and for our after-school snack, Julie and I consumed foods from around the world. One afternoon my mother left baba ghanoosh, for which she had roasted her own eggplant. Another day she turned out *kolacky* cookies, a delicate cookie made from a cream cheese dough rolled out, cut into festive shapes, and dotted with apricot jam; I remember her making these pastries for a Valentine's Day special treat, cutting out the cookies with a heart-shaped cutter. For dinner she turned out tofu, covered with sesame seeds and sautéed in butter until the tofu turned crispy and golden. (I think we were the first ones on my suburban block to check out *The Tofu Cookbook* from the local library, and I fondly recall my mother's tofu-and-onion loaf, which she served in the early 1970s, way before tofu was "hip," at least in my middle-class neighborhood.) Other nights she served an enchilada casserole or an Indian chicken curry. Even though my mother, who was born in 1920, was in her fifties in the early 1970s, she never grew stagnant in her food tastes. She was always willing to try something that was new, experimental, exotic.

The experiences of my family with ethnic foods are hardly unique. Whether it is latkes, red beans and rice, tamales, hummus, or stuffed grape leaves, eating ethnic foods is commonplace in American culture. Often they are taken for granted. Yet, whether we acknowledge it or not, such foods create a powerful social language that speaks of cultural traditions and tastes that have been handed down from one generation to the next and, in some cases, appropriated and commodified by American consumer culture. Ethnic food represents both a source of sustenance and a complex form of communication.

Women, in particular, have been and continue to be attuned to the significance of ethnic food, because they have long been the preparers and servers of such food. Even today, cooking is one of the domestic chores that continues to be most stubbornly associated with women, despite changing gender roles. Thus, the study of food offers a way to understand how women have experienced and lived their lives. This book contributes to that project by looking specifically at ethnic foods and exploring some of the ways these foods have served as markers of identity. Women from all classes, races, ethnic groups, and ages have at one time or another been defined in terms of the foods they prepare and consume.

The book also examines how ethnic foods travel between different groups and how this movement changes the roles and perceptions of such foods. How is it different for middle-class white Americans living in New York City to eat menudo at a trendy Mexican restaurant from what it is for Mexicans to eat it in Mexico? How is the experience of eating Cajun and Creole food different for the tourists who flock to New Orleans and for the Creole and Cajun women who live in Louisiana and have cooked such foods for a lifetime? To what extent has the quest for the exotic, the practice of seeking out new cuisines, changed the meaning of ethnic food, both for those who prepare it and for those who consume it?

Even defining *ethnic food* is no easy task; it is a deceptively simple term. In the United States, if you are a white middle-class urban worker (at least one living in a large city) who is discussing with your fellow workers the possibility of "eating ethnic" for lunch, you are talking, most likely, about one of the countless restaurants, cafés, and other eateries that specialize in foods from around the globe Thai, Vietnamese, Italian, Chinese, Spanish, Mongolian, Mexican, Indian, Korean, Japanese, and many others. But *ethnic food* is a label that many Americans apply to those foods from cultures most clearly demarcated as "foreign." Thus, sashimi will be labeled ethnic more readily than dishes that have been assimilated into U.S. culture, such as British fish and chips or the omnipresent spaghetti and meatballs. Of course, cultural assimilation occurs over time, and the definition of ethnic food is constantly changing. At one time, German and Italian food seemed much more foreign than they do today, now that generations of Germans and Italians have become assimilated into the North American mainstream.

Because of the difficulties encountered when we define ethnic food too narrowly, perhaps the best approach is a broad one. Numerous factors, including social class, ethnicity, race, language, age, religion, and regional location, influence people's reactions to what they perceive as ethnic cuisine.

Take, for example, the role of geography; ethnic foods are strong markers of cultural and regional identity, conveying special feelings about belonging and place. One friend of mine craves the burritos she used to buy in San Francisco taquerias; whenever she visits California, she eats burritos for breakfast, lunch, and dinner. Another person I know who lives in Ohio hungers for the tamales from her hometown in southern Texas; she makes sure that her friends bring her back an ample supply when they visit there. And I remember once carrying from the East Coast an entire long, skinny, straight-as-a-stick smoked eel home to my father on the West Coast because he longed for the smoked eel that he had known as a little boy growing up in a small fishing village in Nova Scotia.

But why study food in the first place? Scholars in the fields of anthropology, sociology, and nutrition have long argued that food offers important insights into our cultural values. As Peter Farb and George Armelagos point out in *Consuming Passions*: "Eating is symbolically associated with the most deeply felt human experiences, and thus expresses things that are sometimes difficult to articulate in everyday language" (111). To some observers, a preoccupation with food is viewed as a guilty pleasure, like reading pulp novels. In her famous cookbook, Alice B. Toklas writes, "Cookbooks have always intrigued and seduced me. When I was still a dilettante in the kitchen they held my attention, even the dull ones, from cover to cover, the way crime and murder stories did Gertrude Stein" (37). Many people are passionate about food, as Elaine N. McIntosh notes in *American Food Habits in Historical Perspective,* "there are few topics which elicit more emotional responses and on which people have stronger opinions, than food" (139). Angela Little comments that, "eating constitutes the most intimate act of our existence. In this regard, I put eating ahead of sex—usually considered the most intimate act—because the substance of food, and food alone, becomes transformed into our own very substance: we are indeed what we eat!" (24). Food has an endless list of meanings for different people. It delights us. It terrifies us.[1]

For academics, despite the recent surge of interest in the historical, social, and cultural meanings of food, there remains a lingering sense that the field of food studies is lacking in intellectual rigor. Food is sometimes dismissed as a subject not worthy of serious analysis. Deborah Lupton writes in *Food, the Body, and the Self:* "Philosophy is masculine and disembodied, food and eating are feminine and always embodied" (3). Some female scholars may be reluctant to think and write about food because to do so would seem to reaffirm the cultural stereotype that a woman's place is in the kitchen. Nevertheless, a number of scholars interested in women and gender issues are demonstrating that the study of food offers important insights into gender roles and into how our culture is structured.[2]

Fewer scholars have focused specifically on ethnic foods in the United States, although much important work is being done. Thelma Barer-Stein observes that "the United States is a nation of immigrants, each ethnic group retaining customs, festivals and food traditions with great pride and yet with a stamp that is unmistakably American" (34). Donna R. Gabaccia's *We Are What We Eat* is a particularly good example of the new scholarship in this area.[3] I hope the chapters in this anthology will stimulate further discussion and give readers a richer and more nuanced understanding of the many roles that food, especially ethnic food, has played for generations of American women.

The chapters in Part I share a personal approach as the writers reflect on their own experiences involving food and relatives, including grandmothers, mothers, and aunts.[4] Paul Christensen opens the book by exploring what making pasta and tomato sauce ("mac and gravy") meant for his Sicilian-born mother. This special meal provided her a way to affirm her allegiance to a tempestuous, romantic, passionate past—a past that appeared far removed from the more prosaic reality of her daily life in the United States. Like Christensen, Cathie English is interested in tracing the roots of food memories. She focuses on the food lessons she learned from her Polish women relatives, writing, in particular, about the pie recipes that were passed down to her. In the third chapter, Leanne Trapedo Sims records the food memories of cookbook collector Dalia Carmel, who discusses the meanings that food has held for her at different times and in different countries—from Israel to the United States. In their lyrical essays, Christensen, English, and Trapedo Sims show some of the ways in which ethnic food culture is embedded in women's memories. These memories suggest a great deal about how women pass on knowledge of cultural traditions and how cooking serves as a conduit for that knowledge.

In the next chapter Lynn Z. Bloom discusses the ways in which her German background continues to influence her cooking and her work as a writer, noting how intertwined ethnic foods are with her experiences as an author. Similarly, Linda Murray Berzok is fascinated by how her Swedish mother's cooking experiences changed and evolved over the twentieth century. Reading her mother's vast collection of recipe cards from a period of decades, Murray Berzok finds that they record much more than recipes— they document a process of cultural assimilation and reveal how food serves as a marker of ethnic identity. Murray Berzok also demonstrates how ethnic recipes change when they are removed from their "original" background, picking up new and sometimes unexpected meanings.

The last chapter in Part I reveals how ethnic food can sometimes build bridges and connections among women of widely disparate backgrounds. Arlene Voski Avakian, an Armenian American, tells the moving story of how food provided a connection between her and her lover's family, especially one aunt. Although this aunt was intolerant of her niece's lesbian relationship with Avakian, food served as a way to bring the aunt and Avakian together, even though they came from profoundly different cultures. Interest in food, Avakian demonstrates, often serves to unify and connect women today.

Where the chapters in Part I are personal essays that show some of the ways ethnic food operates within an ethnic group, the chapters in Part II examine in a more analytic manner the roles ethnic food plays when it crosses boundaries and is consumed by people from different cultural groups. The authors argue that eating ethnic food under such circumstances, even if it seems innocuous, is far from benign. Consumers are implicated in a complex web of relationships between those who make the foods and those who buy them. Moreover, eating foods from different cultures can also suggest certain notions about otherness and the exotic that work to affirm white dominance.

The first two chapters in Part II explore changing views of ethnic food in different American ethnic communities. Meredith Abarca examines how Mexican American cooking has evolved from Mexican cooking. She focuses on how everyday food preparation offers many women a language of self-expression, a language they have access to even if they lack higher education. Abarca argues that numerous Chicana writers use food as a way to tell their stories and those of other similar women. Like Abarca, Benay Blend views domestic cooking as a way that Chicana and Native American contemporary writers resist the larger imperialistic culture of the United States and its pressure for conformity. Abarca and Blend reveal how Chicana and Native American writers use food to form allegiances with other women so as to value and privilege the work that women have always done, work that has traditionally been given little attention and less prestige.

The final three chapters all address what Lucy M. Long refers to as "culinary tourism," which she describes as "the intentional, exploratory participation in the foodways of an Other, participation including the consumption—or preparation and presentation for consumption—of a food item, cuisine, meal system, or eating style considered as belonging to a culinary system not one's own" (181). Doris Friedensohn examines her history as a culinary tourist, focusing on her passion for such foods as *chapulines,* mole, and *pozole.* Moving from Mexico to the streets of New York City, she analyzes what happens when a food shifts from being a "normal" staple of a region to being a "gourmet" item or the newest food trend in a different region. She is ambivalent about such cultural migration, viewing U.S. culture as one that adopts food trends with little or no understanding of their originating culture. She would, no doubt, concur with Amy Bentley's insightful observation about food and politics, that "while food can be an intensely personal experience it is also a political statement, regardless of the eater's intentions or comprehension. Despite the polite prohibition of political discussions at mealtime, politics is rarely absent at the dinner table" ("From Culinary Other" 250).

Like Friedensohn's, the two concluding chapters examine the politics of culinary tourism in the United States and abroad. Lisa Heldke focuses on culinary tourism and Thai food, demonstrating how the Thai craze in the United States (whether in restaurants, cookbooks, or commodities at the grocery store such as lemon grass and coconut milk) implicitly supports colonialist notions of power. Heather Schell takes us to the hot streets and hotter sauces of New Orleans. Fascinated by the food imagery that is such an integral part of the city's reputation, Schell visits souvenir shops and restaurants, as she explores how eating Cajun and Creole food offers the tourist a relatively safe way to experience otherness. Such food consumption, she suggests, is one way that white male power is reaffirmed, since much of the food that the tourists eat is anthropomorphized—described in cookbooks, advertisements, and food literature as possessing female traits or traits of people from ethnic backgrounds other than white.

I hope the essays in this book will leave readers with a keener awareness of the legacy passed along by generations of women. For many reasons, including socioeconomic class and lack of education, our foremothers may have had few opportunities to record their stories in traditional literary forms such as memoirs, novels, and poems, but they passed down a part of themselves in recipe cards and charity cookbooks. They also told their stories through the simple act of making the daily meals and orally passing along cooking techniques and lessons about life. Although I do not wish to reduce the life of any woman *just* to cooking (or any other single activity), it is important to note how cooking has offered and continues to offer a voice to women from many different cultural backgrounds.

This book is equally concerned with disturbing the vision readers may have of ethnic food and its role in U.S. culture. Whether we are grocery shopping for the ingredients to make *pad thai* for dinner or going out for an Indian meal, the connections we have to ethnic food are never as simple as they seem, they carry the weight of political and cultural values and involve us in a much larger global system. All of us have a stake in understanding the dynamics of that system, but unless we are specialists in anthropology, nutritional studies, history, sociology, or other food-related professions, it is likely that we spend little time thinking about food in a critical fashion. Colleges and universities rarely offer classes in food studies, and we know shockingly little about the foods we consume daily. We know little about who grows our food and who prepares it; we know little about the many individuals required to obtain everything from bunches of bananas to cans of Spanish sardines and to place these items on our grocery store shelves.

The last question I hope these essays leave with the reader is, Why do we give so little critical attention to food when it is something that sustains us and is one of the integral and most important parts of our lives? Barbara Haber proclaims, "I think that food—like gender—is a legitimate category of inquiry that can lead to important social and psychological insights" (66). We need to remember these words and bring the study of food out of the kitchen and into the classroom.

NOTES

[1] Important general works that address food cultures past and present in the United States include Belasco, Camp, Counihan and Van Esterik; Cummings, Grover, Hooker, Humphrey and Humphrey; Jones, Levenstein, *Paradox* and *Revolution,* Root and de Rochemont, Sokolov; and Tannahill.

[2] Studies of women and food culture include Bentley, *Eating,* Birkby, Bower, Charles and Kerr, Cline, Counihan, DeVault, Farb and Armelagos, Lupton, Shapiro, and Williams.

[3] Among the significant works on ethnicity, race, gender, and food are Avakian, Brown and Mussell; Goldman; Kaplan, Hoover, and Moore; Pillsbury, and Witt.

[4] For other examples of women authors using reflective narratives about food to explore different concerns, see Colwin, Ehrlich, Lust, Reichl, Ring, and Shulman.

WORKS CITED

Avakian, Arlene Voski, ed. *Through the Kitchen Window: Women Explore the Intimate Meanings of Food and Cooking.* Boston: Beacon, 1997.

Barer-Stein, Thelma. *You Eat What You Are: People, Culture, and Food Traditions.* 2d ed. Willowdale, Ont.: Firefly Books, 1999.

Belasco, Warren. *Appetite for Change: How the Counterculture Took on the Food Industry, 1966–1988.* New York: Pantheon, 1989.

Bentley, Amy. *Eating for Victory: Food Rationing and the Politics of Domesticity.* Urbana: U of Illinois P, 1998.

———— "From Culinary Other to Mainstream American: Meanings and Uses of Southwestern Cuisine." *Southern Folklore* 55 3 (1998). 238–52.

Birkby, Evelyn. *Neighboring on the Air: Cooking with the KMA Radio Homemakers.* Iowa City: U of Iowa P, 1991.

Bower, Anne L., ed. *Recipes for Reading: Community Cookbooks, Stories, Histories.* Amherst: U of Massachusetts P, 1997.

Brown, Linda Keller, and Kay Mussell, eds. *Ethnic and Regional Foodways in the United States: The Performance of Group Identity.* Knoxville: U of Tennessee P, 1984.

Camp, Charles. *American Foodways: What, When, Why, and How We Eat in America*. Little Rock: August House, 1989.

Charles, Nickie, and Marion Kerr. *Women, Food, and Families*. Manchester: Manchester UP, 1988.

Cline, Sally. *Just Desserts: Women and Food*. London: Deutsch, 1990.

Colwin, Laurie. *Home Cooking*. New York: Knopf, 1988.

Counihan, Carole M. *The Anthropology of Food and Body: Gender, Meaning, and Power*. New York: Routledge, 1999.

————, and Penny Van Esterik, eds. *Food and Culture: A Reader*. New York: Routledge, 1997.

Cummings, Richard Osborn. *The American and His Food: A History of Food Habits in the United States*. Chicago: U of Chicago P, 1940.

DeVault, Marjorie L. *Feeding the Family: The Social Organization of Caring as Gendered Work*. Chicago: U of Chicago P, 1991.

Ehrlich, Elizabeth. *Miriam's Kitchen: A Memoir*. New York: Viking, 1997.

Farb, Peter, and George Armelagos. *Consuming Passions: The Anthropology of Eating*. Boston: Houghton Mifflin, 1980.

Gabaccia, Donna R. *We Are What We Eat: Ethnic Food and the Making of Americans*. Cambridge: Harvard UP, 1998.

Goldman, Anne. "'I Yam What I Yam': Cooking, Culture, and Colonialism." *De/Colonizing the Subject: The Politics of Gender in Women's Autobiography*. Ed. Sidonie Smith and Julia Watson. Minneapolis: U of Minnesota P, 1992. 169–95.

Grover, Kathryn, ed. *Dining in America, 1850–1900*. Amherst: U of Massachusetts P, 1987.

Haber, Barbara. "Follow the Food." *Through the Kitchen Window: Women Explore the Intimate Meanings of Food and Cooking*. Ed. Arlene Voski Avakian. Boston: Beacon, 1997. 65–74.

Hooker, Richard J. *Food and Drink in America: A History*. Indianapolis: Bobbs-Merrill, 1981.

Humphrey, Theodore C., and Lin T. Humphrey, eds. *"We Gather Together": Food and Festival in American Life*. Ann Arbor: UMI Research P, 1988.

Jones, Evan. *American Food: The Gastronomic Story*. 2d ed. New York: Random House, 1981.

Kaplan, Anne R., Marjorie A. Hoover, and Willard B. Moore. "Introduction:

On Ethnic Foodways." *The Taste of American Place: A Reader on Regional and Ethnic Foods,* ed. Barbara G. Shortridge and James R. Shortridge. Lanham, Md.: Rowman & Littlefield, 1998. 121–33.

Levenstein, Harvey A. *Paradox of Plenty: A Social History of Eating in Modern America.* New York: Oxford UP, 1993.

———. *Revolution at the Table: The Transformation of the American Diet.* New York: Oxford UP, 1988.

Little, Angela. "An Academic Ferment." *Journal of Gastronomy* 2 (1986). 24–29.

Long, Lucy M. "Culinary Tourism: A Folkloristic Perspective on Eating and Otherness." *Southern Folklore* 55 3 (1998). 181–204.

Lupton, Deborah. *Food, the Body, and the Self.* London: Sage, 1996.

Lust, Teresa. *Pass the Polenta: Polenta And Other Writings from the Kitchen.* South Royalton, Vt.: Steerforth P, 1998.

McIntosh, Elaine N. *American Food Habits in Historical Perspective.* Westport, Conn.: Praeger, 1995.

Pillsbury, Richard. *No Foreign Food: The American Diet in Time and Place.* Boulder, Colo.: Westview P, 1998.

Reichl, Ruth. *Tender at the Bone: Growing Up at the Table.* New York: Random House, 1998.

Ring, Nancy G. *Walking on Walnuts.* New York: Bantam, 1996.

Root, Waverley, and Richard de Rochemont. *Eating in America: A History.* New York: Morrow, 1976.

Shapiro, Laura. *Perfection Salad: Women and Cooking at the Turn of the Century.* New York: Farrar, Straus, and Giroux, 1986.

Shulman, Alix Kates. *Drinking the Rain.* New York: Farrar, Straus, Giroux, 1995.

Sokolov, Raymond. *Why We Eat What We Eat: How the Encounter between the New World and the Old Changed the Way Everyone on the Planet Eats.* New York: Summit, 1991.

Tannahill, Reay. *Food in History.* 1973. New York: Crown, 1988.

Toklas, Alice B. *The Alice B. Toklas Cook Book.* New York: Harper and Brothers, 1954.

Williams, Susan. *Savory Suppers and Fashionable Feasts: Dining in Victorian America.* New York: Pantheon, 1985.

Witt, Doris. *Black Hunger: Food and the Politics of U.S. Identity.* New York: Oxford UP, 1999.

PART ONE

REFLECTIONS ON FAMILY, FOOD, AND ETHNICITY

CHAPTER ONE

Mac and Gravy
Paul Christensen

There were several women circulating inside my mother's body, vying for possession of her personality. I could identify at least three of them while growing up. There were more, but she kept those to herself. She wasn't crazy, she wasn't even what you call unstable. She was crowded with certain possibilities of womanhood that were too entangled, too woven together to be separated. Besides, she needed each of these sisters inside her, and when one came out to dominate her day, the others must have stood back in the darkness chattering and nagging at her.

One of the women was the vamp, a slender, vulnerable southern white girl standing in a homemade but very sexy two-piece suit of green linen, wearing her sister's shoes and flaunting some fox trim on her collar and sleeves—taken from an old coat. Her high heels tilt as she throws out a hip, a white-gloved hand touching her waist as if to say, "I got it, boys." Around her are lugubrious fronds and banana leaves, a white staircase switchbacking up the side of an old colonial brick house, lots of red brick at her feet—all the details of French Quarter culture around 1930.

Another of her women was the dutiful wife, broken of her dreaminess and vanity and made to cut out coupons and look for sales, to tear up canceled checks against nosy neighbors, to sew her own blouses and skirts. This was the flat character, a utility walk-on role she personally hated. It was the source of all her despair and complaining, and it spoiled my childhood. She would fall apart in the role and find fault with everything. A lot of suppers ended in complete silence after one of her tirades about my father's coldness. It was the self she wore most often, and it represented the part of female anger that had grown and festered all through the decades before women's liberation. She was smart, energetic, but with no effective way to use what she knew. She wore this shell of an earlier woman's role in rural society as if it were rusty armor, junk from a museum. But all the women wore it and died in it, and she knew she too would end up wearing it to her funeral.

Then there was the immigrant daughter, the repository of the folklore and food ways handed down to her from her Sicilian mother. When this persona rose into her head, her voice got deeper, rounder, as if she had just smelled the sea breeze coming over the roofs of Agrigento. Her family came from old peasant stock in a little suburb of Agrigento called Villafranca, one of countless hamlets across Europe that sprang up just beyond the tax boundaries of a larger town. It was a farming village with rough mud streets and little one-story houses of dark rooms and outdoor plumbing. The family name was Tramuta, with old Spanish roots in the wine trade. The name comes from the Latin, *transmutare,* the transmutation of grape juice into wine. She considered her heritage sacred; she had gone to Madrid to hunt down the family coat of arms and made a rendering. I have it now—a big shield quartered, with three crowns on top. No grapes.

The Sicilian heritage was superior to my father's. He came from a line of foremen who worked at an iron foundry in a place called Åkland, near Oslo, Norway. The foundry made stoves and implements, nails and brackets. The last of the line, a certain Andrew Christensen left Norway at eighteen to fight in the U.S. Civil War and was naturalized and given a job as guard at the federal arsenal in Rock Island, Illinois. Guns, machinery, iron forges, drop hammers—all the cold logic of the north were concentrated in my father. Wine, bougainvillea, saints, fortune telling were the symbols of my mother's life. She defended herself against my father's cool, analytical style—he looked down his long thin nose at her Catholicism, her peasant origins, her general state of ignorance. She had left school in the tenth grade to go to work, at her father's orders. The Depression was on, and cabinet making was not a going trade in those years. That was her weak flank, no education. My father never let her forget it. And she never let him forget her noble Spanish roots—which included an obscure dauphin or vassal's landholdings, the vineyards of Sicily. Her father's wooden angel, carved from mahogany, was the sign of her family's imagination and art, as against a clan of ironmongers on my father's side.

The immigrant daughter was a powerful presence in our house, and my mother's strongest personality. The green woman, as I called her, from the photograph of her New Orleans youth, was a fragile apparition out of Tennessee Williams's imagination; the crone who ate leftovers three times a week was a product of my father's need for thrift and plainness. The Italian peasant stirring her pot of tomato sauce was a combination of witch, storyteller, and magician. But it was not easy for my mother to clear the stage so that she could emerge fully; the Italian woman always rose out of the confusion of these others inside her, who clung to her even as she put on her apron, got out the colander and pots, sorted through the onions and garlic. It was a slow process getting this recessed, mysterious energy to take form in my mother's consciousness. Let me explain.

We always lived in a place that was an elaborate opposition of my mother's roots. I became aware of my life in a brick row house near the Delaware River, in a neighborhood of Philadelphia known as the Richmond district. Down the block was a rendering plant that boiled horses to make glue, soap, industrial products. The soot rose from the crematory stacks every afternoon, and the thick-legged Dutch wives would be out whacking their marble stoops with buckets of steaming lye water and rags. My mother hated this drudgery under the slate gray winter skies, with its sooty rain always falling over the parked cars and dimming the world. Up the block was another factory with a bright red wastewater pond. The odors of that evil swamp drifted down to us in the fall, when the north winds blew. The roof edges were lined with grimy black antennas, and all winter long the curtains would be drawn over the iron-mullioned windows. Inside sat lonely women watching sitcoms and sewing, ironing, killing time. Kids would swarm the neighborhood at three o'clock, bundles of wool and bright caps, book bags loaded with dog-eared tablets and smudged textbooks, noses red and bubbling, everyone hungry for milk and cookies.

This was the other end of America, the iron world of Protestant thrift and striving. My mother would have spent the day doing chores, in a faded shift and ankle stockings, hair up in a scarf. After a nap, she would make tea and sit in the steel gray glare of the alley window listening to the house settle. A radio would be mumbling in a corner of the kitchen. No sun, no window boxes trembling with geraniums, no vine lazying up the drainpipe. No jazz or creaking shoes, no laughter.

It would take all this sleet and grayness piled on my mother's back for weeks at a time to arouse her Italian soul. You knew it was coming because she would grow very dim and hard toward the end of her crone phase. She was crashing, and she couldn't stand the depression she was in. At some point in her psychic life she would rise, go to the mirror in the bathroom and pull down the rouge and lipstick, pin up her hair to make some curls for the evening, and begin to transform herself. The pallor disappeared in pinks and reds, eyeliner, mascara. Her lips glowed, her cheeks were southern again, her mouth glared with some unspoken passionate desire. She would smile at herself, start singing, and make her way downstairs with a silk scarf tied around her throat. It was then that she would decide to make what she called "mac and gravy," Sicilian style tomato sauce and pasta she had learned from her mother.

This was no ordinary dish. It was like the lineament she made from another of her mother's recipes. It was a sacred rite; only she could do it and make it turn out the same way each time—tasting of religion, of sunny gods and warm, wine-scented cultures bathed in Mediterranean moonlight. She knew it was magic, and her approach to it was with the same matter-of-factness of a potter or sculptor. She had her tools, her ingredients, she had songs to sing. She didn't think any more, she let her hands take over. Her hands were raw and red from chores, but they became sensuous female symbols when she opened a can of Italian plum tomatoes and began to knead them through her fingers in the big steel colander. There was a trick to squeezing the pulp, a certain twist of the wrist as you mashed your knuckles against the holes. The bloodred juice ran out of her fingers, and each time she had a smaller knot of pulp and seeds to press. Her mouth would chew with the effort, as if she were in pain. Her eyes would be far off, her face young looking.

The smell of tomato pulp and raw juice would fill the house. If I came in then, that aroma was the beginning of happiness. The grayness had parted. My mother was in the yellow light of the kitchen returning to her roots. It was necessary to come in praising the smell, exaggerating one's happiness. You emoted broadly and thanked her gushingly. You leaned over the pot far enough to have her brush you away with her shoulder. She would get serious now, more absorbed in her work. Sometimes she would pout at the gratitude and say she was working herself to death. If you offered to help, she would ignore you. Suddenly she didn't have enough room; you had to step back and let her move. She had an iron pot going with olive oil and chopped onion; that smell transformed reality. She knew it. She knew each of her three sons would go through the same ritual of broad smiles, stammers, hugs—and she loved every second of it. There would be my father's entry, and his own way of appreciating the aromas, the unfailing symbol of her good mood.

Everyone seemed to know the Italian daughter was back. She had returned through a thick fog of religion and commerce, through hard winter nights. My father's rigid practicality and dedication to work had been pierced. She had pushed him back, and his laws, his logic and order, his demands for plain living were countered. Even so, there was something terribly fragile about this ritual—we each knew it. It could end suddenly, the illusion collapse in a wrong word, a phone call, some news from the office. It could all vanish as quickly as it had come, because this Italian dream she had cast over us was not rooted in America. It was only her fabrication, her memory.

My father knew it, too. He knew he carried with him from his office that pencil smell, the paper and briefcase odors of seriousness, the genuine business of society. His suit was the embodiment of an official capacity, one that she had no access to. She could re-create immigrant fantasies, but my father's shoes and silk tie were the hard, indestructible laws of reality. Each morning he would restore his authority by shaving, by drinking coffee, by grabbing up his papers and leaving for the brick colossus of government. All day he roamed its power tunnels and talked the language of control, authority. He ate it, drank his martini in a dim restaurant and felt the official nature of his life soak through his blood. He had no need to fantasize anything; he lived his dream and it was made of real bricks and radiators. My father cooked no food, had no recipes, no secrets in his hands. He had no magic. He believed he didn't need any, and because he was certain of this fact, he could come in, lay down his implements of power, and kiss my mother, pat her shoulders or bottom, and lean into the bubbling sauce pot with real admiration. It was her moment.

But I get ahead of myself. We were at the frying of the onions in olive oil. Once started, my mother could go into a trance. No doubt she superimposed her mother onto herself and was simultaneously mother and daughter. She was in a root dream, digging in the earth of memory, myth, aided by the powerful smells she liberated by cutting and chopping. It was no casual thing to be peeling garlic, when you knew that inside the white flesh of the garlic lay something like the lost path of childhood and the sweet fertile immensity of some idealized Sicily belonging to her parents. This was how she communicated with the dead—by dicing garlic with a small knife. Her fingers, red, glistening from the colander, would crowd up to hold the clove while the pieces fell under the blade. She filled her nose with the pungent aroma, her mind drifting back to something blazing with imaginary sunlight.

The room was no longer the kitchen but a kind of loose framework of her expanding emotions. It held her in check, kept her from going into the dark living room. Her preoccupation was so pure that she had forgotten to turn on the table lamps, the outdoor light. The rest of the house possessed the cold winter reasoning of Philadelphia, while in the kitchen, the window misted over and vapors rose like genies from a lost world. There were trees that shook in the sea breeze, and a line of poplars that sounded like applause. Beyond lay vineyards and almond orchards, sand-colored buildings along a white road, and crags of bare limestone breaking up a pasture. Her mother had provided an elaborate picture of Villafranca as remembered by a twelve-year-old child. The image of a day in Sicily—trembling with wind and poplar leaves and loose sand from a neighbor's plowing—was frozen into place in the mind of an anxious girl who looked back over her shoulder as a cart drove her down to Agrigento, to the steamer bound for Palermo and Naples and then to New York. No one had left before, the bones of the elders were heaped in the little cemetery, and the deeds to the land bore links to a much wider past. All this condensed into a single fleeting impression of farewell, with the land serene, innocent, already an Eden fossilizing in the memory.

That was the Sicily my mother had been given—the nostalgic version of immigrants not sure any longer that they had made the right decision. For Italians the life in New Orleans—where my grandmother ended up—was not always easy. The French Quarter of the 1920s was still a kind of ghetto for Catholics, the white Protestant southern elite lived uptown, near Audubon Park and the Garden District. The Italians, considered second-class citizens, were swarthy, crude, pope lovers, Mafia-riddled, with crooked hearts and minds, given to adultery and violence, wife beaters and child molesters, anarchists, and unionists in the factories. They came with Old World notions of socialism, and their Catholic roots made them conspirators in some unspoken plot to take over the South. Eleven Sicilians were lynched in Louisiana in 1891 after the New Orleans police superintendent was murdered. The mayor provoked a lynch mob by vowing to teach "these people" a lesson. Other lynchings of Sicilians occurred at the same time, in West Virginia, southern Colorado, and in Hahnsville, Louisiana, where three Italians were taken from jail and hanged. The pattern of lynchings culminated in Massachusetts when Sacco and Vanzetti were executed in 1927. It was Vanzetti who said before his death, "I have suffered because I was an Italian, and indeed I am an Italian" (qtd. in Parrillo 196–97). Lynchings suggest a parallel with the treatment of blacks in the South, and indeed Sicilians in New Orleans were, before my mother's time, sent to segregated black schools.

As Vincent N. Parrillo describes, "Throughout the nineteenth century the parallels and relationship between Italians and blacks were somewhat unusual. In some pre–Civil War Southern localities futile efforts were made to replace black slaves with Italian workers. In other areas Southerners barred Italian children from the white schools because of their dark complexions. . . . In 1899 five Sicilian storekeepers were hanged in Tallulah, Louisiana, for the unforgivable crime of treating black customers the same as white" (196). John Higham's study of immigrants, *Strangers in the Land,* makes the case that religion was at the heart of the mistreatment of Italians: "Catholic traditions continued to look dangerously un-American partly because they did not harmonize easily with the concept of individual freedom imbedded in the national culture. Americans regarded political liberty as their chief national attribute and supreme achievement.

Observing the authoritarian organization of the Catholic Church and its customary association with feudal or monarchical governments, they were tempted to view American liberty and European popery as irreconcilable" (6).

That made Italians cousins to the blacks, part of the great unwanted. Still, you ate at Antoine's and danced in the clubs, and your brothers played jazz on Bourbon Street with Louis Prima, and there were relatives in politics, and everyone knew everyone in the Quarter. The enforced isolation and suspicion of Sicilians in my mother's city drove them to invent a sense of community not known among the peasant classes in Sicily.[1] They *became* a tight-knit group because of their rejection, which made food, feast days, even religion a defense against abuse and, finally, a source of ethnic pride. The matrifocal foodways and domestic culture of Sicilians, and of Italians in general, fell afoul of the patriarchal system of Protestant mainstream culture, which contributed to their rejection and to an association of Italians with the matriarchal culture of African Americans. New Orleans was a hard town for Sicilians.

You had to load both sides of the scale to know your past—my mother had no memory for my father's facts, but she remembered all the details, all the stories and myths and legends and recipes from her own world. She knew all the branches of her family, all the scandals and gossip. She knew them all the way back to their Sicilian roots—who came over when, who married whom, who cheated, who drank, who got fired. It was an encyclopedia of immigrant lore and bonding. She had listened a good deal in her mother's kitchen in the big wood-frame house on Barracks Street and Bourbon, picking up the stories, the prejudices and feuds. They went directly to her heart. She didn't know why some people were to be hated, but they were and you hated them. You loved others, forgave some. She received her lessons from her mother, who told her everything she could think of *while cooking*! To fill the memory required that there be food in the making, odors hanging over your head, fresh vegetables peeled and chopped. The connection between earth and the soul was dark, very powerful. And the two women talked in the kitchen because it was the female precinct, the ground for telling history.

A man might come in and grab a piece of bread, a drink, listen awhile but figure it was just women talking and leave again. A man might slow the talk or have to be filled in to catch up to the story, and he might stay awhile and then shuffle his feet, consult his watch, and go. It repelled men to hear women sharing such information; it came in languorous loops of words, no respect for punctuation, only pauses while the hands did something, or the mouth chewed sympathetically with the cutting, the peeling, cleaning. Then the words would start up again, as if the cooking and the talking were equal parts of the process. As if without talking you didn't cook correctly, stirring memory meant you could put the ingredients together in the right order. Food and history, memory and taste, knowledge and smell were pairings no man could understand. To not cook and listen was to not participate. You had to do both to be in on the process.

You talked of ghosts and the long dead while you liberated the spirits of the vegetables, which rose in a burst of dying aroma and went up into space. Food had to die to be eaten; the cooking killed and partly digested the things that were so recently in the fields. Now they were cut and diced, and the act of so doing seemed to require sympathetic magic in the form of reminiscence. Such talk lasted the entire cooking time, and by the time dinner was ready and the men and women and children sat down to eat, the women had communed, shared, and satisfied their need to embrace the dead. If the food was good, the men smiled and praised. But they were not part of the mystery, the heat and transformation of separate objects into the colorful liquids that came up to their mouths.

My mother was so completely separated from New Orleans that it now seemed to her a kind of concentrated second Sicily. The Quarter represented the same disappearing past, the fraying links to a diluted memory of Sicily, the older she got and the further away she moved from it. And with my father, she moved a lot, each time going farther east and north, until we left the country altogether and began living in places like Beirut, then Saigon, and later on, when I left for college, Frankfurt, Germany. In each tear of the fabric, she became more isolated, less in touch with her relatives and remaining family.

And when all this travel first began, in Chicago, Chilicothe, Ohio, a stint in West Virginia, then Philly, she had no one to talk to, she didn't trust the other women in the neighborhood. She had learned to be secretive from my father, so she had no confidantes, no alter egos to tell her troubles to. She lived in a house of men, three sons and a husband, and all of them practiced masculine silence. There were few shows of emotion and much stolid mechanical behavior day to day. She absorbed the habits of those around her, and little by little, the transformation of a warm, southern woman took form in her moodiness, her occasional despair, her increasing bitterness about being overworked, lonely, with no way out or back.

To open the skin of a garlic and dice its contents into grains allowed her to become a daughter again, to reenter the female world of her childhood. The stories returned, the joy and pathos of childhood were clear and vivid. The unsolved riddles and torments were alive and harmful. She knew that each time she added to the pot she brought the past to life, and her mother was in the room, hovering, studying her. Aromatherapy? Perhaps. Smell is the strongest of our senses, and the deep wells of memory were pouring out their contents as she prepared her mac and gravy.

The ingredients she used were a combination of history, religion, and the healing sciences. How much she knew about the sources and meanings of the herbs and vegetables she cooked with doesn't matter. The hands knew, and the instincts guided her. The ancient paths by which food came to Sicily, overland from the Silk Road into Italy and by sea from all points of the Mediterranean and beyond, contributed to a vast repertoire of Sicilian food skills, some fraction of which was mastered in Villafranca by peasant wives and passed on.

My mother began the cooking by sorting through her jar of bay leaves, selecting two or three large stiff green ones. The bay leaf is for flavor, for perfuming the tomato juice. It comes from the *Laurus nobilis* or sweet bay, native to the Mediterranean cultures and to Asia Minor. It was the first symbol of woman she put into her pot, for it was the tree Daphne turned into to escape from Apollo. Greek athletes were rewarded with wreaths of laurel in honor of Daphne's agility. It meant good luck, and by extension, a laurel that died brought disaster. One must put luck in the pot, and protect the family from spiritual harm. Next came half a stick of cinnamon, the secret of Sicilian tomato sauce. Cinnamon countered the acids and bitterness; it is among the oldest spices in human use, and is mentioned in the Bible. Frederick Rosengarten, my principal authority in herbal matters, quotes from Exodus 30: 23–25, where the Lord gives Moses a recipe for "an holy anointing oil," which included olive oil, garlic, cassia, cinnamon, and myrrh. The ancients used cinnamon as an air freshener to counteract the stench of burned flesh from temple sacrifices. Cinnamon, from the *Cinnamomum zeylanicum* or "sweet wood" tree, is taken from the soft inner bark of a bushy form of laurel tree cultivated in Ceylon, where the Dutch headed after the last of the Crusades. Hunting the source of cinnamon, Rosengarten maintains, led indirectly to the founding of America—since it was the commodity that spurred exploration on the grand scale. Its presence in my mother's sauce in its true form as bark peels or quills, rather than the more common powder, continued an ancient practice of temple magic, but also darkened the sauce and lent it an exotic aftertaste of remote Indian islands. Cinnamon is not to be found elsewhere in the European diet except in desserts; Sicilian cooking followed the Arab practice of using the spice to flavor stews and sauces.

The word *tomato* comes from *tomatl,* a Nahuatl word, transliterated into *tomate* by the Spanish. Tomatoes began appearing as weeds in the earliest maize fields of Peru and Ecuador and migrated up to Mexico long before Europeans reached the New World. When Cortés arrived, the Aztecs plied him with a variety of tomato dishes used as condiments, garnishes, and also as sauces on tortillas. The Spanish took a yellow variety back to Europe, where it was known as a "golden apple," a symbol of the sun. The French believed it was an aphrodisiac and called it *pomme d'amour* or "love apple" (Stobart 265). By the time it reached Sicily it had acquired the mystique of being the central symbol of a New World Garden of Paradise, with powers to restore youth. But because of expense it did not find common use in the peasant diet until the nineteenth century. Not until 1830 was tomato sauce commonly used as a dressing for pasta, which had long been eaten only with grated cheese; later, butter was added (Montanari 144).

The tomato has always been associated with the female, with an Indian version of Eve, in the wild garden of the New World. Sicily and other coastal cultures of the southern Mediterranean use it the way Maine farmers use jars of dandelion wine—as a taste of summer. Sun-dried tomatoes are steeped in olive oil and sold all year long; a smoky pureed form of tomato sauce, sold in old wine bottles, is the ghost of summer past. Dried or pureed tomatoes supply the table with delicious warmth, and it was this tradition my mother carried on.

Having squeezed the juice from the pulp and poured it over the onions browning in olive oil, my mother added the leaf spices, nearly all of which were remedies for women's ills. Both bay leaf and thyme were regarded in ancient Greece and Magna Grecia as cures for illnesses of the uterus and womb, and for controlling menstrual flow. They also cured nightmares and melancholy. Thyme, like cinnamon, was associated with temple sacrifice; when it was burned, its peculiar light perfume also covered the foul odors of burning flesh. Thyme, from the common weedy plant called *Thymos vulgaris,* is native to the Mediterranean region; there's even a creeping variety called the "mother of thyme." The word itself means to cleanse, to fumigate; a Greek adjective, *thymiama,* means "perfumed." Thyme was considered a stimulant to courage and bravery, and, according to Rosengarten, it was a high compliment in ancient Greece to be told one "smelled of thyme" (410).

But the most important of the herbs was oregano, sometimes called "wild marjoram," the "pizza herb" that American soldiers discovered in Italy during World War II, which eventually made pizza as popular as the hamburger. Like marjoram, with which it is often confused, oregano is from the verbena family, small aromatic shrubs unique to warm climates. The name, according to Rosengarten, is derived from the Greek and means "joy of the mountain" (263).

Garlic (*Allium sativum*) and onion (*Allium cepa*) are varieties of the lily family and among the oldest cultivated plants in the human diet; both were originally grown in Asia—onion in southwestern Asia, garlic in central Asia. But both were common in prehistoric Egypt, India, and China. Rosengarten notes that Egyptian priests used garlic and onion as temple offerings and that they were, like thyme and cinnamon, sacred foods. When the Israelites left Egypt, they complained of missing onion and garlic in their food. But a Mohammedan tradition, recorded by Rosengarten, has it that when Satan left the Garden of Eden after the Fall, garlic sprouted under his left food, onions under his right (310). Garlic and onion are associated with immigrants, a sign of their difference. Garlic especially came to be associated with the "murdering race," the Italian immigrants of the late nineteenth century.

Tomato sauce was a transportable symbol of unity that seemed to celebrate the religions of hot climates, the sense of the sacred by means of powerful smells, and the curative powers of natural plants. Woman is at the heart of the mixture, for the key ingredients whirl around in the Christian and Islamic mythology from the story of the Fall. As Massimo Montanari remarks, such "spices assumed dreamlike qualities, those same qualities that characterized the distant and mysterious Orient: an 'oneiric horizon' onto which westerners projected their desires and utopias" (63). Early maps of the period, he points out, show the Orient as lying next to the original Paradise, and, as the story goes, a few leaves and twigs from the original trees in the Garden, blown onto Asian soil, possessed magical healing powers. Perhaps this is why these same ingredients were, and still are, considered healing herbs for women's ills, as well as elixirs against the evil eye and the poisons of melancholy and despair. The sauce was the essence of what food should be—a sacrificial offering that cured human ills and celebrated the female.

My mother was no different in her attitudes toward religion, which veered toward outright paganism in her fortune telling and in her superstitions, from the indigenous Sicilians she came from. As Vecoli remarks,

> throughout the Mezzogiorno, Christianity was only a thin veneer. Magic, not religion, pervaded their everyday existence, through the use of rituals, symbols, and charms, they sought to ward off evil spirits and to gain the favor of powerful deities. To the peasants, God was a distant, unapproachable being, like the King, but the local saints and Madonnas were real personages whose power had been attested to by innumerable miracles. But in the devotions to their patron saints, the attitude of the peasants was far less one of piety than of bargaining, making vows if certain requests were granted. For the Church, which they had known as an oppressive landlord, they had little reverence; and for the clergy, whom they knew to be immoral and greedy, they had little respect. They knew little of and cared less for the doctrines of the Church. (230)

Montanari notes that the path of spices and herbs into the diets of Europe was from the medicinal sphere to the gastronomic, from healing to nurture.

But the healing had its origins in the sacred sphere, the temple as first kitchen for feeding the gods. This is what my mother re-created each time she cooked tomato sauce in her kitchen—the return of the pagan south, the place of spells and polytheism, and of "spices [that] undoubtedly had a flavour, and a smell, of eternity" (60, 63).

Our peculiar joy was to smell the return of this world into the gloom of our urban lives, each of us stepping into the kitchen with winter-bright cheeks, runny noses, scarf half-done around our necks, gloves in hand, wet shoes, greeting the tropical world and the rule over its fertility by women. Our smiles were a mixture of things—a recognition that our mother's female nature had thrown off our father's domination that day, that she had rediscovered her magic and power. We smiled as if to say, we willingly succumb to you. We acknowledged what she had achieved—the resurrection of the ancient female order, however briefly.

My father's reaction was muted, less acute or demonstrative. He was not abstract enough to understand the myths involved in cooking. He read the literal contents of the pots and knew it meant that his wife was in a good mood and was celebrating something. What, he wasn't sure. He just knew there would be no sullenness, no pouting and arguing. She wouldn't go off as her blood sugar fell, no tirades, no political ranting, no accusations. This was the stable phase, solid and enforced by cooking. He knew that much, but not much more. So he stood about with an awkward inarticulate air of maleness, looking huge and useless in the warm moist kitchen atmosphere. He would go out again, having exchanged a few code words with her about work. He would celebrate in his own way with a stiff drink and the newspaper, and sit patiently until called to the table.

But I looked hard at my father when he came in and did his kisses and pats and pot inspections and then sat under the Chinese table lamp to read the paper. He had that air of being estranged, perhaps excluded from something the kitchen represented. I detected in him a certain defense of his own turf, and behind that, a hurt that he did not understand this side of my mother. What he suspected and what my mother actually knew was that in Sicilian peasant society a man in the house occupies one sphere and a woman the other, and they exclude each other as much as possible. "The head of the family is an autocrat," Salvatore Salomone-Marino explains, "his will is law, and it is carried out on the spot, without comment, unless the housewife grumbles a little to herself. . . . And when the husband does not say anything when factual evidence shows he is wrong, he won't admit he is wrong because he does not intend to lessen his authority in any way. The housewife, too, has her portion of absolute domain; the domestic affairs are hers, and her husband does not interfere with them, nor does anyone else of the family. She sees to the food, provides work for herself and the children, [and] attends to the clothing" (41–42). This my mother knew from growing up in a traditional Sicilian household, where a husband was "truly an absolute master" who took the lion's portion of the dinner and where wives often ate a small amount from the husband's plate (43). Beating wives was common practice in nineteenth-century Sicily, in observation of the old saying, A wife is like a cat: if you pet her she claws you! Something of those values was carried over in my mother, who deferred to my father but not slavishly, and who observed the rights of my father with a certain resentment that occasionally flared. The idea of unequal rights in our house had their consequences in my mother's tirades and emotional storms, which became more menacing as I grew older. But in the kitchen she was on the omphalos stone of her authority, reigning without qualification over nurture and mystery; my father, holding to his own traditions of Norwegian patriarchy, knew when he crossed the border into the female domain.

Something she did caused joy, and yet behind it, in the roots of her skill, was some vague menace, a meaning of some kind that demoted him. Otherwise he would have had advice or offered a hand or appraised the result more vigorously. He would have taken over in some way, claimed his right of education and northern superiority in a look, a gesture. But he didn't. He hunched up his shoulders, and his face became that of a boy, as he stood there unwillingly led into the role of another son, not the ruler of his house.

My mother knew this very well. It came up from her ethnic roots, from the depths of the Mezzogiorno, the southern cultures of Italy where, as Vecoli remarks, "the south Italian family was 'father-dominated but mother-centered.' The father as the head of the family enjoyed unquestioned authority over the household, but the mother provided the emotional focus for family life" (217). Her attitude toward him showed that he had no rights in the situation. He was to go have his drink and come when called. He did this meekly, smelling the odors as they came out of the kitchen. He was hungry; his drink made him feel a little weak and defenseless. The paper depressed him, and the feeling he had as he sat there was that he was not in control. He was merely living now, and the boys, gathered around hoping to taste a meatball or bite a wiggling noodle to see if the pasta was ready—they had a place, a right to be there. He didn't. He provided, but his role now was to exist, not to act. The smell of this southern world wafting up out of the pots reminded him that such tropical fertility followed my mother around. It came with her. It was her dowry, her hope chest. Her Sicilian roots were long tendrils that clung to her as she moved north.

She dropped in the cinnamon stick as the final gesture, after the bay leaves were soft, and the thyme and parsley, the oregano were all swirling dark bluish-green in the bubbling sauce. She put a spoon of sugar in as well; this killed the final acids and created a tight, wine-rich pungency. It would go on bubbling another thirty minutes while the water for the macaroni boiled.

Earlier she had purchased three little packets of meat at the butcher shop, her one major food indulgence. Finely ground chuck roast, lean pork, and veal in three little mounds. She kneaded the meat in the bowl and added an egg, a cup of seasoned bread crumbs (fine grain), fresh parsley finely minced, chopped garlic and onion, salt and pepper. The meat absorbed all the ingredients and became very workable, like moist clay. She would roll a wad in her palms until it was a little particolored ball flecked with green and white and the sawdust color of the bread crumbs. She would fry the meatballs in hot olive oil, turning them quickly as the grease flew up. When they were done, she would drop them into the sauce and stir gently. The mixture was now mature, nearly finished. The sauce would absorb the meat flavors and darken, forming little pools of amber-colored grease. She would slide her big spoon under them and scoop them out, throwing them into a jar on the stove.

It was a curious embellishment to take the darker, mysterious power of the tomato—a member of the deadly nightshade family—herbs, cinnamon bark, pepper, salt, and add in the flesh of a milk-fed calf, a pig, and a cow. The tomato was not only a love apple, but also a heart apple; high in potassium, it is now recommended as a dietary supplement for people with hypertension and heart disease. The meats went against the therapeutic mystique of tomatoes and herbs. These creatures did not fit into a Mediterranean world, either—the pig was forbidden to Arabs and Jews, the milk-fed calf was European, and a cow hardly useful in the rockbound world. Goat would have been more logical. But this was the movable feast of tomato sauce come to the land of plenty, and pork, veal, and beef were gifts of a vast continent's largesse. The meat my mother added to the sauce was foreign to it, not part of the Sicilian foodways, which mirrored the poverty, the skimpy animal protein, the dependence on what grew naturally, abundantly in hard soil. This was a New World addition, the American celebration of excess after an immigrant transcended Old World deprivation.

It pleased my father, and the meats blended nicely so that the veal, soft, mild, insubstantial, was strengthened by the pork, a harder more tangy meat; and the beef, cut from a chuck, came from a lazy, grazing cow on the great grasslands of middle America. It was not a colorful or meaningful unity of animals to put into one's vegetables; it made for a kind of chaos, but the meatball, small and round, compact and heavy was a strange instrument of longings—it seemed to want everything that was not wild in its constituency. The bread crumbs were human artifice, the egg was from the oldest domesticated animal, and the three meats represented the triumph of agriculture. So the meatball was that portion of the dish which constituted human culture in its desire to transcend nature. The ball represented this fact by denying to the ingredients any resemblance to their natural state.

My father knew that this part of the meal was male, made for men to eat. It satisfied their sense of what food should be. He made a special gesture in getting three or four of the meatballs out and attending to them first. He chewed unselfconsciously, and his tongue was very happy being in contact with this form of humanly controlled nature. The wilder sorts of ingredients in the sauce, any part of which could have easily grown in a field without the influence of hoe or watering can, he took for granted, politely refusing to make any acknowledgment. He chewed his meatballs as if they were the principal feature of the dish. My mother ate one and passed the bowl around, refusing any more. She liked meat, had no quarrel with its meanings, but she didn't like much of it. She ate the pasta in the same spirit, for it too represented an unnecessary artificiality—a form of wheat that re-sembled strings (*spagha* means string, spaghetti is little strings of milled du-rum), a dream of symmetry and transcendence unlike the natural flakes of parsley, the bay leaves, and onion bits. These were the stuff of any dry hill-side and lived out of some other will. The meatball and the spaghetti were aspects of the male invasion of food culture and joined the woman's domain of tomatoes uneasily. The meal was unstable, a curious heap of nutritional artifacts from contradictory cultures.

It was one thing in the kitchen to heap up the colander with boiled pasta and pour off the sauce, "gravy" in my mother's words, into a big bowl with a ladle, where the food still possessed the mystique of its female making, and another to cart the food out into the dining room. Why the dining room should change the nature of the food, I can't say. Except that the kitchen was raw and without artifice, the preparations had strewn debris every-where. It was a messy, processual place, the making room. It had magic but no presentation. It was the realm of the lower classes, the peasant dimen-sion. It was where servants once worked, in the heat, with the smells, the scraps, the dogs waiting.

But the dining room was theater. It had special lighting, a cloth with white dishes and gleaming flatware. It had napkins, soft chairs, a cabinet with heirlooms and dressier dishes. It was quiet, and it was a male's domain. The table was where my father recovered his sovereignty. He came to it with lordly slowness, and when he sat, it was the signal for the rest of us to begin. How he ate is another matter; he ate without reserve, total absorp-tion in eating to fullness. He didn't talk, didn't look up, only nodded to questions, buried his great round moon face into the steaming food and didn't relent until his plate was clean. My mother made the effort to speak, but she had relinquished her power. She was exhausted and a little sour about the work. She would often say it took hours to make and a minute to disappear. It bothered her that so much lore and practice could vanish so quickly.

Nonetheless the table had a second more subliminal function; it was the altar at which we took our daily communion. It had the remoteness of an altar, and the way in which things were dished out, it almost seemed that my mother and father were sharing the priest's role. My father would receive, sometimes hand out the portions, and then say grace. My mother would receive compliments with a look of solemn expectation. We each gave praise and then vied for her favor by wolfing our food. The more we heaped up, slurped down, went for more, her eyes would take note and respond tacitly with a dark affection. It was her pay, her due as maker. The wine was poured, and even the kids could have a glass if they chose to. The wine was always there, as if to anchor the ritual in its proper Christian mythology, and behind that, in the deeper wells of pagan myth. The bread came around next, and as it did the meal took on a certain dullness of time, antiquity.

If our friends showed up at that moment, they knew to keep away. They sat on the front step to wait until we were through. They sat there wondering why all the seriousness, all the fuss. They hardly ever sat down to table to eat together in their own houses; the little counters that had sprung up in kitchens were there for quick dinners standing up. The central heating, the television, the snack counters were all part of the dynamo of the twentieth century hurling the family out from the last surviving rituals of domestic life. We kept them, blindly preserved the niceties down to our final motions of sopping up sauce with bread heels.

We kept them because we had to. We had no choice. There was literally nothing else holding us together but these rituals and ties to the deep Sicilian past. My father's evolution out of Norwegian remoteness and Illinois abstractness were such that he had only one direction in his life, deeper into government, his career, his ethic of self-improvement, which replaced emotion, family, nostalgia with the unfolding of some inexhaustible vein of reward. The more he worked, the more loyalty he showed, the more the unfolding would go on, each time revealing something more attractive to him. If the rituals did not call us back from the abyss, we would have floated away like soot in the air. In those houses where no one sat down to a meal, there was still glue—in a friendly, garrulous father, a mother who spoiled everyone, a house that was run down but friendly, dirty without being grim. This was the folk unity we were leaving behind as my father moved up the government ladders, always crisp in white shirt and tie, pressed suit and long black shoes. His road was up, my mother's was in a circle, the daily cycle of events in which she squandered her mortality on ironing, washing, cleaning floors, cooking. The ritual was as necessary to our lives as it was to the peasant whose only relief from drudgery was this moment of sacrifice and communion at the table.

After supper the boys either helped with the cleanup or went off to do homework, but the house had closed in on us and the darkness was heavy. There was the sign of feasting in the refrigerator, in the form of a jar of red sauce, a small container of leftover pasta. But the rest of the house told you we were in the industrial north again, under skies swirling with refinery dirt and chemical plant gases—dark soupy skies with clouds lowering, bringing rain and gray dawn. The other houses had already succumbed to the logic of the city, as neighbors hovered near a radio or TV, or went up to bed early, to lie there listening to the sirens, the silence, the absence of Sicily in the world.

Lying there myself, my dark ceiling looking like a starless sky, I could feel the difference between my father and mother with aching certainty. The day had risen too high; it had almost spilled over into pure myth, into a luxurious fantasy. I could feel its palpable reality as my mother restored her memories through food. The rite was all hers, the equivalent of my father's eating—she had poured herself into it, the tasks were like mantras and hypnotic escapes from the brick world we lived in. She had put her hands down into the red pulp with such determination that the little uneven perforations of the colander scraped her knuckles, and her skin burned with the acid of the tomatoes. She didn't complain. She never did.

But it was all her own world she attended to, as if she had dropped a veil over her life and worked in the dark of some other light, moonlight, which memory casts over the self. She worked by feel, never having to read the labels or weigh things. She went about like a sleepwalker going down a rutted path where there were night lights and sounds of a village near the sea. All of this was plain in the working of her mouth, the lipstick already worn away where she had tasted something, or drank juice, or merely blotted her perspiration with the oven mitten. But it was her poetic escape that had created the idea of festival; such an effect was her special power. Perhaps her only one.

My father created no magic in the house; he assured us there was none to be had. He lived in a strict world of logic and cause-and-effect, and the only benefit of his labors was the money he secretly invested and squirreled away. We never saw it. We saw the new cars, the suits, the shoes, my mother's watch, her new fur coat, her living room furniture, his *control*. That came from the smoldering gold that lay in a safe in the bank, and it had come from living without magic. He let you know by his appearance that he expected nothing beyond his efforts. No miracles, no visions. Only the day-to-day accumulation of small gains, which added to his hill and his future mountain. He lived according to Adam's sentence of exile; paradise, if it ever existed, was in ruins and could never be reconstructed. Forget about Eden. Forget that its remnants were in every pot of tomato sauce throughout Italian America.

For my mother, paradise was no myth or fantasy, but a counterpoint to the killing dullness of her life. Food was the path that led back to it, and each time the pulp was ground against the colander it formed in her mind, and in her senses. She could sense its nearness, as if it crept into the kitchen on the motes of streetlight and came through the blinds in the living room to gather over the stove. It was a real Eden in the sea, shimmering with tile roofs and double exposed with the hot golden sunlight of the French Quarter, with its green fences and the parched, unbearable dazzle of dryers where laundry was hung. She saw Sicily through her mother's eyes, through her father's loneliness and nostalgia, through the deprivations of immigrants who lived in America to find their dreams but who mourned the loss of their roots.

She would sometimes look up over her bowls to say that the tomatoes were not as good as when her mother cooked them. She would use fresh plum tomatoes, which cooked down better, sweeter, thicker, redder. These were factory tomatoes, grown in too big a field with too little care for the nurture of the plants. The skies were not as hot or pure, the sun too weak here to make the tomatoes turn hard and deep with power. She knew that. She knew that her preparations were already adulterated, counterfeited by the lapse of the years. Her sister in Brooklyn was older, closer to the source in the way she lived. Not so well off, but married to another Sicilian, a man in the dry docks who spread that same primal air of Sicilian nature in the house with his cigar, his operas, his low, gravelly voice, his accent. My mother had no such link to the past, having married a Norwegian from Illinois. Now she lived in the middle class, and the middle class ate diluted food—white bread, pale beer, thin soup, frozen peas, canned tomatoes. The stove was never big enough to allow the large skillets full heat; the seasoning was dried and bottled, half the fullness needed to provoke the real Sicily to rise in winter. That is why a certain fragility hovered over her magic; she knew it was borrowed from a dying past, already receding out of focus.

When I taught my wife the recipe for mac and gravy, she followed the steps with a certain interest, but it wasn't her myth. She cooked well and the sauce tasted *almost* like my mother's, but I had the disquieting sensation that the recipe was disintegrating after so many removals from the source. We had begun to put odd things into the mix, to take short cuts, to buy the cheaper brands of canned tomatoes. Still, she and I both make mac and gravy out of deep reverence for its meanings. But then, my wife is German and comes out of German peasant traditions and carries in her soul certain recipes for potato pancakes, *sauerbraten,* calf's tongue which are as magical to her as mac and gravy is to me.

Cooking up a dish of potato pancakes involves a certain amount of passion and quiet, a trance state of memory, a celebration of her now-dead mother, and of tales of cooking when any the kids are about. When we sit down to eat, we are the weaker for our having moved too far from the roots, but the myths are still alive and we honor them. Which is to say no woman comes to a marriage or relationship without her village inside her, all its heritage and traditions, its habits and mysteries. To deny this link to the ancestry and to the folk art for whatever reason—assimilation, individualism, fitting in—harms the soul. My mother would never allow it to happen so long as there was a box of spaghetti in the pantry and some cans of tomatoes around.

NOTE

¹ Vecoli notes that the nuclear family, not the village or "rural city" where peasants lived, was the unit of community: "It was the family which provided the basis of peasant solidarity" (216–17).

WORKS CITED

Higham, John. *Strangers in the Land: Patterns of American Nativism, 1860–1925.* 2d ed. New Brunswick, N.J.: Rutgers UP, 1988.

Montanari, Massimo. *The Culture of Food.* Trans. Carl Ipsen. Oxford: Blackwell, 1994.

Parillo, Vincent N. *Strangers to These Shores: Race and Ethnic Relations in the United States.* 3d ed. New York: Macmillan, 1990.

Rosengarten, Frederick, Jr. *The Book of Spices.* Rev. ed. New York: Jove, 1969.

Salomone-Marino, Salvatore. *Customs and Habits of the Sicilian Peasants.* Ed. Aurelio Rigorli. Trans. Rosalie N. Norris. Rutherford, N.J.: Fairleigh Dickinson UP/Associated U Presses, 1981.

Stobart, Tom. *Herbs, Spices, and Flavorings.* Woodstock, N.Y.: Overlook, 1982.

Vecoli, Rudolph J. "*Contadini* in Chicago." *Divided Society: The Ethnic Experience in America.* Ed. Colin Greer. New York: Basic, 1974.

CHAPTER TWO

Humble Pie
Cathie English

Preserves are fruits preserved with sugar so that the fruit retains its shape, is clear and shiny, tender and plump.
—*The Ball Blue Book*

Pies. It seems like such a trivial place to start developing a plan for self-preservation. But it's a start. It is the beginning of who I am and what I've inherited from two very special women. It is impossible to separate food from love in my maternal ancestry. They are a double cherry. Babka Boro, my maternal grandmother, was never one to show emotion or dole out sage wisdom. She understood the meaning of show not tell. For her, the telling of love was the act of baking. I understood that. I never needed the words. Not that I didn't want to hear them, but I forgave her lack of expression. This faith that work demonstrates love begins with the pies of Anna Wetovick Boro, my Babka, a short, squared-off woman who spoke English a mile a minute and spoke Polish at the speed of light. Somehow, I was lucky enough to keep pace with her and comprehend. Perhaps her lack of expression had something to do with lacking the perfect English words. She was the matriarch and so is my mother, Elizabeth Boro Cave. My mother, however, inherited many of the paternal communication genes and is slow to speak.

Both women are earth women, inextricably tied to the soil; they depended upon a harvest of food to feed their large families. For Babka, it was ten children, for my mother, an even dozen. When I was a child, Babka lived in town, less than a block from a cattle lot and a Pioneer-seeded cornfield; she was a retired farm wife who never left the farm. Babka's grandparents had emigrated from Poland in the late 1880s and had settled and begun farming near the town of Tarnov, Nebraska. Babka and Dziadek farmed northwest of Silver Creek, Nebraska, near what is still called Krakow. Krakow consists of SS. Peter and Paul Catholic Church and a cemetery where Dziadek's parents are buried, including Katherine Cuba Boro, whom I was named for.

Babka was a workaholic. All farmers and their wives are. They work from sunup to sundown. They never once question God if all their labor is in vain in a bad year. They still worked. My mother was a farmer's daughter who kept her roots by maintaining a large vegetable garden. My mother isn't a workaholic. She is not driven to work as Babka was. For my mother, work was a necessity. Babka found joy in her labors; Mom was methodical. She did what she had to do and never complained. It was her duty. Mom daily showed her self-sacrificing love in every meal she cooked, every dish she washed, every pan she scrubbed. Neither woman would ever hear of wasting one morsel. For Babka that was conveyed at butchering time; every part of the hog or chicken was for human consumption. For my mother, waste not, want not was conveyed by the constant presentation of leftovers. For them, waste would have been sinful. The thought of any food not feeding a hungry mouth was sacrilegious.

I am a perfect union of both matriarchs. I am a methodical workaholic. I am driven and because I am, I do what I have to do out of my sense of duty. Like both, I understand that actions speak louder than words, but unlike them, I love words; yet I seldom use them to convey wisdom or emotion to my immediate family. Rather, like them, my family sees my love especially when I take the time to bake that cherry pie, cook the spaghetti sauce from my own special recipe, or bake those fresh cinnamon rolls. I am the farmer's wife's granddaughter, the farmer's daughter's daughter, and I, too, am inextricably tied to the land. I'm not always so careful to give respect back to it, though. I hate leftovers. I discard the gizzards and livers of cut-up chickens. Both women would beat their breasts over this. In their terms, my ties to the land have been severed; they were so close to it they had the scent of wet mud in their nostrils—the scent I smell when I open the windows after a long winter and dirt is in the sills, deposited there by fierce north winds. I am not digging in the soil to plant seed potatoes, tomato plants, or green beans. I am not busting sod like my Polish ancestors, but I know that my sense of identity comes from that indomitable spirit which led them here and kept them struggling despite the hard work, despite the crop losses, despite the hunger. I plow deep into how this agrarian heritage has shaped me.

Both women took their food gathering and preserving very seriously, but they each had their definitive areas of strength. Babka was a talented baker and a professional cook. Mom remembers her mother away for many days at a time, often several weekends in a row, when Babka cooked for three-day Polish weddings. Cooking for Polish weddings was no easy task. Babka made the standard fare: polish sausage, sauerkraut, mashed potatoes, fried chicken, corn, green beans, peirogi, and fresh baked bread. The only thing consumed more than food was pivo or beer. For Polish descendants of immigrants, the food was a part of the celebration of marriage; it symbolized the love, the newly begun union of lives, much like the new lives and prosperity they had been celebrating in a New Land.

Babka had six daughters, my mother being the youngest, and although Mom never has considered herself a very good cook, she certainly mastered and even excelled at frying chicken. That is her signature meal: fried chicken, mashed potatoes and gravy, and whatever vegetable was nearest her arm's reach on the shelf in the cool, canned-goods cellar. That brings me back to me—what cuisine legacy have I preserved from these remarkable women? I've retained their specialties—pies, fried chicken, and the canning process—but I've added a few new traditions of my own. For Babka, there were never recipes. "Just do it," she would say. What I have preserved from her, I learned by observation, trial and error, and a whole lot of patience. That patience has paid off. I learned this patience from my mother.

Let Us Bake Bread Together

Babka Boro amazed me with her ability to peel an apple from top to bottom without breaking the spiral. My childlike wonder inspired me to help her peel apples, but I never accomplished that feat, albeit, grandma's peeling chore was made more enjoyable with company and less work. But it never felt like work, it was a joy. She would get a stool for each of us, and we'd find a shady spot under the sugar maple outside her back door. I would talk and she would listen, or sometimes, we wouldn't say anything. We just tried to get the work done as quickly as possible. We filled the large gray dishpan with peeled and sliced apples. We took that into the kitchen, and she'd add cinnamon and sugar and flour without measuring. We would let that set awhile and have a large glass of ice water. Later, she'd simply throw flour and lard together with a little salt, roll out a crust in less than ten seconds, flip it into a tin pie plate, spoon in the apples, slice thick chunks of oleo onto the apple mix, and cover it with another quickly rolled crust. She repeated this process until she'd made several and started a day of baking.

She always baked her own bread. If she ever ate store-bought bread, it was in the nursing home. She would use a large white enamel pan, red-lipped, that was large enough for two loads of dishes and was filled with a twenty-four-inch circle of dough. She'd go to the big canister in her pantry and scoop in flour to the yeast mixture already in the pan. Her strong hands, forearms, and shoulders would move in a rhythmic motion as she pressed and pressed and pressed. Then we let it sit. The in-between times were our best times. That's when I begged her to teach me Polish or asked her to tell me stories about when she was a little girl. She'd give me a lesson or two in Pohomsku or Low Polish, and tell me stories about my mom's birth—how she gave birth to her alone when she was forty-four because the doctor didn't get there in time. I could have listened for hours; I was awestruck. An hour later, she'd let me do the punching. The large bubble collapsed at my small hand's touch. She grabbed two handfuls of dough and rolled it into a loaf. She let me grease the oft-used rust-and-black-colored loaf pans, and six loaves later, we baked bread together.

The greatest comfort smell in the entire world is bread baking. You can't re-create that in your imagination, it's impossible. We could win wars by baking bread at the front lines. The scent would make men's stomachs growl and render them powerless to take up arms. Instead, they'd pass the rations butter around from both sides, slice off huge hunks of a loaf, and suck in the aroma of steaming warm yeast, then let the yellow warmth glisteningly drip down their chins. They'd lick the butter up after the hunk of bread had been swallowed. Each soldier would know he'd rather be at home and would take his leave.

Chicken, Fried Chicken

When I taped an interview with my son, age three, I asked him what his favorite food was, and he replied with inflection and innocent lust: "Chicken, fried chicken." That remains a constant in his life. In fact, my son, now a teenager, bemoans my limited chicken frying because he knows I know how, very well, in fact, but what I had to explain to him was that frying chicken is like a punishment. I remember frying chickens on Sundays after mass. The A.M. radio would be tuned to KTTT ("K-Triple T"), and despite the static on that worn console stereo, we'd listen to the *Big Joe Polka Show* all morning. Along with sad Polish waltzes, my penance was frying four or five chickens at a time. I remember the charcoal-crusted bottoms of the two cast-iron skillets. I remember the entire can of Crisco in the skillets, melting in minutes over the blue-yellow circle of flames. I remember the hot oven and the two black enamel roasters. The grease, the heat, the smell of fried chicken still nauseates me. Which is all the more reason to canonize my mother as a saint when she steps into heaven. I never understood how Mom could stand it. She endured more heat than Joan of Arc; she survived frying hundreds of chickens in forty-four years of marriage. She has taught me the lesson of long-suffering through her devotion to feeding her family, no matter how sickening or monotonous it could be. Looking back, I think the salvation trick for her was having a can or two of beer handy during the process.

I think, too, it was one of her proudest claims to fame. Mom's fried chicken was far better than Babka's. That was a real compliment to the daughter of an already famous cook in four surrounding counties. Mom somehow had a special knack for the juiciest, most tender fried chicken, a melt-in-your-mouth fowl that would make Colonel Sanders cry. Mom said the trick was to use Crisco—not oil, but shortening. Get it hot, real hot, and then drop in the chicken pieces. No lid for the first ten minutes. Let it splatter! Turn the pieces after five minutes, so both sides get nice and crispy brown. Once the chicken pieces were nice and crispy, you turned the fire down and let it fry for twenty minutes. Once cooked through, you fetched the pieces with the tongs and placed them in the roaster and put that in the warming oven. Round two. Add a little more shortening if it's depleted, and get it hot. All in all, on an average Sunday, two frying pans going, it took five repetitions, or approximately two and half hours. My mother's patience. The patience of a saint. That is her greatest gift to me. It takes patience to sit by a hot stove, grease splattering on your clothes, your hair, your face and arms. That, my friends, is sainthood without the mashed potatoes and gravy.

The Rest Is Just Gravy

Much to my chagrin, I've never been able to make gravy. I can recall only one time in my life that I had success at it: Thanksgiving 1980. I purchased a huge turkey and cooked it slowly all morning. It had rich, brown drippings oozing with butter and injected oil in the bottom of the disposable aluminum pan. I stirred together a little water and cornstarch and slowly poured it into the bubbling caldron of hot oil. It was a masterpiece. Try as I may, and several Thanksgivings later, I've never re-created such a work of art. I did, however, pay attention when my mother fried chicken. Frying chicken is an art and there aren't any short cuts, and I don't buy the precut pieces at the supermarket. I know how to cut up a chicken.

I don't really remember who taught me how to cut up a chicken, but I think my mom must have. She rarely took time to actually teach. She'd just say, "Watch." In her case, you had to watch closely, because she worked quickly. Pull the thighs out of their sockets, cut through the cartilage. Bend the leg and thigh to expose cartilage—slice into it. Pull the buttback off by hand, pull out the wings to expose the joint, slice through the cartilage. Cut the back ribs from breast ribs. Cartilage. That soft clearish white that bends easily, but holds the bones together. That is my mother. She was easy to win over, flexible in all matters, but she was the strength that held us all together. The last step was the breast—the tricky part. The knife must be sharp. Cut the top of the breast from just above the breastbone if you want two pieces, but if you want three, jab the knife into the thick breastbone to split it and then continue the cut through the cartilage. Salt and pepper. Scoop flour into a brown paper bag and shake, and proceed as I just described. I do fry chicken for my son every once in a while as long as I have some homegrown chickens and not store-bought ones that reek of pesticide spray.

I'm not as well known or famous for fried chicken as I am for baking pies.

I used to bake bread, too, but find little reason to do so now mostly because I'd end up eating the whole loaf. I have continued the tradition of Babka's pie baking, but I opt to use Crisco instead of lard. The Crisco is one of my new modern-woman traditions, but mostly it has to do with cholesterol levels and the avoidance of the strokes Babka suffered. I'm the holiday pie baker. My husband's family has always threatened him with bodily harm if he had even the slightest notion of divorce. They would not survive a Thanksgiving, Christmas, or Easter without "Cathie's Pies." It used to be "Anna's Pies" before Babka died a day before my birthday in June 1984. Sometimes I imagine that she is proud of me and my pies. There were times after she died that I felt her presence, guiding me as I perfected my craft, and that she somehow knows I've used my talents for the sake of my family, out of love.

Pies have become so much a part of my holidays that I plan way ahead for flour, pie fillings, evaporated Milk, pumpkin, and plenty of eggs. The usual Thanksgiving fare is two pumpkin, one cherry, and two lemon meringue. I used to make only one lemon until my sisters-in-law got into a fork fight over the last piece and drew blood one Christmas. I've made two lemons ever since. I've become so adept at pie baking and taking pies to family gatherings that I invested a large sum of money in four Tupperware pie takers, so I don't have a mutilated disaster in the trunk of my car. Before raw eggs became taboo, I made my favorite, French Silk Pie. Babka would not have approved. She would have thought it an indulgence. If she couldn't raise the filling in her own backyard, she didn't need to go buy the ingredients at the store. Nevertheless, it will always be my favorite and always an indulgence. Sadly, since I don't enjoy the thought of salmonella-induced cramps, I stopped making it. I miss it. I tried Egg Beaters, but the pie never turned out as high or fluffy with those phony substitutes for the real thing.

Holy Rollers

We each have our areas of culinary expertise, but there is one shibboleth we covet. We don't say it to others, and for a reason: for all three of us, canning is a religious service, dogmatic, sterile with a "women's talk" litany. It is a sacred ceremony that only a few may attend. You have to prepare yourself very well for this celebration of the mass. The mass's hymns are the rattling jars and boiling noises from the blue enamel piano, playing in a key of D minor, rumbling on the bottom at the start of a boil, reaching a key of C when water hisses and spits out onto the burner, bubbling over with intensity. For Babka and Mom, it was a necessary ceremony celebrating what Mother Earth had given them to sustain their children through the fruitless winter months. It was holy. It was their thanksgiving offering. For me, it is the joy of preserving something homegrown, not store bought. It is a work of art much like the turkey. It is the color, the flavor, the smell that factories can't re-create. It is opening a Ball jar of tomatoes, smelling the acidic scent, tasting the salt and sugar, and adding it to beef bouillon for vegetable soup on a Tuesday night in February. Babka and Mom taught me that you have to have the right canner, the right utensils, the right jars, the right rings, the right fruit, the right vegetable, the right processing times—everything must be done with care just as the priest prepares his heart and the heart of his parishioners for communion. For us, it was communion, *koinonia,* of three generations. Canning takes time, more time than the modern woman has, therefore, it is love.

The greatest display of love by these two women was the canning of sweet corn, but it was more like a Pentecostal service. It was an assembly of family slain by the spirit—of exhaustion—by the ceremony's end. Because they had an endless barrage of small children, they understood the fun of having roasting ears in January, instead of just a pile of mush on a plate. It would have been easier to cut the corn off the cob, but they wouldn't hear of it. Two blue canners would belt out July heat like a steamship's boiler below deck. The wallpaper would begin to peel above the stove in mom's airconditionerless kitchen. Like the stoker from a Russian painting, large pink hands would retrieve the corncobs with a silver set of tongs. Cornlog houses would grow in pyramids in large discolored yellow Tupperware bowls. The youngest generation's task was to march the loads to the bathroom, white-hot wisps burning into our tanned faces. The houses of corn collapsed as they tumbled into the icy bath. We ran cold water out of the snake-shaped spout of the deep tub, its enamel yellowed by endless Comet scourings and its antiquated cabriole legs covered by lavender-painted plywood and contact paper. The golden kernels were cooled by clear cold squares from blue bending ice trays. We retrieved the ears of corn from their blanch bath and scurried to the kitchen table where they were stacked into blocks, like one rolling pin on another, and quickly wrapped them in the skating rink–backed, snow-colored freezer paper. The littlest kids always got to add the finishing touch—the sure-fast white freezer tape. Babka and Mom, like pack mules, would load up both arms and trudge to the freezer and shift its contents around to make room for the precious packages of corn on the cob.

Preserves

Polish people really relish their jellies. Last summer my neighbor gave me an ice cream bucket of chokecherries. Little dots of red pressed against the words "Blue Bunny." It was impossible to sieve any pulp out of those little punctuation mark pits. I had planned on jam and made jelly, with lots of sugar—ten cups of sugar. My yield: six half-pint jars. Babka always had several jars of jellies set out on her kitchen table. The apple yellow and cherry red looked like Brach's Sparkle Candies. Amazingly, Babka seldom made strawberry jam. Most of her strawberries were never covered with a paraffin circle. They were tossed with sugar and poured over vanilla ice cream or angel food shortcake. Making preserves seems like such a waste of time. You get so little to show for all the work it takes. But Babka knew this. Mom knows this. I know this. It isn't much. But what you do get is so rich and so good, and its delicate quality stays with you for a long time. Sometimes you don't forget it. Chokecherries: it was worth it for that luscious, purple-colored toast spread. My favorite jelly is wild plum, though it's next to impossible to find wild plums nowadays. My husband, who has done some soil conservation work, informed me that most of the thickets succumbed to herbicides intended for cash crops. There isn't a recipe for the clear jelly Babka made, but if I ever find some honest-to-goodness wild plums, I have a jam recipe on reserve in my cookbook library.

The Crust of It

Really, a good pie depends solely on the crust. That's what I've learned by plenty of practice. I know that you can't play with it. You can't roll it out two or three times to create a perfect circle. Its perfection lies in its imperfection. The jagged edges I roll out for each new pie take on the coastline characteristics of a new continent. But I only roll it once. I cut off the coastlines, letting them drop like California, onto the counter. You can invest in a pastry cloth and a rolling pin sleeve, but a floured board will do. You can buy a pastry blender, but a fork will do. You can add an egg, a dash of vinegar, a little sugar, but a teaspoon of salt will do. None of these things will make or break the pie, but overrolling certifies failure, or at least a cardboard crust.

Crusts. That's the real start. It's the place I've started in passing down a legend's fame to her namesake, my daughter, Anna Rose English. Anna to Anna. Flour dust to dust. We have come full circle, and this time, the circle is perfect. Babka's life was simple; hard work and family love. Mom's life was humble, too, unending work and loving her family. My life is a little more complex because our culture has changed, shifted like the coastlines, and is changing all the time; but my life is devotion to work and family, too. My daughter's life may be similar to mine—at least more to mine than Babka's and Mom's. I'm trying to teach her, too, without words, that work is good and that there is nothing greater than a loving family. She'll learn that you can't play with it. That you have to take it as it comes. When I bake pies, my daughter is always underfoot. When I start rolling dough, she begs, "Please. Let me roll the dough. Can I make those long things with cinnamon and sugar? Please, please?!" I move over, making room for her akimbo elbows, stretching out like wings, rolling out irregular shapes, like me, like Mom, like Babka.

CHAPTER THREE

Dalia Carmel
A Menu of Food Memories
Leanne Trapedo Sims

Prologue

The stories within this work are the threads and patterns of a transglobal Epicurean tapestry. Woven together from phone conversations and interviews at Dalia Carmel's home, these stories serve up a banquet of food memories. It all began at the suggestion of Barbara Kirshenblatt-Gimblett. Dalia is both a personal friend and a colleague of Barbara's. They share an intellectual and emotional ardor for food. So it was in the Department of Performance Studies at New York University where I first caught a glimpse of the determined shoulders of Dalia Carmel. Dalia was a guest and participator in Kirshenblatt-Gimblett's "Food and Performance," a course that drew a formidable cast of characters: food connoisseurs, chefs, scholars, historians, and artists. As a person with a stormy relationship to her own uprooted past, I have always been haunted by storytelling. So, at Barbara's suggestion, armed with my tape recorder, I made the first of many fervent visits to Dalia's home in Midtown. This initial sojourn, slotted for two hours, extended to eight and a midnight cab ride back to Brooklyn.

Dalia, a tall, silver-haired, elegant woman with a guttural laugh, became my informant. She was born in the thirties in Jerusalem to Jewish European parents. As a transplant to America in 1960, Dalia carried with her—her amulet—an ethnically complicated menu of food stories and experiences. Her own layered ethnic past had seasoned her relationship with America.

Dalia's zeal for international and ethnic foods began as a young child's curiosity about her neighbors' customs and foodways. From the roots of this youthful passion, Dalia has traversed to where she resides today, a dignitary of sorts in New York's landscape of food. There she lodges in the intermediary space between the professional and amateur food worlds. Her collection of 4,500 cookbooks, a project with its roots in the sixties, is a library for many food celebrities, collectors, critics, and academicians. Dalia habitually opens our conversations with, "Do I have a food story for you . . ." Not quite a question or a statement, this phrase serves as a canvas for her memories and stories of food. Dalia Carmel can make you smell the aroma behind her words, taste the fusion of spices in her world, and savor the food that lingers in one woman's memory.

Dalia's relationship with food is complicated by her insider-outsider connection with home. Dalia venerates the home and her mother's cooking, yet as a child she defied the confines accompanying them. Her ambivalent relationship to food is evident in our interviews, where the narratives that resist the richness of her mother's cooking live alongside those that romanticize her mother's kitchen.

Food for Dalia Carmel is home. But "home" for Dalia is not an anchored place. This food biography addresses the body, food, and narratives in exile (I am using *exile* in the broader sense to mean not only a physical banishment but a psychological, self-imposed one). The body, the food, and the stories have traveled not only physically across seas; there is also an emotional transportation of the food and the stories, which are stored in the archives of Dalia's memory.

Dalia's food stories are particular to shifting landscapes. At home her initial food experiences were Russian and Hungarian, set against a backdrop of the Middle East. The European Jewish cooking in her home was a menu in contradiction: gefilte fish, matzo ball soup, heavy cream, paprika, and an abundance of *treyf* (food that is not kosher). Even though Dalia loved her mother's cooking, she strayed from the confines of her home into the wanderlust of the street, and Arabic cooking. Dalia was mesmerized by Arabic and Israeli salads, which she introduced into the home of her parents. Her fascination with these salads lay in the method of flavoring—olive oil, lemon juice, and sumac. Dalia was also intrigued by the specialized ethnic functions that identical spices can have; for example, cinnamon in the Mediterranean is a constant companion to tomato sauce, while in Hungarian cuisine it is an essential cake ingredient. Dalia's early food experiences were infused with eclectic tastes, memories, and cultures.

Dalia speaks in food stories—it is her idiom. Her archive of personal food narratives is echoed by her literal archive—her cookbook collection. These volumes—some of which are autobiographical narratives—relate stories, facts, and specific cultural customs to an audience. In a sense, the archive is a theater of knowledge, and the patrons who participate are integral to Dalia Carmel. This assorted slew of scholars, academicians, historians, writers, professional chefs, amateur cooks, and radio hosts is Dalia's community or extended "family." The archive, like the food narrative, is Dalia's surrogate home. Its voluminous body spills into Dalia's literal home, even making its way into her bedroom. Through the archive, Dalia constructs and reconstructs community. The archive is her lifeline; it refines her pursuit of knowledge. It keeps her intellectually curious, and within this theater of pedagogy, Dalia is the "sleuth of cookbooks."

Dalia Carmel is a consummate performer. When she recounts her menu of memories, the experience is always resplendently theatrical. I have therefore chosen to compose this chapter as a dialogue. It would be a shame to rob Dalia's memories of her singular vitality by impersonating her through paraphrase, and so I present her voice verbatim as much as possible. My own voice is the voice of the interlocutor who talks back, in the style of the midrashim (the ancient biblical commentators). I reread Dalia's stories through the lens of my own experience. Like Proust's madeleine, each morsel of Dalia's narrative transports me to my own childhood delectations.

My Mother and the Dirty Pita Falafel

My mother was so awkward standing on the street corner with a pita falafel in her hands. Standing there with the tahini sauce dripping out of the pita. I remember only once in all of my childhood waiting with my mother in a long line winding outside of Melech Hafalafel—*the King of Falafels. He made the best falafel in all of Tel Aviv, so she was prepared to sacrifice her resolute standards. But for my parents, both doctors, street food—particularly in the Middle East—was dirty food. Food to be eaten with the hands. So it was with my friends that I explored this world of forbidden food and the permissive streets. On the way to the beach or a* kumzits *[picnic] we would eat an ice cream cone, corn on the cob, and, of course, the pita falafel. Or we would stop for gasoline in the stifling heat and restore ourselves with some humus at a little café.*

This world of street foods is the world of the "other," a world in which Dalia is both a welcome guest and an outsider. She is a free spirit, and her embracing of the world outside her home is also an act of resistance. Dalia describes the interior of her home, both architecturally and psychologically, as a space that did not exude warmth: "My parents were really old-world. They were older people. I was an only child and they adhered to strict, old-fashioned European values." This old-worldliness extended to food, as Dalia's parents attempted to preserve European etiquette within a home that was surrounded by the larger homeland of the Middle East. They believed their European cocoon would shelter Dalia from the "dirtiness of the streets." For Dalia, the street represented an intoxicating freedom. Dalia, as an only child, was severed from the common language, memories, food, and culture her parents shared. Moreover, the marriage of antiquated Europe with the Middle East was not felicitous.

The Weiser household was fragmented. Later, in 1955, when Dalia was stationed with the Israeli Embassy in England, she was required to change her name from Weiser to Carmel to be easily visible as an Israeli. She held on to Carmel, even when she married Herb Goldstein in 1978. "I was Carmel from 1955 to 1978, so I was not about to let go so easily." The retention and discarding of a name is central to the narratives of the psychological exile. As a child Dalia was sent to a British Jewish Orthodox school where she encountered a tension between having to maintain an Orthodox facade at school—modest dress, prayer, kosher food—and having to shed it in her secular home. In her parents' attempt to fatten Dalia up, cream was a constant companion—so *kashrut* (keeping kosher) was an impossibility. Furthermore, her parents lied about the identities of food.

We were consuming all this treyf. *"What's that, I would ask?" pointing to a rabbit leg. "Oh, that's a chicken leg," my mother would answer. "Well, that's a peculiar-shaped chicken leg." At that point my father would turn to my mother and say in German, "You have to be cautious now. She's getting to identify the anatomy of animals." Of course, I never told them that I could understand their "secret" German.*

Schpitzenbrust *Soup—A Reconstruction in America*

My mother was a fabulous cook and baker. She made delicious beef soup. Our "holiday soup." My father would create a whole ritual out of it. At lunchtime my mother would serve the meat and the soup separately. And my father, the lung surgeon, would tenderly shave off very white, thin slices of fat and place them on a piece of challah with a little salt and horseradish. These precious morsels were then parceled out to my mother and me. What a delicacy—savoring the taste was almost ceremonial. This was one of my favorite soups. I was about seven at the time.

Years later, when I got married to a man who loved soups, I wanted to re-create the taste of my mother's beef soup. Here I was an adult, searching for what I had absorbed as a child at home. So I began to ask various friends' mothers about how they make their beef soups. They suggested soup with short ribs, deckel, flanken soup with onion, turnip, celery root, parsley, dill. I made them all. They were all scrumptious, but they weren't my mother's soup. The childhood aroma was sadly absent. And then one day it was like an epiphany! I remembered that sometimes on my way to school my mother would ask me to stop at the butcher and have him prepare the Schpitzenbrust, which I would pick up later. A day or so later there was soup to die for. The aroma was just heaven. So I turned to the German butchers in Yorkville "Have you heard of Schpitzenbrust?" They had. "Which cut of meat would you sell me?" One said the first cut of the brisket, but he was hesitant, and another said the second cut. Determined to uncover the aroma of Schpitzenbrust, I made my way to Joe, the Italian butcher across the street. From Joe I bought the whole brisket. At home I cut it in half, selecting the first cut of meat, which comes to a point. I set up the soup with all the vegetables and condiments and placed them in a pot on the stove. I went to take a shower. And when I came out. Aah! The aroma of my mother's Schpitzenbrust soup. It was like my mother had come to embrace me from the soup pot in my kitchen.

As I watch and listen to Dalia recounting her father's ritual and the search for her mother's *Schpitzenbrust* soup—I say "watch" and "listen" because it is both a visual and auditory theatrical experience—I am there partaking in their feast. Through her extended sighs, raised eyebrows, and linguistic manipulation, Dalia builds a story like a rare gift. Dalia is able to revive a time that is lost. She has a forte for rendering these food memories in explicit, delicious detail. As the listener, you are transported back to the event, and it carries a whiff of the ceremonial, the sacred. Dalia is absolutely secular as a Jew, but her stories radiate a religious fervor. The stories Dalia dramatizes often appear within Jewish landscapes, wrapped in a Jewish essence.

And so as I was saying, my parents force-fed me like a goose. I was just a skinny beans in those days, skinnier than you! I went to an olive oil lecture and tasting yesterday. My God, all these doctors speaking to themselves about olive oil! I began to think that if these doctors could just see into the bodies, the bodies of the past, there they would meet all the lards and the floating pork fat with paprika. Everything in my home was cooked with butter and cream. The cream became almost like a layer of skin, just another color or a sauce.

As Dalia's stories unfold, I see a parade of historical bodies celebrating the past and the present. Her parents weren't privy to the dangers of excessive fat and cholesterol. Dalia, born in 1935, is a witness to the body in transition, because she follows the changing fashions and aesthetics of food. She was born in Israel, which was then Palestine, a colonial land, which itself exemplifies layers of fragmentation: time, place, culture, and politics. Palestine is a land that symbolizes displacement. It is a country that has lost its name (like Dalia herself)—the plight of many colonial lands in transition. Perhaps this erasure accounts for the rich, concrete detail of Dalia's food memories. Since her past is so tenuous, it is the memories of food that allow her to recall the past with the vibrancy of the present.

Dalia objects to the sobriety I infuse into her food stories. "You have to have fun with food," she admonishes me. "Nor should you imply that food is my entire life, my being. I have other interests, passions. For example, music. Did I tell you that my mother would never allow me to just listen to music without doing anything? So when I began cooking in New York and the opera would come on, on a Saturday afternoon, I would head straight to the kitchen to create. I would fly to the pots and the pans before I could hear, guiltily, her voice in my head. 'You just can't sit around doing nothing!'" This work ethic manifests itself in various ways in Dalia's life. Dalia is an impeccable and rigorous reader of the cookbook. She witnesses stories, philosophy, history, culture, and critique far beyond the words on the page. She admits to disappointment when the recipe fails to include a supporting story.

How I Learned to Gossip in Yiddish

Dalia tells me I am "treading on peculiar ice" by speaking about Palestine as a place that no longer exists. In the Palestinian imagination, Palestine will and always has existed.

I lived in an area in which the State of Israel existed. Palestine didn't mean a thing—it was just a location. The State was "created" as a home for the Jews, and the place was in a constant flux. You can't imagine the type of problems this brought about. Can you imagine all of a sudden there were storekeepers who only spoke Yiddish? The grocery store closest to our house was owned by new immigrants. They were Holocaust survivors from Poland. They spoke to all their customers, older Eastern European Jews, in Yiddish. So there I was listening to "half a challah," "half a bar of butter" in Yiddish. Not to mention all the gossip in that place. The days were hot and sultry. And there was a certain rhythm, a cadence to those particular sounds. There in the grocery store on the corner I learned to gossip. And I learned Yiddish.

> Now there are some people, even scholars and teachers, who you will hear say, Jewish is not a real language. For them, it was inferior. It came out of exile, or the language of exile, for the marketplace. It was for women to talk to children. Not good for big subjects. For these you need Hebrew or Russian or Polish or English. This is nonsense. Jewish we call the mamaloshen. That means more than mother tongue. It is the *mother's* tongue because this was the language the mother talked, sweet or bitter. It was your own. It is a language of the heart (Shmuel, an elderly Jewish man, quoted in Myerhoff 60–61).

Here in the grocery store of Dalia's childhood, Yiddish is perfumed with sensuality. Yiddish is a language that unites the Diaspora Jews. Dalia's parents' common language was German. They never had the privilege of speaking their *mamaloshen* with each other. "My father would speak Hungarian with his friends, my mother would speak Russian to hers. They spoke German to each other and Hebrew to me. My father's Hebrew improved much more than my mother's because he worked in the outside world. When my mother became angry or tired, she would speak the funniest Hebrew, something like this: 'Close the window, there is a private wind!'" Dalia tells me this in Hebrew. The English version limps in comparison.

There are many problems inherent in transcribing another individual's stories. Vincent Crapanzano, in his experimental ethnography *Tuhami,* reveals that a "historical text is often closer to fantasy and the imagination than it is to fact." When dealing with personal histories such as Dalia's, there is a struggle between "reality" (resistance) and "desire," which the author mediates via the idiom. Ethnographer, informant, and audience are all invested in how they perceive "story" and "fact." Crapanzano destabilizes the exchange between ethnographer and informant. He muddies the notion of neutrality. In the exchange between Dalia and myself, and within our revisitation of the text, I notice how neutrality is contentious. Dalia often says to me, "I didn't say that" even though I have recorded her words verbatim. I, as her audience, "hear" the words according to the text of my own life, and, at times, Dalia's words exist in tension with her own imagination. Within the act of recording the story—and her story is intertwined with history—there is a collapse of fact.

The performance of the story is enmeshed with the memory. Dalia engages the performative aspects of storytelling in the timbre of her voice (resonant here, booming there); in the way she reels you in, saving the punch line or the juicy bits for last. She builds toward a climax. She is aware of her position within her environment: how she presents her body within the space, the size of her audience, how she holds her hand, her head. Dalia's stories cascade with humor and delicious pauses. The problem that I, as interlocutor, face when transcribing the stories is similar to the problems inherent in transliteration. I am translating the stories. Somehow the performance, so alive in Dalia's reportage, evaporates, and I am left with the blank pages and the rattling of my fingers against the keyboard.

Restaurant Events Really Don't Last

And you're at one of the best, most expensive restaurants. You're dressed to kill, and the company around you is magnificent. You think you can retain the memory of the aroma, and the taste of that event, that you can grasp it and keep it . . . and it just evaporates. I find that restaurant events really don't last. I recall, for instance, Jacques Pepin was going to cook at a restaurant called La Tulipe *in the Village. I was adamant to go there—he's a wonderful chef and a teacher. I've seen him on TV and I've read his books. So I bugged the restaurant every hour on the hour. Finally, somebody canceled and I got the reservation. I was already married at the time, but I went with a cousin whom I love dearly. We had a very good table—my cousin is six foot seven—so we needed a table that had leg room. Across from me in sort of a diagonal line was James Beard—you know, the father of American cooking. I gasped, "My God, James Beard himself," and he nodded and I nodded. My cousin said, "Do you know him?" I said, "No, but everyone knows James Beard," and my cousin said, "I want another table—we're having dinner together, and I don't want you to make eyes to nobody!" And so we changed tables, which didn't have room for either one's legs! The food was phenomenal. But all I remember were some* quenelles *on the plate. And I thought I would be able to retain every part of that meal because when I finished the meal, I said, "I'm throwing all the pots out and I'm closing the kitchen." The meal was paradise, but do you know, I cannot remember anything I ate? I remember the place, and I remember the table, and I remember James Beard, and I remember that to our right was another couple who had been neighbors of Pierre Franey. These neighbors kept on peering at our food, and they just about got into our plates and ate with us. I just don't remember what we ate. But I do remember—it was divine.*

In Dalia's humorous recounting, it's ironic that the food itself is absent, divorced from the memory. What remains paramount in Dalia's memory is the physical landscape or architectural decor surrounding the meal. But the food itself evaporates. Dalia remembers the particular day and its happenings—the restaurant, Franey's intrusive neighbors, James Beard—the theater of the event. Then why is she unable to retain a memory of the food? I am arrested, taken off guard. Whenever Dalia speaks about food, her memory is as crisp as fried bacon. And here at La Tulipe, the food floats above us—a phantom. Dalia's restaurant memories, except for Byblos, a Lebanese restaurant near her home, are evanescent.

Within the theater of the restaurant, the character of food drops out, assuming backstage to the environment. In the restaurant Dalia is just one of the multiple personalities in the frequented set design. But what about the backdrop of her personal kitchen? Here Dalia is the professional, the leading lady. Memories of the kitchen are not fleeting. I enter Dalia's kitchen and imagine the creations that occur here in this compact place. An eclectic display of kitchen magnets adorning the refrigerator catches my eye. Pans, pots, skillets, all dark and sturdy, hang from the ceiling in a neatly aligned chaos. Oh, the array of knives! Dalia's kitchen is aesthetically more about the hidden than the visible. "When we moved into this apartment, I was more concerned about a living room to accommodate these Klipsch horn speakers," says Dalia pointing to the monstrous stereo equipment. "I wasn't paying attention to the kitchen." Yet within this diminutive space, where there is barely room to turn around, Dalia has managed to find a home for butcher blocks, an army of implements, and an alluring display of spice jars. Within this tiny space, magic and memory are created.

The memory of food becomes really alive for me when I am in my own kitchen cooking one of my mother's recipes which I love, like creamed spinach, chicken paprika, brisket soup. In my re-creation, I am guided by a discernible memory of aroma and taste. A taste which was plentiful. An aroma which I visited and do visit often.

The Spitting Seeds

Home is a central character in the makeup of Dalia Carmel and in the presentation of these food narratives. I ask her: Where is "home" for you? I know you were born in Jerusalem—so is that your home, or is New York City your home after so many years?

I have a house in Israel, not a "home." Yet, my sense of going home is always to Israel. But I hated Ramat Yitzchak (a suburb of Tel Aviv), where we moved when I was fifteen. Ramat Yitzchak, an ugly-looking neighborhood, was chiefly an Iraqi town with old men sitting on the corners, cracking seeds and spitting them onto the streets. I hated the place. But it's ironic, I befriended this guy down the street who had muscular dystrophy, and it was because of him that I kept finding myself back in the neighborhood. This Meir Iny was a prisoner of his body, and it was through him that I came to terms with this neighborhood and the house. Meir's mother was Iraqi, and she would invite me into their home and into the meals of God. She made the most wonderful M'juddara—you went to heaven and you didn't need an elevator. Cooked rice and lentils, sprinkled with fried onions, fried garlic, topped with an egg, sunny-side up—all served in a bowl with this wonderful yogurt on the side. It was sort of a Lent dish used on the first nine days of Av. I remember one Friday night during the Yom Kippur War. I was supposed to go there for dinner, and then I received this urgent call to return to New York. Meir's mother insisted that I stop at the house on my way to the airport. And there she was at the doorstep, urging me to ladle overflowing spoonfuls of M'juddara *down my throat.*

Meir's and Dalia's parents, who are all now dead, are ghosts residing in her memory. Even though they cannot exist in her present, through food Dalia can retain their essence. This reconstruction of the past in the present is not only attained through food, although food is a tangible tool, it can also be re-created through a memory of a gesture, an idiosyncrasy. Dalia says that often when she is walking upstairs, she feels her mother walking behind her, because her own gait and footsteps are identical to her mother's. I am aware how Dalia's stories move over and through each other. Now, after having interviewed Dalia on separate occasions, I realize how particular, yet interconnected the stories are. And in my attempt to render them, they leak into one another, wearing the transient character of memory.

Steam rising from the pot and a little bubble of smoke like in the cartoons. A caricature. Now within the blurb of steam is a story, a memory. Poof. It's just like a cloud. Light and Wispy.

Baguette Beurré avec Jambon

In 1955 I went to Paris. It was my first time out of Israel. I was sent by the army to London and I decided to stop in Paris. In Porte de Clighancourt there was this lively flea market. I stopped at one of the sidewalk cafés. It was during Pesach. *And I had a* baguette beurré avec jambon. *It was divine and really, really "kosher." And somehow I have always remembered the taste. It was like drinking that celestial first drink of water after being parched. I have always wanted to revisit the taste of the baguette beurré avec jambon. And so, when I went with Herb to Normandy many years later, guess what the first thing I wanted to taste was? But it was never quite the same. I think the accordion player was missing.*

Dalia's desire to reconstruct the baguette beurré avec jambon is connected with her tenacious thirst for independence. This type of memory is corporeal, connected with everyday life. The food itself is a simple food, in contrast to the fancy French cuisine at Lutèce or the experience at La Tulipe. The baguette beurré avec jambon is a food of sustenance, like the drops of water. This rustic experience is minimalist compared to the stylized restaurant experience. Dalia's virgin taste of the baguette beurré avec jambon, inscribed in the mise-en-scène of her first expedition away from home, is a rite of passage.

The Soup That Never Turned Golden

My mother was a wonderful cook. When I left home I didn't know how to boil water. When I came to the United States, I got a studio apartment and I set up home. The first thing I did was to run out to Woolworth and buy a beautiful set of one-ply aluminum pots and pans. I readied myself to become a gourmet cook. The first thing I remember wanting to cook was soup, and a curry chicken with rice. In our home rice was never cooked, only potatoes. I remember my mother put bones in her soup, with an onion and some greens—so I bought that. I took out my new shiny pot, put in a few bones, an onion, salt, lots of pepper, lots of water, and I cooked it for hours. But nothing happened. I said to myself, this is very strange. My mother's soup was always so golden. And here, this thing—this peppered water—is white, with none of my mother's delicious fragrance. That was my first soup.

I now want to tell my own story, about the yellow gefilte fish. I grew up in South Africa, and my Lithuanian maternal grandmother, Anita, always made the gefilte fish. They were round and solid, very yellow, with carrot nipples perched on top. When I came to America, I was horrified at the flat, lengthy, white pieces of gefilte fish drowning in a gelatinous, repugnant mold. At the age of thirty-four, I said to my mother on the telephone:

"Mom, I miss Granny's gefilte fish." "When you come home, I will teach you how to make Granny's gefilte fish from scratch." "You know, there is something I have always been puzzled about. Where did Granny get yellow fish? Why don't they have it in America?" My mother laughs. "Leeky, darling, you mean to say you didn't know it was food coloring?"

War Stories: A Lentil Is a Lentil Is a Lentil

I have to tell you about the supermarket. Around the same time as I bought these Woolworth pots and pans to begin a new life as a gourmet cook in New York, I decided it was time to pay a visit to the supermarket. I went on Friday to D'Agostino, which was on 36th Street and Third Avenue. D'Agostino was pretty small at the time. It was Friday and hectic, and I was embarrassed to stop and read the labels on the cans. But I was unfamiliar with the items. Growing up in Israel, a product of the War of Independence generation, my mother had always taught me: "You have to have cans of meat, chicken, potatoes—two of each in the pantry, in case of war." So I went to the can aisle and bought two beef, two chicken, two of this, and two of that. As I was waiting to check out, I was thinking to myself, only these peculiar Americans would have a picture of a cat or a dog on their cans. So with my robust cart, I proudly prepared to check out. The cashier said to me, "I see you have a kennel." I smiled. Kennel, I didn't know what a kennel was. To this day I still don't know all the words. When I came home and finally read the label on one of those cans, I laughed to myself. Now I know what a kennel is. So back to the supermarket I went, to return all the cat and dog food for my pantry security blanket.

Dalia inherits her mother's anxiety about war. She carries this anxiety, which is deeply connected with food, as a talisman with her to America. In the same way that her mother's footsteps linger with Dalia on the stairs, so does her mother's advice. Dalia often speaks about experiences with her mother as "lessons."

During the Second World War, my mother bought a sack of lentils and it came into use years later during the siege on Jerusalem. At the time we had no food, no water, no electricity, no gas—nothing. So my mother used to cook on the terrace. My mother had a samovar, which she used to fill with bits of wood that she collected outside. She would cook something up in the samovar from the lentils. We would have lentils forever—lentil soup, lentil patties, lentil puree. The aroma of lentils was imprinted lit-

erally in my mind. Usually the mind attempts to block out unpleasant memories, but traumatic things are indelible. We came out of the war and life was fine. But whenever I would come to somebody's home, even to deliver a letter, and there would be the aroma of lentils cooking, that night I would have nightmares of sirens and bombs. Because we were forced to eat lentils day in and day out, it remained as a sign of grief.

Some of Dalia's stories are situated around wars, so within the recalling there is often a simultaneous absence and excess of food. The deprivation accentuates the poignancy of food in Dalia's life and memory.

In the midst of her animated stories, Dalia will often use untranslatable sounds that reflect her cultural identity. When she tells her tale of lentils, harsh, clucking sounds inflect the painful association. I gradually notice how sounds infiltrate and inform our conversations. Often these resonances speak far beyond formal language.

Eggs were rationed during the War of Independence, and I've always loved eggs. So one day my mother and I deliriously promised each other that when the war was over, we were going to cook dozens and dozens of hard-boiled eggs and eat them with abandon. We were invited to a Seder in 1950. The relatives of my father were Hungarian and moved to a place, which was called Beit Dagon, *with an orchard where they raised pigs and chickens. They were a family with three proper Hungarian daughters—Kato, Lizl, and Magda. The farm was across the street from the police station and voluptuous Kato used to like to sun herself naked in the orchard. You could see the policemen with binoculars on the roof leering at the brown, solid Kato. We went to the Seder, and I was wearing a navy blue dress with a white collar and a belt pulled tightly at the back, which made your waist as tiny as possible. The white collar was decorated with flowers.*

We entered the room where the Seder was going to be held, and there was a bowl of hard-boiled eggs. I mean eggs three times as many as the people around the table. And my mother and I exchanged glances that said, "We're going to do it today!" We had all the trimmings, the matzoth, the harosset, *and then we arrived at the eggs—Aah, eggs and salt water. So I had one and I had two and I had five, I had seven and I had nine. My mother stopped at I think four or five, but I had nine and my father said, "There's still a whole meal!"* (Dalia collapses in a chorus of laughter.) *Then we had the Seder meal, and I didn't leave anything on my plate. I*

helped bring the stuff from the table to the kitchen, and there in the bowl was the hu-
mongous hard-boiled egg—a duck's egg. I was not going to leave that, and so I ate
it with tremendous relish. And all of a sudden pop . . . my bra . . . the whole room
heard it. I had ten eggs and the duck's egg was the biggest of the lot. Never again
have I eaten a boiled duck's egg!

I try to imagine Dalia as that fifteen-year-old girl with the snapping bra. She
inserts me emphatically into the scene and I desire to see it in my mind's
eye. All those bodies in abandonment—the three Hungarian sisters, and
Dalia gorging herself on a boiled duck's egg.

The Sleuthhound of Books

You know, I think we have really missed something in this project and that's my
cookbook collection. To understand my connection to food, you have to look at my
own collection. I'm not a mother of six, and I don't cook to entertain large groups as
I used to do before Herb became ill. But I am a sleuth of cookbooks. Let me give
you an example. There's this magazine, The International Cook Revue, *pub-*
lished in Spain. It is a glossary of sorts, which annotates cookbooks of various na-
tionalities and languages. For me, it is a treasure because I use it in the sport of find-
ing cookbooks, not for its scholarship. So for example, a year ago, I spotted a picture
and a title called Traditional Slovenian Cookery. *Listed below was only the pub-*
lisher, with no city, address, or contact number. Can you imagine? It's mind-
boggling—all they have to do is write one extra line. Well, I was intrigued because
as far as I know there are no Slovenian cookbooks published in English, and I know
very little about Slovenian cooking. So I contacted the Yugoslav consulate here in
New York, and they provided me with the address of the publisher. I've been fax-
ing and writing the Slovenian publisher for a year. I write in English and so I ex-
pect the whole world to read English, but this is not so. I persevered because I don't
like to fail, and finally . . . the Traditional Slovenian Cookery *book arrived two*
days ago! A one-year job of sleuthing accomplished. There are all these peculiar-
looking dishes with Slovenian names. Listen to this one—fried sauerkraut. Can
you imagine the aroma of that? I could just jump out of the window. Salad of hop,
an ingredient I've never heard of—but I'm going to investigate. So this is my
Slovenian success. Now I'm onto a new sleuth.

Dalia ferrets out cookbooks from all the corners of the world. She admits that some places hold little fascination for her. She needs to be intrigued by their aesthetic. She is also attracted by the strange. Anything that carries a scent of the obscure or the undiscovered appeals to her. The focus of her collection is on ethnic and international books—she doesn't collect American cookbooks and has eliminated most of Great Britain.

Dalia's vast collection, in a sense, is a solace for the fact that she herself can no longer cook as prolifically as before. She has retired into a more private sphere as an entertainer. She expresses a wistfulness over this loss because she adores cooking for large groups: "When I was in my twenties, on Saturday afternoons, I would listen to the direct-broadcast opera from the Met. I'd feel so creative, turning raw ingredients into all this bounty. And then the opera was over, and I'd say who the hell made all of this? So I would round up the neighbors. It was such a fun time."

"To Dalia Carmel. 'A cousin born in Jerusalem who exemplifies the Arab virtues of generosity and kinship. One's cousin is like a wing to a falcon. Can falcons fly without wings?'" So reads the dedication to Anne Marie Weiss Armush's book *The Arabian Delights Cookbook: Mediterranean Cuisine from Mecca to Marrakech*. Dalia glows as she shows the dedication to me. These epigraphs left by friends attest to Dalia's reputation as a lover of food. They also are testimony to her privileging of friends, who indeed become family. Dalia gives, and these epigraphs return. They document memory, the past, and serve as links to the future. These words, like the books themselves, will remain behind. A legacy.

I like sharing knowledge, cuisines, names, contacts. It is the act of sharing, giving, and partaking that attracts me. I would never become a professional chef because I'm just too old. The work is too arduous, standing on your feet for so many hours. But I had and still have my dreams about having a nice little café.

Mothers and Grandmothers

Every year my mother would make the most delicious, fluffy matzo balls. Every year without fail she would serve them to my father. And every year without fail my father would say, "Mmm good, but when I was a child my mother's were lighter." My father's mother, Mrs. Weiser, moved to Milwaukee when I was still a child in Israel. I never really liked her. She was a cold woman. When I moved to New York, I decided to visit her in Wisconsin. I did everything I could think of in my desperate attempt to make her like me. So I began to talk about my father. I told her about the past Seders, cautiously making my way to the matzo ball story. Do you know what she said to me? "I never made matzo balls in all my life!"

One of my favorite cakes that my mother used to make was a mocha hazelnut torte. It was flourless, with a smattering of breadcrumbs and a fabulous mocha butter cream. We came upon this cake in 1951 in Neve On, near Tel Aviv, and it later became our family's signature cake. We were invited to this young Hungarian couple's house in 1951. The husband was a resident in my father's hospital. Food was still rationed then. I remember that I was sixteen, and I distinctly remember the young bride's name—Mrs. Gaspar. Well, she baked this cake that was like a trip to heaven. I remember my father just about swooned and called it something in Hungarian. For him it was like a journey back to his own mother. My mother asked Mrs. Gaspar for the recipe, and we just about died when she told us it called for nine or ten eggs. Nine or ten eggs was unheard of in 1951. I think during the rations we were only allowed five eggs per week. When life became "normal," my mother would bake the hazelnut torte every year for my father's birthday on May 3 and my own birthday on September 1. It truly was a cake from heaven. In those days we had these old small refrigerators with ice trays, and there was no aluminum foil or plastic wrap. Well, my mother would always save me a piece of the cake when I was away from home. And one of my most vivid memories is enjoying that cake accompanied by the metallic aroma of the refrigerator, absorbed by the mocha butter cream. I wouldn't give up my piece for anything, so I learned to relish it with the refrigerator aroma. Every possible September 1 I would return to Israel for my cake. Until 1968, when my mother was struggling with breast cancer, and I told her I was coming home for my birthday cake. And when I returned, there was a cake but it wasn't my cake. And my mother didn't know what I was talking about. I couldn't believe that she couldn't make the cake.

After my mother died, I found her recipes. I tried to get a couple of my friends to bake the cake, but it was never right. You see, I could never make it myself. My mother really knew how to bake. Her recipe is full of holes and missing links. And I don't want to fail. If I make it, it has to be exactly like it was.

Just as Dalia quested for the *Schpitzenbrust* soup, she hungers also to reproduce the mocha hazelnut torte. The cake is written by its originator, Dalia's
mother, and so it is canonized in a sense. The soup recipe is an oral recipe,
reproduced through trial and error, sleuthing and approximation, elimina-
tion and improvisation. Within the subtext of Dalia's mother's torte recipe,
fear and loss are inscribed. The recipe for the mocha hazelnut torte, with
its many holes and silences, evokes a ghostliness. Dalia cannot bake her
mother's mocha hazelnut torte.

Epilogue

I think about the irreverent act—my inhalation of Dalia's stories into the far
reaches of my belly. The stories linger inside of me. They move around, fox-
trotting here and there with the stories of my own life. Here, they meet my
grandmother's yellow gefilte fish with the orange carrots perched on their
very yellow bodies. Here, they mutate, don a new timbre, before I exhale
them out onto the white page. I listen to the dull click of my computer keys,
no longer rattling. They are pallid in their reverberation of what once was and
is no longer. Dalia's voice and face perch high above my computer screen. Her
river face. Her peanut-brittle laugh. She has another story for me.

*The cake is elusive. It should remain elusive. Certain things are nicer when they
remain as memories.*

WORKS CITED

Crapanzano, Vincent. *Tuhami: Portrait of a Moroccan*. Chicago: U of Chicago P, 1980.

Myerhoff, Barbara. *Number Our Days*. New York: Dutton, 1978.

CHAPTER FOUR

Writing and Cooking, Cooking and Writing
Lynn Z. Bloom

Writing and cooking are two of the things I like to do best. Indeed, they're a lot alike—a messy mix of knowledge and improvisation, experience and innovation, and continual revision with a lot going on between the lines. For years I've toyed with writing a cookbook. But although I'm willing to revise my writing indefinitely until I get it right, I'm not willing to revise my cooking the way Rose Levy Beranbaum did when she wrote *The Cake Bible*. She baked draft after draft of yellow cake, the subject of her master's thesis, until it floated out of the oven, light as a whisper, flirting alternately with sweet and with tart. Fifteen versions in two weeks, or so I imagine.

That's about right for revising a manuscript, but what would my husband and I do with a cake a day? We had enough trouble getting rid of the Friendship Bread, a millstone in doughy disguise. I've never learned to make bread because Martin does that so well I don't need to know how. Today he's making sourdough baguettes with sun-dried tomatoes from our own garden. A dozen years ago, returning from the Sierra Nevada where I had gone to edit the wartime diary of Margaret Sams, I had carried back to Virginia her gift of a sourdough starter, a bubbly descendant of pioneer stock. Margaret's great-grandmother had transported it to Sacramento in a covered wagon 140 years earlier. Mine made the return journey by jet, its adolescent vigor threatening to break the Mason jar in transit. A neighbor once gave us, in desperation, we later realized, a starter for Friendship Bread (aka Hermann Bread, aka Amish Bread), a sweet, yeasty concoction

calculated to create enemies because it doubled daily in bulk and had to be
fobbed off on still other neighbors. They grew as quickly sick of it as we
did until we hustled it off to the compost heap where for weeks we'd catch
glimpses of it creeping, amoeba-like, from beneath rotting cabbage leaves.

But I digress. This is much easier to do when I'm cooking than when
I'm writing, unless I'm writing about cooking, a continual digression, for
every recipe is full of stories. Although writing, like cooking, demands an
audience for the finished product, the dialogue in my head when I write—
with other writers, readers, myself—is spoken aloud when I cook. If no
one's in the kitchen with me, I'm on the phone, a cordless model in perpetual danger of dropping into the dish du jour while I talk with students,
family, friends, editors, and colleagues. The night before last, for instance, I
peeled ten cups of Ida Red seconds for a pie while helping a grad student,
herself a pie baker, explore a dissertation prospectus on working-class auto-
biographies. During the next conversation of substance I'll peel and sauté
the onions for the onion soup I've been contemplating making for several
wintry weeks. In fact, writing this sentence has impelled me to call the
butcher to make sure he has beef bones in stock. He does, but how many
pounds? A frantic flipping through Julia Child yields only vague clues, but
there, on page 40 of *The New All Purpose Joy of Cooking* lies the answer: five
pounds. I'd guessed six, and I can relax. I'm planning to make the salad for
our impending dinner party during a long-distance call to my mother.
"What are you cooking this week?" she invariably asks, anticipating the ob-
bligato of chopping and dishwashing.

But the cooking is more fun when the kitchen is full of those very people
who make the phone calls, as it has been since the day my German grandmother wrapped me twice around with an apron and I climbed up on a
chair to pinch fanciful shapes from leftover strips of pie dough stretched on
the floury red vinyl counter. I learned to cook by watching my grandmother and my mother and through considerable experimentation, as well
as from a stew of cookbooks. My recollection is that Mom did all the fun
parts while assigning me to peel the potatoes and scrub the carrots, but since
I have always loved to cook there must have been pleasure beyond root vegetables. I learned to write by total immersion in a broth of books and a lot
of practice and false starts and careful attention to the sounds as well as to

the sense. So I absorbed Dr. Seuss, my earliest favorite author, followed soon by Louisa May Alcott, and later by Dr. Spock, subject of my first après-dissertation book. If to write was to join the conversation of mankind, to cook as an adolescent was to join the conversation of womankind, expanded in adult life to a colloquy with the world. Scraps of that communion over the years remain in the exchange of recipes, and the resulting recipe file, a history of friendships over time and distance.

As I write this, I flip through my bulging recipe file, crammed with recipes like rings on a redwood. The scent of chocolate wafts up from clippings and cards written in diverse hands. A card with a patina of tomato-y fingerprints is labeled Lentil Soup from Fifi, a neighbor in Indianapolis thirty years ago. This succulent concoction includes lots of carrots, dried mushrooms, "a slug of red wine," and seasoning with basil and vinegar instead of salt in deference to Jim's—her husband's—high blood pressure. It remains the gold standard of lentil soup and memento of a golden friendship, imbued with the absent presence of Jim, who has since died. Indeed, this recipe file contains a movable feast, my lifelong dialogue with fellow cooks, a history of friendships. The card for Kleff's Kale is suspiciously clean. Could wariness of that aggressive leaf have kept us from re-creating this standout from the marathon Middle Eastern cooking sessions in our Williamsburg kitchen? With Ramsey Kleff, Martin's social research colleague, as impresario, we always made so much food we had to call up extra guests on the spot to share the overrun. I learned the labels—Dolma, Baba Ghanoush, Kibbeh, Tabbouli—long after the orderly chaos in our kitchen had subsided. But when Martin and I visited Ramsey's mother in Haifa, we came to understand essence and substance alike, for she stuffed us with food and tales of compassion, Christian and Jewish, Arab and Israeli, and blessed us with two baskets of savory leftovers for the road.

On a besplotched index card is Jerry's Salad Dressing, vinegar-and-oil with two surprise ingredients, onion juice and Worcestershire sauce. Along with Chicken-Sparerib Adobo, this is a lagniappe from my research in 1965 in Cleveland, where I began to edit Natalie Crouter's *Forbidden Diary*, a record of her family's imprisonment in a Japanese camp in the Philippines during World War II. Natalie herself could scarcely boil an egg, even when her life really did depend on it; Jerry, her husband, did the cooking in prison camp and invented these recipes that survived two world wars. When the prisoners were weak from hunger they would "spend hours talking of food," feeding their imaginations with prewar repasts. "Gingerbread with whipped cream or hard sauce, apple sauce, whole wheat bread with gobs of butter—endless lines of dishes parade in our talks," Natalie wrote, "each talker going the other one better. Clara copies British cookbook recipes all day and reads them out to us" (November 4, 1944). My own children, Bard and Laird, didn't dare complain about the food at home, for they knew I'd retaliate with paragraphs from the Crouters' starvation diet at the end of the war, two handfuls of dirty, moldy rice garnered bit by bit from "cracks in the storeroom floor" (November 12, 1944). Writing long accounts of camp life daily in her clandestine diary, an activity punishable by death, was for Natalie as life sustaining as eating. "This diary," she wrote after eight months' incarceration, "is a safety valve! It is a rock through the window!" (October 5, 1942).

As I write this I am interrupted by a phone call from Waldo, Martin's colleague, "What can we bring for dinner?" "Dessert," I say without hesitation, hoping secretly for a rhubarb pie from the fruit of their garden. Even if it's technically a vegetable, rhubarb works like a fruit. Turning again to the recipe file, I encounter Polly's Microwave Risotto with Asparagus. She'll be at dinner next week, too. She's an economist and collector of antique children's books, and I am as grateful to her for giving me a book sale find of Julia Child's *Mastering the Art of French Cooking,* first edition, as I am for her lucid explanation of the euro. I don't know how she found such a pristine volume. In my kitchen, good cookbooks get so sticky and spotted from service on the front lines that I don't dare borrow library copies. The cookbooks likely to turn up at library sales run to specialized exotica, *The Whole Anchovy Cookbook;* outmoded tastes, *The Joys of Jell-O;* or astounding concoctions, *Radio Recipes,* heavy on combinations of canned mushroom soup, ketchup, fake bacon bits, and crushed potato chips. Good cookbooks, tattered and grubby from honorable use, stay home where they belong.

How happy I've been to have a second chance for rapprochement with Julia. When I was writing *Doctor Spock. Biography of a Conservative Radical*—my futile hope to end the Vietnam War—with my preschool sons playing in the same room because I couldn't say, "Go away, don't bother me, I'm writing about Doctor Spock," I gave Fifi my copy of Julia Child. (Julia salts with discretion.) This was the very bonus I'd joined Book-of-the-Month Club to get, along with the *Compact Edition of the Oxford English Dictionary* in the two hefty volumes. So absorbed was I, however, with my children and my writing ("Move over, Ben," Martin would say night after night as we climbed into bed) that I could scarcely even read Julia's long, detailed recipes straight through. Everything I tried was a failure, for she demanded a concentration and devotion to nuance at a time when I needed to get to the point in a hurry. So I relied at the time on two svelte paperbacks, Peg Bracken's *I Hate to Cook Book* and Marion Burros's *Elegant but Easy.* With the children grown, I am happy to return to the kitchen with Julia, even though Boeuf à la Bourguignonne takes two fat pages to one skinny column of Beef Stew with Wine in *The Joy of Cooking.* I usually make this toothsome dish two days in advance of the day my grad students come to dinner, a recompense for reading their term papers aloud, and reheat it in the oven so the succulence will permeate the house when they arrive. I want their reading to be imbued with the subtle essence of the climactic dinner-party scene in Virginia Woolf's *To the Lighthouse,* Mrs. Ramsay's gift to the guests and family she loves and, with her own death imminent, will never see again.

What recipe did Mrs. Ramsay give her cook to use, I wonder. Probably none at all. For the language of food is not the language of recipes but the language of cooks, communicated as surely and eloquently through their creations as the most sophisticated discourse emerging through scholarly articles. Neither my grandmother, who went through eighth grade, nor my college-educated mother relied much on cookbooks. The only cookbook in my mother's house to this day is a 1944 *Woman's Home Companion Cookbook,* its daunting advice (cook spinach, brussels sprouts, and cauliflower a full forty-five minutes) ignored. That their breads were light, their piecrusts flaky, their pot roasts tender, and their chicken soups full-bodied with falling-off-the-bone chicken chunks and golden homemade noodles attests to the wisdom of long years of practice—and Mom's desire to beat her mother-in-law at her own game. They never wrote down recipes, never tried to transform an art into a science, in tacit acknowledgment of the fact that most good cooks regard recipes the way good writers regard dictionaries, as sources of inspiration, with license to improvise.

Although grammar books would be a closer analogy to cookbooks than dictionaries are, such comparison would be not only infelicitous but inaccurate. I don't know any real writer who reads grammar books or even uses them for reference, though I've met a couple who have written them. In a moment of weakness, over a very elaborate, very costly lunch in Manhattan, I once agreed to write a very large handbook of grammar and mechanics for a very large publisher. It was to include all the rules college freshpersons would ever need to know, and many they would not. Over dessert, Chocolate Damnation, a seductive blend of chocolate and raspberry I recall to this day, I agreed to write a workbook, and over espresso I said sure, I'd do a teacher's manual as well. Today, with further infusions of butter and sugar I'd have agreed to prepare a CD-ROM and a web site, too. Once I was safe at home, however, and on leaner cuisine, I found many other projects to write on the new computer that came with the contract. Journal articles, book reviews, conference papers, forays into autobiography, even another whole book, *Fact and Artifact: Writing Nonfiction.*

While my professional vita grew fat, the folder labeled "Handbook," never more than a generic name, remained thin. Every time I thought about all those rules, I found compelling reasons to go into the kitchen and reaffirm my burgeoning relationship with Elizabeth David. Her cookbooks, embodiments of summer—*A Book of Mediterranean Food, French Country Cooking,* and *Summer Cooking*—were an emblematic choice, for her impressionistic recipes call for a backbone of experience, a deft hand, and a willingness to take risks, to experiment and invent. Lemon Chicken, for instance, begins, "Poach a chicken with turnips, carrots, onions and a large piece of lemon peel," clearly an invitation to improvise. As I read it, a chicken of any size will do. One can omit the turnips or substitute parsnips, expand or contract the ratio of onions to carrots in the poaching stock, use more (or less) wine, white or red, tarragon and parsley instead of watercress, and on and on. Just the way real writers do it. A little of this, a little of that, add and subtract and move things around until the result is elegant simplicity—or abundance if that's what you're after. Exactly the advice I'd given in *Fact and Artifact.* Just as Huck Finn couldn't pray a lie, I couldn't in honesty write a handbook of rules. I canceled the contract, the only time I've ever done such a thing, and returned the advance. They let me keep the computer, but it was already obsolete. Then I celebrated by making David's Cold Chicken Véronique, which begins with her characteristically casual enticement. "Divide a carefully boiled chicken into several large pieces." What, I wonder, does it mean to boil a chicken "carefully," or recklessly, for that matter?

My grandmother was not a reckless cook, but she was a generous one. When I was growing up in New Hampshire, heavy wicker hampers would arrive from Grandma in Detroit right after Thanksgiving, redolent of cinnamon, ginger, and anise. Pfeffernüsse, springerle, lebkuchen, gingerbread, mandelplaetzchen, and Christmas stars with red and green sugar marked the delicious days of Advent. Their essence is so powerful in memory that I have had to get up from the computer—right in midsentence—not only to tend the beef stock that has to simmer for three more hours before it will be ready to make onion soup, but to eat a leftover Christmas cookie, a snowman made of two stacked nut-studded balls rolled in powdered sugar. (I eat when I write but I never even taste anything when I cook, for the process provides its own nourishment.) Yet no recipes corroborate this legacy or Grandma's other specialties—Dutch apple pie and sauer klops, ground meatballs in a sour cream sauce with whole allspice. Or is it klups? I have never seen the name written down, and indeed had to look up the German cookie spellings in a cookbook rather than a dictionary. Writing about this abundance is the best way I know to preserve it, whether I get the spelling right or not.

Our immediate family dotes on recipes even as we recognize that much of their meaning, as with any other writing, lies between the lines. We knew Sara was destined to marry Laird when we saw the pictures from her first Christmas visit to our house in rural Connecticut. Martin, Sara, and I are bending over pots on the stove, heads atilt at the same angle, spoons astir in right hands, a cheerful chorus of cooks. They commemorated their marriage by making a three-tiered wedding cake from *The Cake Bible,* chocolate cake with chocolate frosting, raspberry ganache, and fresh raspberries. And the next Christmas we began what has become a family tradition, extended to Bard and Vicki when they married six years later, the annual purchase of a cookbook that we can all share. Because each household already had copies of *The Joy of Cooking,* 1975 edition; Jane Brody's *Good Food Book,*

Marcella Hazan's *Classic Italian Cooking;* and Claudia Roden's *Book of Middle Eastern Food*—each with a distinctive literary flavor that complements the food—we began with the Silver Palate's *New Basics Cookbook. The Joy of Cooking,* 1997 edition, is too indispensable to share; we've given copies to one another. Bard and Vicki keep Madhur Jaffery's *A Taste of India,* Bard having been influenced at a critical age by a month's apprenticeship to our houseguest from Bombay, Grace Chellam, truly a mistress of spices and of amazing free-form aromatic cookery. Bard and Vicki are also custodians of the parent *Moosewood Cookbook* and its offspring and of *The Thousand Recipe Chinese Cookbook,* a fat book with a thin one—a dozen basics—inside yearning to escape. Laird and Sara have the *Bon Appetit* subscription, whose relevant issues promise sustenance, both literary and culinary, during family vacations. We trade back and forth Judith Olney's *Joy of Chocolate* and Maida Heatter's *Book of Great Chocolate Desserts,* inspired by Laird and Sara's annual gift of diverse homemade chocolates, in which their children, two-year-old Beth and five-year-old Paul, now have a hand. Indeed, in our annual orgy of Christmas baking it was Paul who assembled and rechristened the Snowman cookies—aka Mexican Wedding Cookie, aka Pastelitas de Boda, aka Pecan Butter Balls, only we like walnuts better. But none of us can cope with Marcel Desauliners's opulent compendium of lavish desserts from our favorite restaurant in Williamsburg, Virginia; Chocolate Caramel Hazelnut Damnation, Tuxedo Truffle Torte, Pillars of Chocolate with Cocoa Thunderheads all seem to require costly ounces of Valhrona chocolate (Sam's Club, our chocolatier, purveys ten-pound bags of Gitard bittersweet chips at $15. 95) and four days' preparation time. The pages of this gift from Maureen, a Williamsburg friend and fellow cook during ten years of collaborative monthly dinners, got stuck together during a dishwater spill and we have been too intimidated by the contents to pry them open.

Vicki, a food scientist, has provided enlightened redemption from the only formal cooking lessons I've ever taken, obligatory domestic science in eighth grade. There we were taught to prepare bland, colorless, mushy foods that have never since blighted my kitchen—custard, tapioca, and tomato aspic, oatmeal, Cream of Wheat, and omelets that everybody burned. Mrs. Wilcox, who also taught grammar, another complexity of rules that we had to follow to the letter regardless of the literary flavor, imposed comparable rules on our cooking classes. We had to make sure the kitchen was spotless before we began. What a waste, since we were only going to mess it up. We had to suit up, in calico aprons and despicable hair nets. We had to arrange all the utensils and ingredients in the order in which we expected to use them, and we had to turn the oven on to preheat, even if what we were baking wouldn't be ready for an hour. When we finally got to muffins, the only redeemable recipe in our repertoire, we had to sift the flour three times before measuring, and once again after adding the salt and baking soda. Teaspoons, tablespoons, cupfuls had to be level or the results would be doomed to disaster.

When I began my first full-time teaching job, I hired a volunteer from among my freshman English students as cook's helper. It would make literary sense to say that I taught Susan how to cook every Friday afternoon for four years until she graduated, but in truth she was a home economics major and we taught each other how to cook. I don't remember the exact recipes except for Fifi's Lentil Soup and Linda Kraus's Brisket—they probably weren't very exact—but we laughed a lot and spilled a lot and often had to adapt what was simmering on the stove to compensate for crucial ingredients omitted because, as Mrs. Wilcox would have chided, we were talking too much instead of concentrating on what we were doing. One year Susan gave us a yogurt maker for Christmas, but Martin and I soon backslid to our oven method. When Susan and her husband came to dinner years later, I served the brisket—a flat cut of beef slathered with chopped onion and garlic, baked for four hours, then covered with a mixture of chili sauce (one 8- or 12-oz. bottle), Worcestershire sauce (2 tbsp.), dark brown sugar (½ cup), and studded with whole cloves and baked another hour with parboiled potatoes and carrots. "Whoever finds a clove will have good luck," I would tell Bard and Laird, who understands why and now lures Paul and Beth to the dinner table with the same enticement. A recent e-mail correspondence tells me that Susan's daughter Laura, now a college sophomore—an English major, and an aspiring professor—will be joining our household for a summer internship and a taste of what it's like to prepare a book manuscript for publication. I will be surprised if our collaboration doesn't spill over into the kitchen.

Vicki explains the chemistry that underlies the recipes, reinforcing the intuitive wisdom of my ancestral cooks; why jelly jells better when you add pectin; why water ruins melting chocolate; why a food processor turns potatoes into a glutinous blob instead of mashing them. In *CookWise: The Hows and Whys of Successful Cooking,* a fortieth wedding anniversary gift from Vicki and Bard, Shirley Corriher, research biochemist turned cook, adumbrates further cooking conundrums. None of us, however, knows the verb for what happens when the yogurt is done. We make four big tumblers every week. In the interests of economy and elegance I have deleted extraneous ingredients, such as condensed milk and softened gelatin, from the recipes others have given me. Although I work from memory, in the recipe I give people I always say, "Blend together five cups of nonfat milk powder, 3½ cups warm water, and 2 tbsp. live yogurt start, fill the glasses, and keep in a warm water bath at a constant 110 degrees, the temperature of a gas oven pilot light, until the mixture *yogs.*" *Yogues* might be a better spelling, although my computer spellcheck resents both versions. Even Claudia Roden, who recommends wrapping the bowl in an "old shawl" and letting the mixture sit overnight, circumnavigates the verb with "thick like a creamy custard."

It has taken me four days, much faster than my usual writing pace, to write "Writing and Cooking, Cooking and Writing." But then, I actually began this piece in 1990 and revised it four times in 1991. While this has been simmering for nine years, out of sight and conscious mind, I have concentrated on researching and writing other scholarly articles, books, and creative nonfiction. Yet all the while I've been writing I have also been cooking, a practice continued during the writing of this piece. I've interrupted this text to stir the soup bones and vegetables browning in the oven, then gone back to the computer, transferred the soup mixture to the stove top and added liquid, returned to write more, and finally strained the cooled beef stock at midnight before going to bed. *The Joy of Cooking* promised that the congealed fat would form an airtight seal that would preserve the stock. I checked this morning, and so it had. I could postpone slicing and slowly browning the onions for the soup until I'd finished this writing.

Because of its long simmer, I thought that "Writing and Cooking" would be a piece of cake to finish. But as I tried to knead it into shape I realized that during the intervening years, without even looking at the 1991 version, I had cannibalized it for parts of other essays. So I started again from scratch. I am a better writer of personal essays now than I was nine years ago, less fearful of spilling the beans, more willing to improvise with a pinch of this, a soupçon of that, confident (originally I had "condiment," a Freudian typo) that what begins as potluck will, with proper seasoning, provide a feast for the eye and nourishment for the mind.

I always try out my academic writing on readers before I send it off to editors. Martin and a colleague or two can be trusted to give tough critiques, smart and thorough. After the editors and reviewers have weighed in and the work is published, I usually receive congratulatory e-mail messages from a few friends, and gradually the citations of my work appear in others' publications, missiles launched in the wars of the words. Such is the way of the academic world. My creative nonfiction, however, stories embedded in stories like raisins in scones, is intended for a much wider audience—anyone who likes stories. And who doesn't? Accordingly, I've given earlier drafts of "Writing and Cooking" to friends and colleagues, cooks and noncooks alike. Everyone likes to eat, and I have yet to find someone who doesn't like to read about food. I asked them the same questions I always ask, "Is this clear?" "Do I need to add anything? Omit anything?" "Have I avoided sentimentality?" But what I really want to know is, "Do you love this piece? Did you savor it? Would you come back for a second helping?"

What I don't dare ask for is, fortunately, what I get. Whereas the reader response to my academic writing, even the hot topics, is invariably cool—intellectual if not disengaged—the reaction to my personal essays sizzles. Writing about food whets the readers' appetites. They reminisce about good cooks in their own families. They revisit the menus of family gatherings. They correct the seasonings. They try out the recipes embedded in the text. I had a long conversation with Lori, who had copied the yogurt recipe, on why you only use 2 tablespoons of yogurt start. (Any unpasteurized yogurt will provide one, but I gave her some of mine.) More than 2 tablespoons crowds the growth of the culture, the mixture won't yog properly, the result is too runny. "My yogurt came out very firm and shrank to half its original volume. Why did it do that?" I don't know. "Can I add fruit or

flavoring to the mixture as it yogs?" I don't know that either, for thirty years
I've only made additions after the yogurt was done. "Vicki will have the answers," I say. "Let's send her an e-mail." Or readers counter my favorite
recipes with recipes of their own. Jenny's Mint Chocolate Chip Cookies
calls for, and I've never seen this anywhere before either, ¼ cup of dried
mint—"if grown in your own garden, all the better." Those who know my
essay is coming in the mail salivate in expectation.

    Whether I am a better cook now than I was nine years ago is incidental,
as long as my family and guests are satisfied. I was going to add, "after all,
my life doesn't depend on it." But writing this essay has made me realize that
in many ways my life, and the lives of those I love, do depend on the cooking even more than the eating. The morning after Thanksgiving we were
at Laird and Sara's in Boston amidst a houseful of other relatives, including
a dozen children under ten. Beth got up at six, and I got up with her to keep
her from waking everyone else. After an hour's reading, we grew tired of
Double Trouble in Walla-Walla, a wild and wonderful book whose rhym-
ing principle is signaled in the title; *Cloudy, with a Chance of Meatballs,* food
rains from the sky and nearly swamps the village's satiated inhabitants; and
June 29, 1999, a small book about giant vegetables. "Let's make something
good for breakfast," I said, "scones." "What are scones?" she asked. "Flattish
biscuits with raisins in them." Beth pulled a chair up to the kitchen counter,
I wrapped an apron twice around her, propped open *The Joy of Cooking* to
Classic Currant Scones, and measured the flour and sugar while she stirred.
Then she dropped in the butter, a tablespoon at a time, while I stirred, and
then the raisins. I beat in the egg-and-milk mixture, and together, my hand
on hers, we began to pat out the dough. "Take your hand off, Grandma
Lynn! I can do it myself!" she ordered. "Gently," I said, "don't pound it
flat!" and showed her how to fit the cookie cutter shapes—stars small,
medium, and large—efficiently onto the doughy rectangle. After the stars
got boring, we switched to pigs and Scottie dogs, and by the time Beth was
sprinkling the tops with cinnamon and sugar the rest of the family was fil-
tering into the kitchen ready to snatch the scones from the oven before
they'd even cooled. "Let's do it again," said Beth the next day. She beamed
when we gave her nested real measuring cups for Christmas, with match-
ing measuring spoons for Paul.

During our most recent visit to Boston, Paul presented us with a large flat cardboard box carefully wrapped in paper of his own design, with P-A-U-L crayoned over it in his favorite color, green. "You can't unwrap it until you get home," he said, "but your clue"—he has discovered mystery stories—"is sticking out the top." An 8-ounce raspberry yogurt cup, filled with the wad of black Polartec that had transformed it to a flowerpot, sprouted a large red carnation. "A flower," he assured us, "*not* an umbrella." When we tore off the paper, what to our wondering eyes should appear but a miniature garden: a green felt rectangle expanded by a sheet of paper colored green, with bright felt vegetables taped to the surface, carrots, tomatoes, cucumbers, eggplant, green beans, pumpkins. No kale. "Exactly what we grow in our garden," Paul said when we phoned to thank him, "and exactly what we cook." We did not discuss the two untethered genuine movie theater tickets resting atop two of the pumpkins. "Admit one," says each. We have given the garden pride of place on the pass-through counter between the kitchen stove and the center hall; anyone who enters the house will spot it on the instant. With this Eden in view and tickets to get us in, I finish making the onion soup.

WORKS CITED

Barrett, Judi. *Cloudy with a Chance of Meatballs*. New York: Atheneum, 1978.

Berenbaum, Rose Levy. *The Cake Bible*. New York: Morrow, 1988.

Bloom, Lynn Z. *Doctor Spock: Biography of a Conservative Radical*. Indianapolis: Bobbs-Merrill, 1972.

———. *Fact and Artifact: Writing Nonfiction*. 2d ed. Englewood Cliffs, N.J.: Prentice Hall, 1994.

Bracken, Peg. *The I Hate to Cook Book*. New York: Fawcett, 1960.

Brody, Jane. *Jane Brody's Good Food Book: Living the High-Carbohydrate Way*. New York: Norton, 1985.

Burros, Marian. *Elegant But Easy: A Cookbook for Hostesses*. New York: Collier, 1960.

Child, Julia, Louisette Bertholle, and Simone Beck. *Mastering the Art of French Cooking*. New York: Knopf, 1961.

Clements, Andrew. *Double Trouble in Walla Walla*. Brookfield, Conn.: Millbrook, 1997.

Corriher, Shirley O. *CookWise: The Hows and Whys of Successful Cooking*. New York: Morrow, 1997.

Crouter, Natalie. *Forbidden Diary: A Record of Wartime Internment, 1941–45*. Ed. Lynn Z. Bloom. New York: Burt Franklin, 1980.

David, Elizabeth. *Elizabeth David Classics: Mediterranean Food, French Country Cooking, Summer Cooking*. New York: Knopf, 1980.

Desaulniers, Marcel. *Desserts to Die For*. New York: Simon & Schuster, 1995.

Hazan, Marcella. *The Classic Italian Cook Book*. New York: Knopf, 1979.

Heatter, Maida. *Maida Heatter's Book of Great Chocolate Desserts*. New York: Knopf, 1980.

Jaffrey, Madhur. *A Taste of India*. New York: Macmillan, 1985.

Katzen, Mollie. *The Moosewood Cookbook*. Berkeley, Calif.: Ten Speed, 1977.

Miller, Gloria Bley. *The Thousand Recipe Chinese Cookbook*. 1966. New York: Grosset & Dunlap, 1970.

Olney, Judith. *The Joy of Chocolate*. Woodbury, N.Y.: Barron's, 1982.

Roden, Claudia. *A Book of Middle Eastern Food*. New York: Knopf, 1972.

Rombauer, Irma S. and Marion Rombauer Becker. *Joy of Cooking*. Indianapolis: Bobbs-Merrill, 1975.

Rombauer, Irma S., Marion Rombauer Becker, and Ethan Becker. *The Joy of Cooking*. New York: Scribner, 1997.

Rosso, Julee and Sheila Lukins. *The New Basics Cookbook*. New York: Workman, 1989.

Wiesner, David. *June 29, 1999*. New York: Clarion, 1992.

Women's Home Companion Cookbook. New York: Collier, 1944.

Woolf, Virginia. *To the Lighthouse*. New York: Harcourt, 1927.

CHAPTER FIVE

My Mother's Recipes
The Diary of a Swedish American
Daughter and Mother
Linda Murray Berzok

On a sweltering August day, I made several trips down to our basement to deposit a dozen boxes of index cards with my mother's recipes, literally hundreds, most handwritten, covering a forty-year span from 1952 to 1992. I had carried them back from my mother's house after she died, with the intention of going through them to look for personal favorites. Some were metal boxes, others cardboard, falling apart where the edges met because the cards were packed so tightly. There was even an overflowing shoebox full. There the boxes stayed for two years, archaeological artifacts, gathering dust, another layer in the history of women and their relationship to cooking. When I finally went through them, I discovered that my mother had used her boxes for a complex task—a combination of recipe development, diary/family Bible, and social notes. Each container was labeled: Cake, Cakes/Cookies, Chicken, Cookies/Candy/Frostings, Desserts, Hors d'oeuvres, Meat Casseroles, Menus, Muffins, Soups/Beverages/Pickles, and two Miscellaneous, one with cards filed alphabetically, the other randomly. The outsides of the index boxes were annotated with notes on masking tape. The Muffins box, for example, noted, "Muffins shelf 'C' (third from bottom) 400 degrees, 20–25 minutes." The Cakes/Cookies box was almost completely covered with notes. In 1985, she wrote, "Try an oil cake but follow d's [directions]. Don't beat oil & sugar?" Another read, "Cut squares in 2½. For picnics 1 ½ × 2." On an inscription running around three sides of the box, she had written in October 1990, "Elfy's Frosting [referring to an Austrian Yale faculty wife who lived next door]: "Melt 1 c. semi sw. choc. bits (*Don't use dd [*sic*] bits. Frost. doesn't get smooth!) ½ c. butter or 1 stk *together* over hot H2O & stir. (Is best)."

Each recipe card was also heavily annotated. My mother never met a recipe she liked—at least, not at first. Consequently, she kept detailed notes on the outcome of every dish and how she planned to modify the recipe next time. She recorded not only the menus she served when entertaining, but also the dates, who was there, and what she would do differently next time. ("Our party December 27, Sunday, 5 to 7. Next time just say at 5." For a 1972 barbecue, she notes, "Maybe instead of creamed carrots, just buttered. Everyone seems to be dieting.") I unearthed the menu for the little home wedding reception she gave for my first marriage. She documented many of the meals she ate at other people's houses and restaurants. Even a department store lunch or dinner at my father's business club was carefully recorded. ("Salad at Club—Red cabbage, slivered cheese, croutons, Romaine lettuce, carrots, garlicky.") High-volume production of Christmas cookies was very important to her. For the holiday season 1982, she recorded having baked 941 cookies and gave a breakdown of how many of each variety. In 1983 she topped out at 1,350—most of which she gave away. She also noted food preferences of my brother, father, and me, and our heartfelt dislikes for certain foods. (Scalloped tomatoes—"Kids don't like— gooey." Spaghetti and lobster casserole—"Average. Kids don't like lobster." Date oatmeal cookies—"Bill and Bill R [my father and brother] don't like."

This meticulous, almost obsessive approach to food is what gives life to my mother's "manuscript cookbook," the appropriate term for this recipe collection, according to Barbara Haber, curator of Radcliffe's Schlesinger Library culinary collection. My mother turned it into a monumental work. The sheer volume of recipes, the process of soliciting, collecting, and modifying them was the work of a lifetime, involving a vast, far-flung network of women. My mother gathered recipes wherever she found them—from her three sisters, patients in the hospital where she volunteered, at the dentist's office, beauty parlor, from neighbors, and from her primary school teacher colleagues. All these sources were given careful credit on the cards. I smiled at one recipe I found that recalled an important childhood relationship of mine. When I was in high school, my best friend was named

Rita Esposito. Her mother made a particularly good chocolate frosting. Of course, my mother solicited the recipe. It became known forever after in our family simply as Esposito Frosting. And there was the card and recipe for this delicious concoction!

As I picked my way through the cards, reading each one, I began to realize that there was a story here—one that could be read through the cards. Some women leave diaries, I thought. My mother left recipes. The story was hers as the daughter of Swedish immigrants, a woman who had lived through the difficult years of the Depression and World War II and had emerged as a mother and housewife in the late 1940s and '50s. Like many other first-generation American women, she was trying tentatively to establish an identity in a world that was at best unfamiliar—a world for which her own Swedish-born mother could provide no preparation.

Minnesota Beginnings

My mother, the third of five sisters, was born in 1909 in Minnesota to Swedish immigrants, Ida and Axel Pierson. Her sisters were Gertrude, Dorothy, Astrid, and Mildred. Swedish was spoken at home, and the style of cooking was that of the old country—hearty peasant fare. My grandparents were part of a steady influx of Swedes in the middle of the nineteenth century who contributed to the development of Minnesota (Neirdle 90). Given this ethnic background, I expected to find a treasure trove of Swedish recipes in my mother's file boxes. This was not the case. On a folded, yellowed, and torn page from a small three-ring notebook was a recipe for *Dolmar,* an entree I remember from childhood that I always thought was Armenian. My Aunt Mildred, my mother's only surviving sister, tells me it is Swedish. In this dish—which has versions in many cultures—cucumbers, tomatoes, and cabbage leaves are stuffed with a mixture of ground beef, rice, onion, and parsley, then simmered in broth. My brother, father, and I loved it. On this well-worn recipe written in black ink, my mother had over the years made notes in lead, red, and blue pencil, red and purple fountain pens, and blue ballpoint. Significantly, she has noted on the lower version that she attributes to her mother ("Ma's"), "Just an average dish!" On another card where she recorded having made it for company in September

1985, she notes, "Didn't seem to go over well." At a certain point, *Dolmar* simply disappeared from her culinary repertoire. A recipe for a dish called *Root Mos,* a combination of yellow rutabaga and potatoes mashed together and topped with bits of pork, was totally unfamiliar to me. Aunt Mildred confirmed that *Root Mas* is Swedish and was one of my mother's favorite meals. But I never recall her having made it. Swedish meatballs, traditionally part of a Scandinavian smorgasbord, I do remember from childhood, but I note that they were relegated by my mother to a cocktail party hors d'oeuvre. Swedish cookies, including *Pepparkakor, Spritz,* and *Mandel Skorper,* were also rare treats, part of the annual frenzy of pre-Christmas baking that is a Swedish tradition. The *Pepparkakor* recipe, however, is from a *McCall's* magazine cookbook, and in the *Mandel Skorper* recipe, my mother has eliminated the traditional almond flavoring, which she did not like.

Clearly, my mother had moved away from ethnic culinary ways. One reason may be the fact that my grandmother did not work from written recipes. "How much sugar?" my mother and aunts would ask. "Oh, not too much and not too little," my grandmother would reply. Most surviving Swedish foods made by my mother and her three sisters—and eventually even by my grandmother herself—were culled from the *Swedish American Cook Book,* a community cookbook compiled by the West Hartford (Connecticut) Ladies Aid Society, published in 1941. My grandmother was especially happy to find there a recipe for *Blitztorte,* a dessert with double layers of yellow cake, topped with meringue and almonds, filled with whipped cream and crushed pineapple. My grandmother's failure to use recipes could partially explain the scant number of original Swedish recipes in my mother's collection, but there were other reasons as well. In her essay "Ethnic Foodways in America," Susan Kalcik suggests that the process of acculturation is a combination of the pull of the old and the push of the new (38). One influence on that process is how society views ethnicity. Alice Ross writes of a period of strong anti-immigrant feeling between 1884 and 1922 when most mainstream Americans were more concerned with preserving native-born traditions than exploring new "foreign" foods (170). This was a time when my mother was entering her teen years. She and her sisters had to struggle with the fact that their old ways were disdained by the culture at large. "The livelier tastes and traditions that still flourished in immigrant families and communities were supplying the nation with more adventurous perspectives on food, but scientific resistance was strong," writes Laura Shapiro about the turn-of-the-century movement known as domestic science (212). In an article titled "Queer Foreign Foods in America" that appeared in *American Kitchen* magazine in 1901, the author chided the immigrant for preferring ethnic foods, "even though coarse and unsavory compared with the food of his adopted land" (qtd. in Shapiro 212). Between World War I and the 1960s, that is, for about half a century, "generations of women were persuaded to leave the past behind when they entered the kitchen, and to ignore what their senses told them while they were there" (215–16).

Alongside the desire of the children of immigrants to forge new American culinary patterns, there was a simultaneous wish to leave old patterns behind because of their painful, conflictual associations. From family oral history, I knew that my grandmother's life as a pioneer wife was extremely arduous. Cecyle Neirdle notes that this "pioneer generation" of women was a special group, "subject to a larger share of insecurity and anxiety than was the lot of other women" (86). The agricultural life in the new country was simply a continuation of the old. My grandmother had been born into a poor Swedish Lutheran family, one of six children living in a rural one-room cottage on land where her father was a tenant farmer. She came to the United States when she was eighteen, speaking no English. Living conditions in the rural Swedish ethnic communities in the Midwest were primitive, and women increasingly had to work at demanding farm labor. The insecurities of life became their primary concern. My grandmother suffered an enormous tragedy when she lost her second daughter, Dorothy, at the age of two. Left in the care of my grandfather while my grandmother attended church, the toddler ate an overdose of bromo quinine pills and died.

Many of the pioneer women suffered mental instability. "Insanity seems especially frequent among immigrant women, because they had less power of resistance," Blegen wrote about Norwegian immigrant women living in Minnesota (qtd. in Neirdle 96). It is, therefore, not surprising that my grandmother suffered a nervous breakdown (possibly two). During the months my grandmother was hospitalized, my mother, only nine at the time, took charge of her younger sister Mildred. My aunt took to calling her Lille More

(Swedish for "Little Mother"). For all these reasons, it becomes clear why my mother and her sisters would look back on their childhood with mixed feelings. Perhaps no other generation in American history has experienced such a huge culture gap in relation to their parents. The immigrants remained isolated from mainstream America in ethnic communities. Yet their children had to learn to cope in a new world for which their parents were helpless to provide preparation. My conclusion about the lack of heritage recipes was that this particular group of first-generation American women had a strong need to dissociate from past (peasant) food traditions and create a new—read American—identity. Consequently, when my mother wrote, "Just an average dish" or "Didn't go over well" about Swedish *Dolmar,* she was not simply moving away from the traditional food, she was rejecting it. "As in many ethnic communities, in the Scandinavian ones it was only a generation or two before the vast majority of food consumed became mainstream American in character," wrote Richard Pillsbury. Ethnic dishes were saved for holidays as "celebrations of the past" (148).

Where Swedish foods did survive in my mother's collection is in the disproportionate number of sweets. (This was true of my three aunts as well.) Five of the twelve index boxes are devoted to cakes, cookies, frostings, and desserts. If there was a focus to my mother's cooking, it was her preoccupation with baking. "Large quantities of cream and butter and comparatively small quantities of flour tend to make the cakes and cookies light and fragile," Pillsbury notes of Scandinavian baking (148). Thelma Barer-Stein observes that "Swedes prefer to take their grains in the form of pastries. . . . The Swedish sweet tooth is well-satisfied by all the delicately sweet baked goods that accompany the many daily cups of coffee. A supply of these in any Swedish home is considered as much a staple as bread for the table" (497). I can hardly remember a time when there wasn't a homemade pie, cake, or cookies in the house. If my mother lapsed, my father, brother, and I put up a great hue and cry. We considered it cruel deprivation!

The Making of a Perfect Generation

As my mother moved further away from her Swedish roots, she was edged along by the culture toward a strange new standard of culinary perfection, the first definition of femininity for this motley generation of American women culled from so many ethnic backgrounds. No object or recipe better symbolizes this approach to food than the molded Jell-O salad. It is difficult, if not impossible, to understand today what could have been so compelling about a shimmering molded construction of Jell-O, studded with colors of various fruits and perhaps marshmallows, all perfectly aligned, served with mayonnaise dressing. Yet, for a long period of American cooking, this concoction reigned supreme. The number of my mother's cards and notes concerning these towering gelatinized masses indicates that they were not simply a novelty item. It is also true that they were not everyday foods. The molded Jell-O salad in all its incarnations was an occasion salad and its presence was de rigeur for every celebration—Christmas, Thanksgiving, dinner parties, the Fourth of July, Labor Day, birthdays, my father's retirement party. There was no menu my mother recorded that didn't include this essential item. Apparently, the party didn't begin until the salad was on the table. A recipe for Cherry Salad Supreme that she clipped from the August 1969 *Better Homes and Gardens* uses both raspberry and lemon gelatin, a can of cherry pie filling, and the ubiquitous miniature marshmallows. My mother wrote "Ex!" (for excellent) on the card, and noted that it could be served as a dessert by eliminating the mayonnaise dressing.

Molded salads are complex constructions. They require a number of different sizes and shapes of molds, the exacting placement of each kind of fruit in its designated spot, sometimes indicated by the mold itself, and finally, the careful unmolding and presentation of the completed masterpiece. On my mother's recipe for Tomato Aspic, she has drawn a diagram of the unmolded ring, indicating that cottage cheese should be placed in the center, and round slices of dill pickle arranged around the outside. For a Lemon Jell-O salad, she includes a diagram showing where the halved pineapple rings, the peach halves, and the cherries (all canned) were to go. This "arduous approach to salad making became an identifying feature of cooking school cookery and the signature of a refined household," comments Shapiro (97). "Salads proliferated magnificently in number and variety until they incorporated every kind of food except bread and pastry" (97–98). This "Art of assemblage" approach provided a measure of control over food, and using gelatin held things in place. Control was very important. Huge uncertainties were looming on the horizon. Meals had to be finessed as quickly as possible with predictable results. Between World War I and the Depression, Shapiro relates, the kind of work involved in cooking changed more dramatically than it would again for another half century (222). Thanks to electric appliances, the burden lightened considerably. At the same time, the use of canned and packaged foods was growing steadily. These prepared foods enhanced the possibility of perfect, if boring, fail-safe meals. "Culinary idealism," as Shapiro calls it, took hold in the later part of the nineteenth century and held sway for several generations of women, meaning that it was still in force in the mid-1940s, when my mother was well into her culinary life.

This approach simply reflected huge social changes. During the Depression, large numbers of women went to work because "their homes needed every bit of cash they could bring home" (Halberstam 588). My mother, after attending normal school (teacher training), taught in a poor Italian neighborhood in Meriden, Connecticut, where her family had moved. The professional gains for women during the Depression were double-edged because once a woman married, she was discriminated against. When my mother and father decided to marry, they did so secretly for one year because employment of married women was forbidden by law. My mother's meager income was essential. She continued to live at home and contribute to the family funds.

World War II brought another set of changes. For one thing, I was born in 1943. Two months later, my father was drafted, even though he was already thirty-five, blind in one eye, and paralyzed in his right index finger. His term of duty—fortunately not overseas—was two years. My parents rented out their home, and my mother and I moved back in with my two youngest aunts, grandmother, and grandfather. My mother went to work again, this time in the war effort, working a drill press in a factory, making parts for planes. This period of living back in the family home must have produced some tension in my Americanized mother, who found herself once again eating the food of immigrants. There were two roles for women during the war. Amy Bentley has identified the "politics of domesticity," the creation of the patriotic image of woman as wartime homemaker, created by the government and media to mobilize women in their kitchens, magnifying their position of domestic helpmates to best serve the interests of the state. Messages about food, she notes, were clear. "Women's most important battlefield was the kitchen. There women could—and should—fight the war and prove their patriotism by cooking and serving the right kinds of foods in the right kinds of ways. Every meal served was a political act" (30–31). When the war ended, these women had few adjustments to make to conform to the postwar definition of femininity—fostered by private industry, TV sitcoms, and the pervasive women's magazines—that a woman did not work but kept house immaculately and cooked perfect meals efficiently (Halberstam 590). But for women like my mother who followed the Rosie the Riveter role model and worked in the war effort, there was a sharp split between their wartime and postwar-time roles. In all, 8 million women joined the workforce during the war. When the war was over, the jobs for women disappeared as returning soldiers were given priority. Within two months after the end of the war, some 800,000 women had been fired; two years later, 2 million women had lost their jobs (Halberstam 588–89). Suddenly, these women were in the home full-time—the suburban home. It was clearly in the best interests of the state to remold these women, so to speak, to give them a new role, and what better tool than the Jell-O mold?

As early as the 1940s, advertising was reflecting the image of cooking as a nuisance. By the '50s, it was viewed in the light of technology as an "arm's-length" relationship with food. Food was simply a necessity, "one that ought to be manipulated and brought under control as quickly and neatly as bodily functions were handled by modern plumbing," Shapiro writes (228). Assembling meals took the place of working from basic ingredients. Meals were "constructed," pouring a can of condensed soup over other canned and packaged items such as tuna fish and noodles, hamburger meat and stewed tomatoes, or combining mushroom soup with frozen green beans and a can of onion rings (the classic Green Bean Bake, introduced by Campbell's in 1955). Other convenience foods included Jell-O, of course, Bisquick, Cool Whip, Dream Whip, store-bought cakes, pudding mixes, cake mixes, canned and frozen fruits. My mother's recipe collection is full to overflowing with "constructions" featuring these foods.

I remember in particular one Jell-O salad my mother made in a loaf pan, using lemon Jell-O and grated carrots. Before pouring in the liquid Jell-O, she carefully created a flower motif on the bottom, using canned pineapple chunks for petals, half a walnut for the flower's center and green pepper strips for the stem and leaves. This tedious attention to detail reminded me of the ritual preparation of the *obento* lunch box for nursery-school children during the 1980s in Japan, described by Anne Allison: "Customarily, these *obentos* are highly crafted elaborations of food: a multitude of miniature portions, artistically designed and precisely arranged, in a container that is sturdy and cute" (22). Two different periods and cultures, both requiring the manipulation of food, creation of particular designs, careful ordering, and laborious, time-consuming work. What could be the larger purpose and meaning of this exercise?

Allison uses the concept of the *obento* box as a gendered ideological state apparatus. "I conclude," she writes, "that *obento* as a routine, task, and art form of nursery school culture are endowed with the ideological and gendered meanings that the state indirectly manipulates. The manipulation is neither total nor totally coercive, however, and I argue that pleasure and creativity for both mother and child are also products of the *obento*" (297). It could be similarly argued that the Jell-O mold that occupied such a prominent position in post–World War II culinary habits, was also invested with a gendered state ideology. In other words, it served the best interests of the state to encourage this trend, principally to stimulate the postwar economy. Certainly, the companies that produced gelatin and the women's magazines that were constantly developing and promoting new recipes for the packaged and canned foods gave a big push to this trend. This "politics of domesticity" directly benefited the postwar economy. "The new culture of consumerism told women they should be homemakers and saw them merely as potential buyers for all the new washers and dryers, freezers, floor waxers, pressure cookers, and blenders" (Halberstam 589). The appliances meant that women had more time on their hands and few options for doing anything very meaningful or fulfilling with that time.

The difficulty with perfectionism, of course, is that perfection is not attainable. Just as the daily production of the *obento* box was so demanding that Japanese women were unable to also hold jobs outside their homes, and they were kept in a constant state of anxiety, so the new post–World War II compliant femininity kept women off balance. The purpose of the Jell-O mold as well as the *obento* box seems to have been to keep women in a perpetual state of striving. They served their purpose well. As Stanton Peele and Archie Brodoky, in a penetrating analysis of this generation, observe: "Perhaps owing to such forced narrowing of larger aspirations and talents, these were nervous people who insisted on keeping control of their homes" (121). This striving to stay in charge is indicated in my mother's manuscript cookbook by the perpetual modification of recipes in an effort to "get it right." No recipe, it seems, was set in cement. Instead, they were set in Jell-O!—subject to endless tinkering. On a dessert recipe called Food for the Angels in which a store-bought angel food cake is torn apart and mixed with a filling of frozen strawberries and pink-tinted whipped cream, my mother records that when she tried it on January 13 (no year), "a liquid oozed from bottom layer. I used margarine. Next time use butter and half amount. Save crumbs for top! In filling, use half amt. butter. It looked curdled. Sometime try without putting strawberry juice into whipped cream. Try on us [meaning my brother, father, and myself—the proverbial guinea pigs]! And rewrite. Maybe, melt butter?" In a second example, my mother made a note on a muffin recipe from her sister Mildred. "Don't ever make Mil's recipe again. They have big holes and tough . . . Took 30 mins. at 425 degrees and stayed white . . . Impossible to get out of paper cups."

Food Habits Die Hard

Although individual recipes were subject to endless revision, the overall schema of the new American food habits in place by the 1950s was set in something more solid than concrete. It endured until the end of my mother's cooking life in the early 1990s. Her recipes and menus from the '70s and '80s are just as likely to include molded Jell-O salads, tuna casserole, and potato chip dips as those from the '50s. Kalcik comments that foodways seem particularly resistant to change. "It has been suggested," she writes, "that this is because the earliest-formed layers of culture, such as foodways, are the last to erode" (39). The new fragile American identity was perhaps not secure enough to accommodate innovative culinary techniques and unfamiliar ingredients such as spices. Women, she finds, are particularly resistant to changes in food habits (40). Although Kalcik refers here specifically to ethnic food habits, her thesis can also be applied to my mother's manuscript cookbook. Julia Child began the *French Chef* series in 1962 (Shapiro 230). But my mother barely acknowledges her existence. The single exception is a curious hors d'oeuvre recipe attributed to Child. It amounts to little more than grilled ham and mozzarella cheese sandwiches, cut into "finger food" slices. It can easily be seen how this atypical Julia Child recipe fit right into my mother's culinary scheme of things.

Sometime in the late 1960s or early '70s, I gave my mother a subscription to *Gourmet* magazine. But there is no evidence in her collection of any recipes having been derived from this source. I also gave her recipes from *Gourmet* that I had made and recommended. She tried them—most only once. On a recipe I passed on for Chicken in Champagne Sauce, she notes that it "Takes long." She intentionally left out the dried mushrooms, which would have been unfamiliar to her. For a cocktail party, she notes that she "tried L's dish [Liptauer cheese] with pumpernickel but didn't go over so big." A Baked Stuffed Shrimp recipe she found "Good but very expensive." And a *New York Times* Christmas plum pudding recipe was dismissed with "Don't make. V. Expensive—Lots of wk.!" Three of these dishes required cooking with wine or beer, something much too exotic for my mother. The "foreign" influences that she did allow into her cooking were those bland Americanized dishes accepted as "legitimate" by the culture as a whole. These included "Mexican" represented by Chili con Carne and southern Italian represented by Spaghetti and Meatballs, Lasagna, and Chicken Cacciatore, which came from my Aunt Mildred, who married an Italian. Pillsbury notes that these two ethnic traditions were overwhelmingly accepted into American cuisine, although it was not until the end of World War II that "Italian cooking and particularly food of southern Italy, swept across the country and conquered the mainstream palate" (110). There were also some Americanized Chinese dishes in the collection, and one for a very simple Korean Barbecue that my mother acquired from her Korean American daughter-in-law.

The one truly adventurous departure, which defies explanation, is that my mother took an adult education course in Chinese cooking. She even bought a wok and a steamer! Even more remarkable, for Thanksgiving dinner 1980, she recorded serving egg rolls and what she called "Chinese crackers" as hors d'oeuvres! This is all the more jarring because the rest of the menu for this quintessential American holiday proceeds traditionally with turkey and stuffing, mashed potatoes, squash, carrots, cranberry and orange Jell-O salad (naturally), squash and apple pies. A Labor Day celebration in 1981 included "Chinese pickles." At a dinner in November 1981, she served Chinese Shrimp Puffs and Sweet and Sour Pork. She also notes having served my cousin and her husband a chicken, baby corncob, and cashews stir-fry that she made in her wok! Sometime before, I had brought home some homemade Chinese dumplings and demonstrated my steamer. This was at a time when, Shapiro notes, "Americans may have started to reverse the lemming-like culinary trends of the previous century" (230). One of the signs of this hopeful change was the "new ethnicity," a passion for ethnic food that took hold in the 1980s. It wasn't long, however, before my mother passed the wok to me and returned to her entrenched mode of cooking.

The Great American Recipe Quilting Bee

After my mother died, I reflected on her oeuvre, her manuscript cookbook, on how much time and energy it had taken to create and maintain this work. It was a dynamic process, never complete. This was, of course, a specifically female activity that had two goals. The first was relational—to perpetuate and deepen existing relationships and make new ones. The second was personal—the activity had intrinsic meaning and significance to my mother and provided some measure of satisfaction.

The relational goal. Most of the recipes in my mother's collection came through relationships. They were acquired from relatives, friends, neighbors, and casual acquaintances. Each recipe, carefully and laboriously copied by hand—and sometimes accompanied by a sample of the food itself—became a kind of gift. This process, binding together a huge network of women, is similar to other examples of what anthropologists call "reciprocity" in different cultures. For example, Anna Meigs explores how exchanges of food among members of the primitive Hua people in New Guinea are used to develop social relationships. "In particular, I explore how food and eating (and the rules associated with both) are understood as means that unite apparently separate and diverse objects and organisms" (95). Meigs refers to Marcel Mauss's *The Gift,* a treatise on economic systems based on reciprocity: "Mauss focuses on how reciprocal gift exchanges, often of food, bind members of a society together in relations of mutual participation and unity" (102). It works, Mauss says, because the obligation to repay comes from the undeniable fact that the gift is a part of oneself. Isn't this exactly the case with a recipe that has been developed and nurtured over time, nudged along on the road to perfection? Although the concept is carried to an extreme in Hua thinking, in which to eat a food produced by another person is to experience that person, both physiologically and emotionally, the fundamental analogy is apt. Food acts as a vehicle for symbolizing and expressing ideas about the relationship between self and other. "Through his or her continual acts of food exchange [read recipe exchange], both as producer and as consumer, the individual is constituted as part of a physically commingled and communal whole" (Meigs 104).

In the case of my mother's manuscript cookbook, this whole had no geographic or temporal boundaries. The process of collecting, soliciting, copying, and exchanging recipes took on a life of its own. It involved and defined a vast community of middle-class women—my mother, her mother, my mother's sisters, me, her daughter-in-law, her nieces, her aunt, cousins, friends, neighbors, and colleagues, members of a great many ethnicities—all together in a kind of free-floating recipe quilting bee. These women may well have experienced what Anne L. Bower calls "greater comfort within a *female* culture, and a *women's* world" ("Cooking Up" 31). In one communication, Kammy Loo from Hawaii, who identifies herself as a schoolteacher, sends three recipes with personal notes to my Aunt Gertrude's best friend, Ruth Ogren. Ruth apparently passed it on to my aunt, who sent it along to my mother, and it ends up in her recipe box. Kammy Loo's recipes feature convenience foods—lemon Jell-O, yellow cake mix (any brand), and Swansdown Lemon Flake. They are also annotated with personal notes: Jell-O Yellow Cake is "Earl's favorite [my Aunt Gertrude's brother-in-law] Aileen and Lynette baked the cake for his birthday." For Mary Harrison's Orange Cake, Kammy Loo says to "take a package of cake mix, Pillsbury or any other brand," and tells Ruth that Mary Harrison teaches at the same school she does; "You'll love this," she writes.

A second round-robin recipe is for Cheer, a dessert or ice cream topping of brandied fruit in a crock, which originated in Kirbyville, Texas, according to the anonymous donor. The preparation *requires* that each new participant acquire a starter of the fermenting liquid as well as the recipe from the giver—surely the ultimate quilting bee recipe.

The personal goal. Since women historically have not been encouraged to write their own stories, "feminist scholars have used the 'verbal artifact' approach" to demonstrate that such items as quilts, needlework, gardens, diaries, and letters "have provided women with an important outlet for their creativity and a forum for expressing their view of the world" (Bower, "Cooking Up" 30). Bower adds community cookbooks to the list, which, she says, "can be read as literary texts whose authors constructed meaningful representations of themselves and their world" (30). The women who contributed recipes to these works had a story to tell—that of women "asserting themselves as middle-class assimilated Americans" (3). The plot is what Bower calls "the integration plot"—the story of "achieving assimilation and status through their acceptance of the larger society's conventions and standards" (38). The community cookbook, then, provides a community portrait as well as portraits of individual members. This is certainly one aspect of my mother's manuscript cookbook.

However, the community cookbook and autobiography part company in the realm of the personal. Bower defines autobiography as "a story of how a life came to be what it was, or a self became what it is" ("Cooking Up" 31). My mother's manuscript cookbook is far more personal and autobiographical than a community cookbook. In some sense it is a kind of diary, defined by *Webster's* as "a record of events, transactions or observations kept daily or at frequent intervals" (qtd. in Franklin, xv). Penelope Franklin describes a tremendous flexibility in format ranging from entries on sheets of paper, backs of envelopes, between the lines of an almanac, and even on the end-papers of a novel (xv). Certainly, a recipe collection qualifies. A diary, she says, is a "safe place, a sounding board for ideas, a testing ground for creative experiments, a record of progress and growth, and a place where the past, present, and future live together all under one's control" (xix). What a perfect description of my mother's manuscript cookbook! Franklin points out that although women's social roles have changed, their responses to the roles have a repetitive quality, namely, the fear that they don't measure up to society's current ideal of womanhood. A diary provides a refuge for gaining perspective and control (xxiv–xxv). That fear is expressed in my mother's copious notes. But who could match up to the image of compliant and perfect femininity propounded during the 1950s?

My mother's recipes, in their particular detail, tell a personal story. In their broader scope, they tell the story of an entire community and generation of women who struggled to shape an American identity and protect that fragile sense of self. It was a generation whose mothers had been born in other countries and perhaps never saw their homelands again. As their daughters struggled in isolated suburban kitchens to fashion a new life, they learned to create unique documents and reach out to other women in new and innovative ways to exchange gifts, share experiences, and lend support. All of these women whose mothers lived in such radically different circumstances were "bound together by recipes" (Bower, "Bound" 14). Just as the stories of quilts can be read, so can manuscript cookbooks. As I observed earlier, some women leave diaries. My mother left recipes.

This essay is dedicated to the memory of Doris Pierson Murray, 1909–1996.

WORKS CITED

Allison, Anne. "Japanese Mothers and *Obentos:* The Lunch Box as Ideological State Apparatus." *Food and Culture: A Reader.* Ed. Carole Counihan and Penny Van Esterik. New York: Routledge, 1997. 296–314.

Barer-Stein, Thelma. *You Eat What You Are: A Study of Ethnic Food Traditions.* Toronto: Culture Concepts, 1980.

Bentley, Amy. *Eating for Victory: Food Rationing and the Politics of Domesticity.* Urbana: U of Illinois P, 1998.

Bower, Anne L. "Bound Together. Recipes, Lives, Stories, and Readings." *Recipes for Reading: Community Cookbooks, Stories, Histories.* Ed. Anne L. Bower. Amherst: U of Massachusetts P, 1997. 1–14.

——. "Cooking Up Stories: Narrative Elements in Community Cookbooks." *Recipes for Reading: Community Cookbooks, Stories, Histories.* Ed. Anne L. Bower. Amherst: U of Massachusetts P, 1997. 29–50.

Franklin, Penelope, ed. *Private Pages: Diaries of American Women, 1830s–1970s.* New York: Ballantine, 1986.

Halberstam, David. *The Fifties.* New York: Villard, 1993.

Kalcik, Susan. "Ethnic Foodways in America: Symbol and the Performance of Identity." *Ethnic and Regional Foodways in the United States: The Performance of Group Identity.* Ed. Linda Keller Brown and Kay Mussell. Knoxville: U of Tennessee P, 1997. 37–65.

Meigs, Anna. "Food as a Cultural Construction." *Food and Culture: A Reader.* Ed. Carole Counihan and Penny Van Esterik. New York: Routledge, 1997. 95–106.

Neirdle, Cecyle. *America's Immigrant Women.* Boston: Twayne, 1975.

Peele, Stanton, and Archie Brodoky. *Love and Addiction.* New York: New American Library, 1975.

Pillsbury, Richard. "Imported Tastes. Immigration and the American Diet." *No Foreign Food.* Ed. Richard Pillsbury. Boulder, Colo.: Westview Press, 1998. 136–63.

Ross, Alice. "Ella Smith's Unfinished Community Cookbook: A Social History of Women and Work in Smithtown, New York, 1884–1922."

Recipes for Reading: Community Cookbooks, Stories, Histories. Ed. Anne L. Bower Amherst. U of Massachusetts P, 1997. 154–72.

Shapiro, Laura. *Perfection Salad: Women and Cooking at the Turn of the Century*. New York: Farrar, Straus and Giroux, 1986.

West Hartford Ladies Aids Society, ed. *Swedish American Cook Book*. New Britain, Conn.: Privately published, 1941.

CHAPTER SIX

The Triumph of Fassoulia, or Aunt Elizabeth and the Beans

Arlene Voski Avakian

The license plate read "ALMOST HEAVEN"—almost heaven for whom? I wondered, when Ashley asked me to go with her when she visited her family in West Virginia. It was the second summer we had been together, and I knew she wanted me to see her mountains, to breathe the crisp air, to experience her home just as I had wanted her to see my New York City— the uptown neighborhood of Washington Heights, where I was raised, and Greenwich Village, where I was a voyeur of bohemianism and other "different" life styles. But I had great trepidation about taking my Armenian American, 1960s feminist, antiracist, lesbian political self to the South and to a small town at that. I knew that West Virginia had come into existence during the Civil War when it had separated from Virginia and fought on the Union side. Ashley insisted that it wasn't really the South. It was a border state. That distinction did not matter to me. It might be a border state, but Ashley had gone to segregated schools. She had told me that about the year her mother had taught in a school at the bottom of a hollow where two one-room schoolhouses sat side by side. Her mother had ridden the haulage every day with a black woman, the teacher of the other school. West Virginia was definitely alien territory for me, but Ashley wanted me to go with her, so I agreed.

When we crossed the border from Virginia with its beautiful rolling hills, Ashley broke into song, her voice lilting, caressing the words praising the West Virginia hills. I could see that we were truly coming into a different topography. The rounded tops of the mountains turned to sharp peaks, more and more rows becoming visible as we climbed higher and higher. Having never been good at lying, even while engaging in simple chitchat, I was relieved to be able honestly to exclaim over the truly spectacular vistas before me.

The landscape was the easy part. When we got to her family home in Lindon, Ashley's mother hardly noticed me—she was totally absorbed in her younger daughter. While they were talking, Ashley's father, Harry, a big man with dark hair and a nose large enough for him to fit comfortably into my Armenian family, tried to make conversation. I appreciated his effort, but try as I might, I understood only every third or fourth word he uttered. Listening to him was like having a conversation in a bar with a very loud band playing. You might understand what the person is saying, but you might also totally miss the meaning by hanging sentences onto the few words you catch. I smiled a lot, nodded my head at what I hoped were appropriate moments, and stole glances at Ashley who was enveloped by her mother. Well, at least he was trying to relate to me, and I did remember Ashley's saying that her father's accent was particularly strong, one that even she and her sister did not always understand.

Thankfully, we could go to bed soon after we arrived. We had driven fourteen hours from our home in western Massachusetts, and it was late. Soon we were snuggling together in Ashley's double bed in her old room in the attic. No one mentioned the sleeping arrangements.

I had made it through the initial encounter, but I knew the next day would be important. We were to have dinner at Aunt Elizabeth's house, the woman who had nursed Ashley's beloved grandmother when she was dying of cancer more than two decades earlier. Still living in her mother's house, Aunt Elizabeth now reigned in her mother's place. Ashley had told me a lot about this aunt. She was an accomplished seamstress, making clothes and quilts for her children as well as other relatives. But mostly Ashley talked about Aunt Elizabeth's food, how Aunt Elizabeth had learned to cook from her mother, who had been well known in the small town as an excellent baker. When Aunt Elizabeth married Tony Tucci, a Sicilian, she learned southern Italian cooking from her mother-in-law.

One afternoon early in our relationship, when we were wondering what to have for dinner, Ashley told me that her Aunt Elizabeth made the best meatballs in the world. I wanted to try them, so Ashley called for the recipe. The mixture of beef, pork, and veal combined with lots of grated cheese, bread crumbs, beaten egg, and oregano resulted in the most flavorful meatballs I had ever had—maybe the best in the world, after all. I hoped that her accent was not as thick as her brother's. If I could understand Elizabeth, I hoped that I could engage her in some conversation about food.

The next night in Elizabeth's dining room I tasted her wonderful meatballs, but they were served to me with a full helping of hostility. When I raved about the dinner, her response was monosyllabic. Good, she said, as she turned away from me to ask her sister Betty if she had had enough to eat. She had decided to make this meal, she said, because she knew how much Ashley liked Italian food. She went on, raving to Betty about what a wonderful cook Tony's mother was, and that everyone around there, all the Italians, knew she was the best. Stopping for a minute to take a breath, she turned to Ashley and asked her if she had ever made those meatballs. I moved closer, hoping to get in on this conversation, but Elizabeth walked away when she saw me. Ashley shrugged, turned to her Aunt Betty, and told her how we had called Aunt Elizabeth for the recipe and now made her meatballs frequently. Arlene, she said, is a great cook. Betty smiled at me and said she hoped she would eat my food someday.

After a dessert of peach pie, we moved outside to Elizabeth's yard. Ashley showed me the trees she had climbed when she was a kid and where her grandmother's asparagus patch and perennial garden had been. I heard Grace's voice calling Ashley, and when she went to meet her mother, I was alone. I stood near the beautiful stone wall enjoying the cool of the evening and wondering why Elizabeth seemed to hate me. Just after we had cleared the dishes, we had been alone together for a minute. Trying again to make a connection, I asked why it was that people in West Virginia called their grandmothers "Mamaw." I had never heard that expression before I met Ashley. That was the way it was done, she said. Then she said that people from the North understood nothing about what people from "around here" know so well. I knew she was talking about race, but I bit my tongue. This time, I was the one who had no response. I had promised Ashley that I would not talk about black people or racism while we were in West Virginia.

On our trip home Ashley and I talked about Aunt Elizabeth. While Ashley was not out to her family, they knew that she had "special friends," and that sometimes she and these "friends" even lived together. The last "friendship" had lasted for twelve years. Mary Beth was a West Virginia girl, born and raised only a short drive from Lindon, and she had visited Ashley's family often. Like Elizabeth, she loved to sew, and Ashley had told me that she and Aunt Elizabeth had shared their projects and sewing secrets. Maybe I was just not feminine enough for Aunt Elizabeth. Or maybe the fact that I had children and that Ashley and I had recently bought a house together made our "friendship" a little more serious. Maybe her problem was that I was from the North. After all was said and done, maybe the fact that I was an Armenian, a feminist, a lesbian just did not matter. Maybe what was really important was that I was a New Yorker, a Northerner, a Yankee.

We decided that Aunt Elizabeth was really not that important. Ashley's mother mostly ignored me, but we did not think she disliked me. Her father talked to me whenever we were together, and I did manage to understand most of what he said one evening when we were alone together. Grace had gone to take a casserole to a sick friend, and I had decided not to accompany Ashley, who had gone to see an old high school friend. Harry had hurried through dinner to go to a cemetery board meeting. I was looking forward to a little time without having to relate to anyone, and had just settled myself on the couch with my book when I heard Harry come in. The meeting had been real short, he said, and now he could have the second cup of coffee he had not had time for after dinner. Wouldn't I like to join him in the kitchen? Not wanting to risk insulting Ashley's father, I smiled, put down my book, and followed him out of the living room. While he measured out the coffee and water into the old percolator, he was talking to me. When I repeatedly caught the words *plant* and *Carbide,* I realized from what I knew about him that he was telling me something about Union Carbide, the major employer in the area and the place where he had worked as a chemist for most of his life. When he came to the table to sit with me, I understood that he was talking about his relationship to the black workers in his plant. He wanted to be fair to them, he said, and he had decided to eat with them. He told me he was the first of the white professionals to sit with black workers in the lunchroom. I nodded my head, hoping he would not notice my puzzlement. He began to talk about particular people and suddenly rose from the table and went to the basement for photographs of the black men he had known, pointing out the three whose families had asked him to be a pallbearer at their funerals. The issue of race again. Was I wearing a sign? Maybe my being Armenian was part of it for Harry. I was an "other," but for him a positive one. He told me about the wonderful food Tony's Lebanese in-laws ate. He had found out where they shopped in Charleston, and whenever he was there he stocked up on Lebanese food. He said he particularly liked a kind of cheese they ate and wanted to know if my people ate that kind of cheese, too. I thought from his description of the crumbly, salty, white cheese that it was Feta, and I assured him it I grew up on it. After hours of very hard listening, I managed to understand most of what Ashley's father was saying, and from the inordinate amount of attention he was giving me, I realized that he liked me.

Over the years, Ashley and I have become familiar to our respective families. Though we never talked about my relationship with Ashley, my family took her in as they did all in-laws. They knew we were a couple, that we made a home together and that we were raising my children, their grandchildren, together. Harry also seemed to have no trouble with me or my children, but Grace went through a process. I was different from Ashley's other "special friend," nothing like the nice, quiet woman from the next town whom Ashley had known since college. My New York ways must have seemed brash to her, perhaps even rude. I learned to soften my edges, as Grace learned not to be so put off by my directness. We have finally come to enjoy our differences, and I think she has come to accept Ashley's "difference." Especially in the years after Harry died, she has visited us at least once a year, and we have gone to West Virginia, making the trip twice with our adult children. Grace talks to me when she calls if Ashley is out. She asks about my children and, best of all, calls me "sugar."

Only Elizabeth remained aloof. She was never as cutting as she was the first time, but she definitely had a problem with me or with seeing Ashley with me. For many years she was full of anger, mostly at men. It erupted from time to time, apropos of nothing but her own inner conversations. After her husband died, her anger dissipated, but I was still wary.

So, when Ashley suggested that we invite her mother and Aunt Elizabeth to visit us in the summer house that we had just bought in New Hampshire, I agreed but was worried. The place was tiny, especially the kitchen.
I had not even cooked a proper meal there. We had bought the place on a
whim in April. Ashley had seen pictures of a lake in New Hampshire, had
heard a house was for sale, and had come up with the startling idea that we
consider buying it. A call to the realtor confirmed that a house at the end
of the lake was available and that the price was very reasonable—cheaper
than some people's cars, Ashley kept saying. We went to see it in the depths
of winter and fell in love with the small lake surrounded by hills, and the
funky little house right at the edge of the water.

The first summer we owned the house we spent lots of time there, but
all of it was devoted to the work of renovation. I cooked at home and
warmed our meals in the little microwave that the old couple who had sold
us the house had left for us. All of our time was spent doing the small car-
pentry jobs Ashley could manage, wall boarding and painting endless coats
over old wallpaper. She and our friend Alec had knocked down the walls of
the three small rooms, which had closed in the downstairs, and opened the
area up to the view of the lake. The space felt bigger, but the kitchen was
still just a galley with only Ashley's Aunt Ruthie's old enamel table and one-
foot slivers of counters on either side of the sink for work spaces.

I had to prepare meals from this space for seven people for three days.
Besides Elizabeth and Grace, we invited Ginny, Ashley's older sister, and
Ginny's son Jeb and his lover, Sam. Ashley, Jeb always said, really knew how
to be an aunt. She had always been an important person in his life. When
he came out as a gay man, that bond deepened and I was brought into the
circle. Jeb brought most of his lovers "home" to meet us, and after he and
Sam had known each other for only three weeks, they made the trip from
New York City to Massachusetts. I felt instant rapport with Sam, whose
mother's family were survivors of the Holocaust. We laughed at each other's fears—survivors' descendants   his the well-known and mine the still-
unacknowledged genocide. I was so glad that Jeb and Sam were going to be
part of the weekend.

I worked over the menus for weeks. Everyone but Elizabeth had eaten
my food and expected wonderful meals—all but desserts. Not liking

sweets, I had not learned to bake and I did not particularly care about the end of the meal. Ashley usually got something from a bakery, or we had fruit and frozen yogurt. Breakfasts were not a problem. Jeb and Sam were staying at an inn and would eat there. Everyone else could help themselves to cereal, toast, bagels, and fruit. I did not worry too much about lunches either. Ginny, Jeb, and Sam, always conscious of their fat intake, would be delighted with sliced turkey sandwiches, but I did want to have something to make lunch special. I decided on tabouli for one day, not the hippie kind with carrots and red peppers, but tabouli made with lots of garlic and so much chopped parsley, scallions, and mint that the grain is like a garnish to the greens. For another day, I planned on soup, harvesting our sorrel patch for the requisite four cups and using low-fat yogurt instead of cream. Making it a day ahead would work well. The laborious task of washing and chopping heaps of greens for the tabouli could be done at home, as could preparing the bulgur. When ready to serve, I would only have to mix them together. The greens would stay fresh and crisp while the bulgur continued to absorb the garlic, oil, and lemon.

Dinners, on the other hand, presented more of a problem. Weekends always meant drinks and appetizers before dinner. I could not make anything as elaborate as the cheese-filled Georgian breads I sometimes made for Christmas, decidedly not low fat but eaten with gusto just the same. Nor would this little kitchen allow me to cook *lahmajoon,* a kind of open-faced meat pie made by spreading a thin round of yeast dough with ground lamb mixed with tomatoes, onions, pepper, garlic, and lots of cumin, basil, and parsley. The *lahmajoon* were baked until the dough was brown and the meat cooked. Usually a main course, I had lately made them as appetizers. They were a mess to make and took lots of room—a surface to roll out the dough, another to spread the meat on the rounds, and another to cool the finished *lahmajoons.* The dinners, too, would take some thinking. Not a vegetarian by principle, Grace just ate little meat. But she was easy. She had learned to love Armenian string cheese wrapped in lavash—a soft, thin Armenian bread—and my rice pilaf. Her appetite, diminished with age, opened wide for the mild cheese dotted with black caraway seeds and the rice laced with butter and flavored with chicken broth. I would make lots of pilaf, and serve it with *fassoulia,* string beans cooked in tomato sauce, both staples from my childhood. Chicken, marinated and cooked on the grill, would complete that meal. I wanted to have the pilaf on the first night, so Grace could have her favorites right away.

I had done as much as I could in my well-appointed and roomy kitchen at home, but I was still worried about how I would manage in the little, untried kitchen at the lake house. Ginny was driving up from Connecticut to our house with Elizabeth and Grace in the morning. They were to arrive around lunchtime and Ginny had offered to bring sandwiches. I was grateful because I knew that the job of organizing and packing the food for the trip would take most of the morning. After lunch, Ashley drove Ginny's car and I drove our pickup with the two coolers filled with marinating chicken and lamb, sorrel soup, caponata, tabouli, cheeses, bags of bagels, bread, fruit, snacks, and all the other ingredients necessary for the weekend. I was happy to delay family time for another couple of hours. The trip alone also gave me the space to ruminate on everything that could go wrong, all the things I had probably forgotten and the sharp looks and comments that Elizabeth probably would throw my way.

When we got there, I unpacked the food while everyone exclaimed over the beauty of the lake and the cuteness of the house. Luckily, the refrigerator was new and big, and, to my relief, all the food from the coolers fit easily. I had already done everything for dinner except to make the pilaf and the string beans, so I could relax for a few hours. I changed out of my sweaty clothes and got into my bathing suit just as Jeb and Sam arrived from New York. After more hugs and oohs and aahs over the house and lake, we all settled into the afternoon.

I was lying half asleep at the edge of the lake on one of the chaise lounges we had gotten for two dollars each at a tag sale, when I heard Elizabeth's high-pitched voice and the slam of the back door. She was telling Jeb and Sam some Lindon gossip, news she had from her daughter Vicky. I turned over to look at them, now sitting on the back porch in the five-dollar director chairs from another tag sale. Jeb knew the people Elizabeth was talking about and occasionally threw back his head in laughter, but Sam was also engaged in the conversation because Elizabeth would often turn to him and fill him in on the relationships among the people. Now, you know, Sam, Tammy is Rosser's daughter, Rosser Greene, the lawyer who was in Harry's lodge.

Clearly, Elizabeth did not seem to have trouble with gay men. Of course, Jeb and Sam were not out, but they were obviously a couple, had been to West Virginia often together, and had been living together for more than five years. I remembered then Jeb's telling me that the first time Sam had gone to Lindon with him and the first time he had met Elizabeth, she had talked endlessly about mixed marriages and how Christians and Jews just could not make it for very long as couples. Was she really worried about Jeb's mixed "marriage"? I then wondered if Elizabeth might have been particularly sensitive to this issue because she had married a Sicilian. But that idea was overtaken by my delight in thinking about Ashley's Aunt Elizabeth as a "fag hag." Smiling to myself, I turned back around to stare at the lake, watch the loons and their baby, wait for a glimpse of the heron.

Things seemed to be going fairly well. Ashley and Ginny canoed out to the swimming rock and when they came back, Sam and I went out to the rock for a swim. Jeb held his post in the sun, maintaining his tan. Grace and Elizabeth sat on the porch chatting. Before long, my stomach told me it was time to think about eating. I went into the kitchen to get the appetizers out of the refrigerator. Caponata, braided cheese pulled into thin strings, feta chopped with lots of fresh tarragon and dill, lavash and olives. I had just begun to unbraid the cheese when Sam came in and as usual gave me a hand. He washed his hands and picked up a strand of cheese to work on. I called Ashley to make drinks, and handed her the beans to string and snap.

A breeze had come up over the lake and the late afternoon sun fell behind the house, shading the porch, so I was not surprised when I heard Elizabeth's voice coming toward the kitchen and the back door slam. Grace said she felt a little chilled. Ashley was in the kitchen area making drinks, and Grace gave her a hug. She was so happy, she said, to be here. Looking down at the enamel table she saw the appetizers, now in their serving plates and ready to be taken to the picnic table outside. Grace's eyes twinkled and she smiled at me when she saw her favorites on the tray. Elizabeth gave a passing glance to the array on her way upstairs to get their sweaters. When Elizabeth came back down, Grace was working on her second piece of cheese, exclaiming to Elizabeth how good it was and how she had to have a piece. Elizabeth responded that she would wait until she had her drink before eating anything.

By that time, everyone had drinks and we all went back outside. Elizabeth did have some cheese and asked what kind it was. Never heard of that kind of cheese before, she said. Didn't think they had it in Lindon? Maybe she could get it at the big Krogers in the next town, and she turned to Ginny to fill her in on the size and grandeur of the newly remodeled supermarket. She did have more cheese, though, and some caponata, asking before her second helping if I had made it myself and almost smiling when I said yes. I thought maybe she would ask me more about it, but she leaned over the table to ask Grace if she had some and then was engaged in a conversation with Jeb.

Ashley went into the house to make a second round of drinks and I followed to start the pilaf and beans. We had a moment of evaluation. It seemed to be going well. Everyone was getting along. The day was beautiful. The swimming and canoeing had been great. Wasn't this a wonderful place we had? And everyone was enjoying the food already, even Aunt Elizabeth. She thought the fire would be ready soon. Should she start the chicken? I said it was time. She went back out laden with drinks and returned for the chicken that had been marinating for a couple of days in lemon, a little oil, and herbs.

I got out the rice jar, measured three cups, and began to wash it, when I heard the back door slam again. Elizabeth and Grace were back inside. It had just gotten too cold for them, Grace said, so they were coming in to keep me company. She was going to sit at the table and look out the window at the beautiful lake. She just loved it here. Elizabeth walked over to see what I was doing. Why in the world was I washing that rice, she demanded. I explained that it was basmati rice from India, and I always washed it, explaining that my mother had always washed her rice before she cooked it. She did not respond, turned and walked to the table to join Grace. They fell into the easy chatter of women in their eighties who have talked to each other every day of their adult lives. Wasn't this a pretty place? Elizabeth was so glad Ashley had a camp. She remembered how much Ashley had enjoyed the place she and Tony had had on the Greenbrier River in Pocahantas County. Now that her Vicky's Tom had fixed it up, the grandchildren were enjoying it just as Ashley had. Grace assented, not taking her eyes off the lake.

I drained the rice, and as I melted large quantities of butter and slowly sauteed vermicelli noodles until they were golden brown, the fragrance filled the room. I added the rice, stirred until the grains were all coated, and poured in the chicken broth. When it boiled, I turned the heat down to simmer and started to sauté onions in oil for the *fassoulia*. When they became translucent, I added chopped garlic, stirred for a minute before pouring in tomato sauce and some dried tarragon. The familiar smell rose to my nostrils and calmed any apprehensions I might have had about this meal. I felt Elizabeth's eyes on me. Was that tomato sauce for the string beans, she asked, her question an honest inquiry rather than a rebuke. I smiled and said yes. I smelled the sauce again, added salt, pepper, a little more tarragon, then put in the beans, brought it back to a boil and lowered the heat to a simmer. Elizabeth said she'd bet that those beans were going to be real good, and that she sometimes made beans with tomato sauce. Tony's family liked it that way. She hadn't had them cooked like that for the longest time. She was getting ready for dinner, she said. She turned to Grace before I had a chance to respond and asked if she was getting hungry? Grace, still looking out the window, nodded. I looked over their heads to the lake that by now had turned pink as the reflected clouds gathered the setting sun's rays on their undersides. I stopped for another minute and noticed that the mountain at the other end of the lake was now a cool, slate gray with a tinge of purple. Just as I was turning back to the stove, I saw the heron flying across the lake to land on the little island in front of the house. I hoped I had called out in time for Grace and Elizabeth to see it in flight. When I looked at their smiling faces, I knew they had caught the magnificence of its glide.

I cleaned up the mess I had made to this point. Now for the salad. The dressing was made; I had washed the many different varieties of lettuce at home. They merely needed to be torn into the salad bowl. I added a few tomatoes and some chopped fresh parsley, basil, and dill. Ashley called to have me come and look at the chicken. As I was going out, Ginny, Jeb, and Sam were coming in, carrying what was left of the cheese and bread. The caponata was gone; only a few crumbs of feta and strands of braided cheese remained. Everyone was inside now. My job was almost done. I turned the chicken for the final time and when I came in, Ginny and Jeb were setting the table, and Sam and Ashley were putting away the drinks and the few leftover appetizers. I went to get the chicken and when I returned everything was on the table. Dinner was on.

They all raved about the food, especially Elizabeth, who had three helpings of *fassoulia*. For the rest of the weekend, she talked to me—about food and the importance of having a place to relax, and what a good friend Grace had been to her over the years. And now, when she writes to Ashley, she always adds a little hello for me at the end of her letters.

Something about the beans got me over. Sometime while I was cooking the *fassoulia*, I went from being "that woman" to Arlene, Ashley's friend, who really knows how to cook, and maybe is a nice person. I will always be grateful to that *fassoulia*.

Cooking can sometimes keep women in "our" place and sometimes help us out of a place. If you are a cook and want to move from one place to another with a difficult in-law, relative, or friend you might try not cooking at all, but if you think some *fassoulia* and pilaf might help, here are the recipes.

FASSOULIA, STRING BEANS IN TOMATO SAUCE

1 pound fresh string beans, snapped or frenched

1 16-ounce can tomato sauce

1 medium yellow onion, thinly sliced in half moons (my grandmother did this holding the onion in her hand—a cutting board will work)

1–2 cloves garlic, finely chopped (not put through a press)

1 tablespoon olive oil

¼ cup red wine, optional

dried or fresh basil, to taste

dried tarragon, to taste

salt, pepper

Heat the oil over medium heat and add the onions and a little salt. Stir and cook slowly until the onions are translucent, and then add the garlic. Stir to mix garlic into onions, and add the wine. Raise heat and cook until wine has almost evaporated. Then add the tomato sauce. Bring to a boil, add herbs, salt, and pepper. You should be able to smell the tarragon. Lower heat and simmer for about 10 minutes, then add the beans. Bring to a boil again then lower to a simmer, check seasonings, cover and cook until beans are cooked through—about 25 to 30 minutes. If you are not fond of tarragon, or want another taste for a change, use fresh dill and add it about 5 minutes before the beans are cooked. The taste is very fresh and quite different from the licorice-like tarragon.

For thousands of years Armenians have lived under various rulers in different countries in the Middle East. Armenians living under the Ottoman Turks experienced a number of pogroms in the late nineteenth century. Early in the twentieth century the Turkish government perpetrated a genocide on the 2 million Armenians living within its borders, a genocide that was keenly watched by Germany, Turkey's ally at the time. The response to these cataclysms by Armenians living in diaspora was divided into two bitterly opposed political camps, each eventually creating its own community organizations including two separate sees for the Armenian Apostolic Church. While the rivalry between the two parties, the Ramgavars and the Tashnags, raged in Armenian communities from Beirut to California, Armenian American families were split into two other opposing camps: the Uncle Ben's and Carolina rice divisions. Each side insisted that only their rice made pilaf properly, the other rice resulting in something that could not be called pilaf. My family was clearly on the Carolina side of the divide, but some of my best friends were on Uncle Ben's. The only other rice we had in our house was kept in a large glass jar and used on very special occasions. That rice came from Persia. It was hidden in each shipment of rugs for the family Oriental rug importing business. My memory of pilaf made with this rice is that the grains were very long and it had a distinctive fragrance. I now imagine it was basmati or a similar rice. The availability of basmati, which has recently appeared in my supermarket, has made the Carolina/Uncle Ben's war moot since it easily bests both brands. Any Middle Eastern or food specialty store will have basmati rice. If you have the misfortune to live where no such stores exist, you will have to revert to the American brands, and I, of course, recommend Carolina. If you do use basmati rice, be sure to wash it until the water runs clear, and drain it thoroughly.

RICE PILAF, TURKISH ARMENIAN STYLE

1 cup rice

1 cup very thin egg noodles

1⅔ cups chicken broth (you may use water)

salt, pepper

¼ cup butter

As with any rice, you need a heavy pot with a good, tight cover. Melt the butter over medium heat and add the egg noodles. Stir constantly until noodles turn a golden brown. Do not leave the rice at this point. If the phone rings or a long-lost lover comes through the door, take the rice pot off the heat before you do anything else. If the noodles burn, you have to start again. Once the noodles are golden, add the washed and drained rice and stir to coat each grain with the melted butter. Add the liquid—chicken broth or water—salt, and pepper, and bring to a boil. Taste the liquid to check the seasonings. Lower heat, cover and cook for 25 minutes. Do not ever open the pot while the rice is cooking. If you are not eating immediately, when the rice is done, open lid, fluff rice with a fork and put lid back, but do not completely cover pot. The rice reheats beautifully in the microwave, one of the few things a microwave does really well.

These two dishes are wonderful with chicken, lamb, or even fish. They do not really communicate well with beef. Vegetarians may want to add half a can of rinsed and drained chickpeas to the string beans. The *fassoulia* tastes great when piled on top of the rice.

PART TWO

CHANGING RELATIONS TO ETHNIC FOOD

Los Chilaquiles de mi 'ama
The Language of Everyday Cooking
Meredith E. Abarca

> Cuando me casé las hermanas de tu papá y su mamá hacían las tortillas
> bien feas. Y cuando vi que ellas hacían unas tortillas feas, ya no me dio
> vergüenza. Yo me acuerdo que quise demostrarles que yo sabía hacer
> las tortillas mejor que ellas. [Ellas] hacían las tortillas bien feas, feas.
> ¡Uy me lucía yo haciendo mis tortillas, las ponía así en un canastito!
> ¡Uy—y mis tortillas me quedaban bien delgaditas y se inflaban
> bieeeen bonito! Las que yo hacía. Este, sí, sí les ganaba yo pa' hacer
> tortillas allí. Sí, ellas hacían unas tortillas feas, panzonas, agujeradas.
>
> My mother, Liduvina-Vélez[1]

Not long ago, my mother, my older sister, Alma Contreras, and I sat around
my mother's kitchen table having *charlas culinarias* (culinary talks). We all
talked about our earliest cooking memories, our favorite dishes, and the
dishes that have circulated in our family for generations and how each generation has added its own *chiste* (twist). In the course of our conversation, the
older gourmet cook of the family was mentioned numerous times: my
mother's sister, who lives in Puebla, Mexico. Presently, I hold the title of the
young gourmet *cookbook* cook. While my kitchen has a special bookshelf for
all my international and vegetarian cookbooks and my years of subscription
to *Bon Appétit,* their kitchens do not contain even a box to keep the recipes
we exchange. Since my Aunt Esperanza had been mentioned so often during
our conversation, I decided to have a *charla culinaria* with her by telephone:

> Cooking classes I never took. What happens is that I like to cook. I
> *do* like to cook. I don't know that much, but people say I have a
> good hand for cooking. But I never took cooking classes. The truth

is that I like to make a dish and to see that my family enjoys it. It is a form of showing love. Or of showing affection to your family, right? To dedicate to them the time in the kitchen and prepare something delicious for them and hear them say: "Ah, how wonderful this is!" I like to cook something for the people I love. For my sons, for my nieces, for my sisters. For my brother-in-law. I like to cook for them when I see that they enjoy what I cook, and I enjoy seeing them enjoy what I have cooked for dinner.[2]

The previous passages, from our *charlas culinarias,* are in response to general questions I asked each person: What is your first memory of cooking? How did you learn to cook? Their answers reveal the different personal relationships they have or have had toward cooking. For my mother as we see at the beginning of this chapter, making tortillas was a way of reclaiming and reasserting her own presence as a teenage woman in a household governed by a matriarchal authority. Making tortillas was also a way of defining her own aesthetics. For my aunt, cooking represents knowledge based on experience, not on cookbooks—textual knowledge—and is a vehicle for transforming food into gestures of love. My sister, Alma, understands cooking as a necessity, but also as a duty she must perform:

Well, I don't know. I have never liked the kitchen. I would be interested in wandering around. Cooking never caught my interest. There are people that from the time they're children, they have notions about cooking, and others don't. Cooking never caught my interest, and to this day, I don't like it. I do it because I have to do it. But to like it, to say: "I'm going to go into the kitchen." No. I don't like to cook. Well, I don't know much about cooking.[3]

For all these women cooking represents much more than just feeding a hungry stomach. Cooking is a language of self-representation.

Cooking Discourses

The language of food serves different needs; it is spoken in public kitchens and in private ones; it is a language spoken by many women. Many are working-class women like my mother, my sister, my aunts, women whom I rarely see represented in the pages of books, but who speak the language of everyday cooking to express artistic creation, manifestations of love, self-assurance, and economic survival. Therefore, in my desire to understand the discourses of quotidian cooking and how a working-class woman's sense of self is refashioned through such practice, I do not wish to limit this culinary language to literary interpretations. I am seasoning my work with ethnographic as well as poetic analysis. As my Aunt Esperanza says when speaking of the right etiquette for selecting a daily menu:

> If you make a fried noodle soup, you have to make either a veg-etable or a cream soup. So it will combine because you can't make fried noodles and noodle soup, right? Meaning, noodle soup and fried noodle soup, both noodle soups. These are things that you are constantly learning throughout life, right?[4]

My aunt's articulation of soup combinations and her knowledge of an etiquette based on an evolution of specific cultural practices parallels theorists such as Stuart Hall, Aron Rodrigue, Anna L. Tsing, Emma Pérez, and other critics who ground the analysis of their subject research within its own cultural and historical specificity. Their rationale (their etiquette) for such grounding gives justice and merit to culture-specific practices. For Rodrigue to analyze tolerance in the Ottoman Empire, it would not serve him well to employ analytical methodologies based on the Aztecs' structure of power. These theorists argue that cultural practices have their own strategic order of production governed by their own specific historical evolution.

Following cultural studies methodology, the only fiction in this chapter is from Chicana women writers, since a similar cultural reference exists between these writings and the *charlas culinarias* I have had with Mexican women who live here in the United States or in Mexico. Chicana writings and the ethnographic research share a cultural specificity, or in my aunt's words, they share the same cultural etiquette. Therefore, the legitimacy of my analytical juxtaposition is the same legitimacy that governs the protocol of serving "sopa de pasta" with "sopa ya sea de verduras o . . . sopa de crema" (fried noodle soup with a vegetable or a cream soup). While my analysis shares cultural specificity, my theoretical framework is what Chicana critic Tey Diana Rebolledo calls "salpicón," a bit of this and a bit of that, just as recipes are put together (5).

The language of everyday cooking is another avenue for both Chicana writers and working-class, nonwriter women of "seizing . . . subjectivity—evolving into speaking [and] writing subjects" (Rebolledo 4). Yvonne Yarbro-Bejarono says that Chicana writers "search . . . for a language that consciously opposes the dominant culture." Yarbro-Bejarono states that a number of Chicana critics, including herself, understand that a woman's "self-empowerment" comes through writing. She also claims that the "Chicana subject as writer" is a central focus in Chicana literary creation. "Writing," writes Yarbro-Bejarono, "emerged as the medium for the definition of individual subjectivity of the Chicana writer through the articulation of collective experience and identity" (213–18).

While I agree with Yarbro-Bejarono, writing down stories regrettably requires something that working-class women often do not have: the luxury of time. The majority of working-class women do not have a "room of their own" in which to sit peacefully and quietly, privately writing out their lives. However, many women do have a kitchen in which they often make their own food and inscribe their life experiences—through the seasoning of it, through the sharing of their recipes, and through the time spent in other women's kitchens.[5]

The language of cooking, with its gendered discourse, also opposes the dominant culture. A literary and cinematographic example that illustrates this defiant act is Laura Esquivel's *Como agua para chocolate (Like Water for Chocolate)*. In this film, the act of preparing, cooking, and serving food is a multifaceted, gendered discourse of health, pregnancy, sensuality, sexuality, retaliation, and liberation (see Leonardi; de Valdés). The simultaneous co-existence of such discourses coming out of the kitchen has a subversive function. A cultural and familial tradition confines Tita, the protagonist, to life in the kitchen. The matriarchal power subordinating her denies her the right to love. Nonetheless, Tita, as the agent of these discourses, learns to overcome such obstacles by constructing alternative forms of expression. For instance, eating *codornices en pétalos de rosas* (quail in rose petal sauce) becomes for her and her beloved the very act of sexual intercourse. Tita "in spite of many troubles, a brush with insanity, jealousy, repression," all the outcome of a familial tradition, "manages, through her cooking, to develop her own language that combines erotics with independence" (Lawless 271).

The act of resistance in culinary discourse is governed by an embodiment of sense, smell, taste, touch, and texture that yields the right *sazón* (taste). The logic governing this language is based on sensual forms of knowledge. Such knowledge, with its disregard for the absoluteness based on empirical knowledge, on scientific evidence, presents a challenge to the dominant culture. For instance, during a *charla culinaria* with my mother, I asked her how I would know the quantity—empirical means of knowledge—of lime to add to water when soaking *maiz* for making *masa* for *tortillas*. She looked at me with an expression that made me feel I had asked a rather obvious question. She did answer my question. Extending one of her hands, she showed me her palm while with the other she made a motion as if gathering lime out of a sack and pouring it into her open palm and said: "Te la pones así, la sientes pa' calcular" (you put it in like this, you feel it in order to calculate). My sister did something similar when she gave me a recipe for *pozole*. As she gave me a list of "add this and add that" to a boiling pot, I—the academically trained one—stopped her and asked her for quantities: "No sé decir yo de cantidades porque es algo que yo le calculo" (I don't know how to speak about quantities because it is something I just calculate). However, culinary knowledge is not grounded only on intuition or pure senses. This type of argument only reinforces the binary split of the mind (men) and body (women) process of knowledge. The point here is to establish the notion that knowledge (just like the process of writing stories) is obtained through a diverse realm of experiences. Sor Juana Inés de la Cruz, a seventeenth-century Mexican nun, eloquently articulates the cooking experience as follows:

> What could I tell you, my Lady, of the secrets of nature I have discovered while cooking! That an egg holds together and fries in fat or oil, and that, on the contrary, it disintegrates in syrup. That to keep sugar liquid, it suffices to add the tiniest bit of water in which a quince or some other fruit has soaked. But, Madam, what is there for us women to know, if not bits of kitchen philosophy? . . . And I always say, when I see these details. If Aristotle had been a cook, he would have written much more. (Lawless 269)

Culinary practices not only have their own distinctive epistemology; they transform into culinary creativity.

Helena María Viramontes interconnects the power of the written word and the power of creative expression found in the kitchen:

> We *mujeres* are inventive people. My mother, for example, faced the challenge of feeding eleven people every evening. Time and time again, I saw her cut four pork chops, add this and that and this, pour water, and miraculously feed all of us with a tasty *guiso*. Or the *nopales* she grew, cleaned, diced, scrambled with eggs, or meat, or, chile, or really mixed with anything her budget could afford, and we had such a variety of tasty dishes! (292)

Viramontes attributes her mother's talent in the kitchen to her skills of invention, innovation, and imagination—crucial elements for the creation of written fiction. On a similar note, Rosario Ferré challenges the dominant culture in the realm of academic theoretical debate in regard to the supposed superiority of either female/male or male/female writing. Ferré demystifies the dichotomy of such essential gender differences vis-à-vis our mothers' cooking practices. She concludes her argument on gendered writing differences as follows:

> What is important is not to determine if we as women have to write with an open or closed writing structure, with a poetic language or with an obscene language, with our heads or with our hearts. What is important is to apply that fundamental lesson that we learn from our mothers, the first ones, after all, who taught us to fight with fire: the secret of writing, like the secret of good cooking, has nothing to do with gender, but with the wisdom with which ingredients are combined. (154)[6]

Viramontes and Ferré thus find new creative expressions to challenge a dominant ideology that denies women creative and intellectual outlet. Both of these critics see the power of the written word and the power of the practice of *our* mothers' cooking as part of the same continuum, as part of the same process of writing women's stories.

The sharing of women's stories takes place through the process of sharing recipes. But like a story that yields different possibilities with each new reading, so do recipes yield new stories with each new retelling. Susan

Leonardi describes a recipelike narrative that is "reproducible, and further, its hearers-readers-receivers are *encouraged* to reproduce it, and, in reproducing it, to revise it and make it their own" (Leonardi 344). Consequently, a new story is narrated. The process of telling different stories that I speak of, however, is not in the hands of a re-creator (the reader) of recipes. The narration of a story is not in the recipe per se, but in the actual act of expressing the process of making a meal, of creating unique and distinct recipes, of adding a personal *chiste* (twist) to an old recipe. A recipe's composition, according to Debora Castillo, "is not a blueprint. It is less a formula than a general model; less an axiom of unchanging law and more a theory of possibilities" that allows the recipe teller the ability to express multiple narratives (xiii). The ethnographic emphasis of this project is not to write out recipes so the reader can appropriate them through a process of re-creation. Such appropriation changes the meaning of the story. Within the frame of my analysis, if others revise the process and recipes conveyed by the *charlas culinarias,* the cooks' own *chiste* in their cooking will be obscured. Each recipe, as Goldman says, is "an individual authority"; therefore, the appropriation of an individual's recipe becomes the appropriation of that person's authority and self-assertion. In the ethnography of *charlas culinarias,* these women's voices are articulated through their own personal *chiste,* so the revision of their practices and recipes detracts from their moments of seizing subjectivity (Goldman 188).

Writers as Cooks and Cooks as Writers—Marinating an Identity

In a theoretical analysis of the historical evolution of female identity construction in Chicana literature, Rebolledo observes: "In the process of formulation [of] an identity both ethnic and female, one area that is distinctly original is the concept of the writer as cook. It seems that one way to express individual subjectivity (while at the same time connecting to the collective and community) is by reinforcing this female identity as some one who cooks. One of the spaces traditionally construed as female is the kitchen, and Chicana literature is filled with images of active women preparing food (130). Culinary imagery in poetic expressions is one way Chicana writers, or the writers as cooks, negotiate their individual as well as their collective subjectivity. Culinary discourses can be deciphered if food, like language, is treated as a code. Therefore, "the message it encodes," as Mary Douglas observes, "will be found in the pattern of social relations being expressed" (250).

An example of this is la Chrisx's poem "La Loca de la Raza Cósmica." La Chrisx's poem is a search for an identity in different and simultaneous registers of the social body. The poem is a recognition of the vast diversity of women within the Chicana (and Latina) community, therefore, the social relations expressed through culinary references in the conceptualization of an identity are the religious self, the keeper of tradition, the dutiful wife and mother, the socially and politically racialized other, and the modern liberated woman.

> Soy tan simple como la capirotada . . .
>> soy la comida en la mesa cuando llegan
>>> del jale
>> soy la que calienta los TV dinners
>> soy tamales at Christmas time . . .
> soy Coconut[7]

"La capirotada" has religious implications: *La capirotada* is a traditional Mexican dish that carries with it a relation to one of the fundamental cultural identities for many of us (Chicanas/Mexicanas), Catholicism. *La capirotada* is a dish prepared only during *cuaresma* (Lent), the period of the crucifixion and resurrection of Jesus Christ.[8] This line in its entirety connotes food as the embodiment of the self, the offering of the self through food.[9] In la Chrisx's poem, however, the act of self-giving for the formation of an identity resonates with an array of possibilities:

> Soy love-maker to my main man . . .
> living to love and support
> my husband and to nurture and teach
> my children . . .
>> soy la Revolucionaria . . .
> soy la chicana en los conferences . . .
> soy wondering if there is a God

> soy la Virgen de Guadalupe
> soy la community organizer . . .
> Soy achieving a higher status en la causa
>   de la mujer . . .
> Soy finding strength from within
> my Chicana soul.[10]

The act of self-offering is also symbolically charged in everyday culinary practices. In the cases of my Aunt Esperanza and my sister Alma, their sense of self is tenaciously sustained by the validation of their emotions, by the convictions of their thoughts, and by the right to their creative expression. They enter a third space where the act of self-offering is an active and conscious choice of identity assertion rather than a passive and submissive acceptance of the domestic space, the kitchen, as the proper woman's place.[11]

When she serves her *comida en la mesa* (food on the table), my aunt is serving the gift of her love and emotions.

> It's a way of showing love. At least this is how I feel about it. And I
> feel that you also see it this way. And you like to cook. And I believe
> that you understand me because you also—I have seen you, when I
> come you cook, or someone that you love comes, you cook for
> them. Because you also like the kitchen. We enjoy it [cooking].[12]

Not only does my aunt address the importance of her emotions toward her family with the offering of food, she also connects the gesture of self-giving as a communal act for women's emotional expression. Self-giving here becomes a communal act of showing gestures of love through plates filled with food. Yet my aunt's or my own act of self-giving does not follow the traditional implication of religious self-sacrifice: the denial of our individuality for the benefit of our family, community, and culture. Cooking for either of us is not an obligatory performance but rather a celebration of our own affectionate and creative expression.

Furthermore, my aunt's choice of words in speaking about her culinary practices claims her authority and knowledge. Her way of speaking about cooking indirectly questions the Western tradition of logical rationale. She affirms her knowledge not through a process of what she thinks about the act of offering her love through food, but through a process of how she feels: "así lo siento." She could have easily said "así lo pienso" or "así lo veo" (this is how I think, or, this is how I see it). One could argue that such choice adheres to an objective development of knowledge since "feelings" are subjective and often dismissed as less valuable. Yet this is one source of her intellect, knowledge, and creative expression. If women "professionals who can cook should never admit it if they want to maintain credibility," as Leonardi says, because "cooking can be a dangerous thing for a woman" (341), my aunt's culinary expression has yet another dimension for those of us working within the boundaries of the academic world. For those of us who are also cooks, affirming our culinary knowledge based on the observation of "chemical interactions, physics, and even philosophy while cooking," as did the erudite seventeenth-century nun Sor Juana Inés de la Cruz, will only add to our intellectual merit and growth (Rebolledo 133).

For my sister Alma, culinary knowledge foregrounds her creative identity. In her case, even though she mentions more than once that she does not like to cook, when she speaks of what in our family is known as "sus famosas enchiladas" (her famous enchiladas), this conversation takes place:

> *Alma:* "Okay. The majority of people dip the *tortillas* in oil first. Then in the sauce. Then they put cheese in the middle and fold them. And this is how they do it. I did it this way once, and I didn't like them. They tasted only like wet *tortillas* in a sauce. What I do, I dip the *tortilla* in the sauce first and then I fry it in oil. It's more of a mess. Which means everything gets dirty. One more thing. Many people, for instance, they're going to eat dinner together, therefore, they make many *enchiladas.* They put them in the oven, and then they put everything out and everybody serves themselves. I don't like it this way. I like to prepare them as people are eating them."
>
> *Me:* "But in this other way, everyone sits and has dinner together."
> *Mom:* "Well, just because it's more work to have to be making them. But the flavor. The steamy flavor."[13]

Alma's connection to her family at this moment is through time, devotion, and labor in the kitchen. However, this labor within the woman's place is a temporal, conscious, and discursive action. Alma's culinary practice at such moments serves to transform the dismissal of her cooking ability to the assertion of her cooking creativity as she adds her own personal *chiste*.

> One time I made a salsa with oregano using a mortar and pestle, and
> I thought of putting it in the middle before putting in the cheese
> and folding the *tortillas*. One day, I thought of this, and it tasted
> good, and now this is how I do it. Which means, I have already
> changed my recipe. To some people I tell them, and they say, "But
> those are not *enchiladas*." I know how I like them, and this is how I
> make them.[14]

Alma's affirmation of her right to creative expression becomes an affirmation of her agency. The narration of her process in adding her own *chiste* when making *enchiladas* conveys the story of a woman who at certain moments sees cooking as more than a wife's duty and obligation. The confidence in Alma's practice tells the story of a woman who no longer feels apologetic about her supposed lack of culinary knowledge toward her younger—academic gourmet cookbook—sister. As a matter of fact, she even goes so far as to question my use of measuring utensils and cookbooks: "I never write down measurements. You also cook only be calculating. Or do you use measurements? I don't think you go and look at the recipe. [I] don't base my cooking on a book and looking at what must be added from a recipe."[15] The tone of suspicion with regard to measurements and cookbooks stresses and validates knowledge based on her specific lived experiences. Thus, my sister's claim of agency comes from her creative interventions.

I wish to be careful not to romanticize the culinary practices of these women, or their lives for that matter. Their marital relations are still very much governed by old, traditional, and culturally gender-specific codes of behavior. However, although *machismo* often governs, *marianismo* does not always submit.[16] Women like my aunt and sister are not devoid of agency and a sense of self, which is articulated through the narratives of their cooking practices. My sister's style of making *enchiladas* and of normally eating when everyone has finished could tempt some of us to argue that she is not "at *will* the taker and initiator, for her own right," as Hélène Cixous advocates women should become by taking a pen and writing poetry (880). If this is all we are able to hear, what happens to Alma's statement: "Yo sé como a mí me gustan y es como yo las hago" (I know how I like them and that's how I make them)? The self-assertiveness in this comment must not be dismissed just because Alma is standing over a hot stove. Alma and my Aunt Esperanza, nonacademic women, are working within and against social and cultural structures of power to rearticulate their subjectivity by adding their own *chiste* to the meaning and function of their cooking. My sister and my aunt as cook-writers are, like most writers as cooks, working in processes of re-vision.

Adrienne Rich foregrounds the importance embedded in the act of re-visioning for women writers. "Women writers, even when they are supposed to be addressing women, write for men; or at least they write with the haunting sense of being overheard by men, and certainly with the inescapable knowledge of having already been defined in men's words. That is why 're-vision' . . . is for women 'an act of survival'" (qtd. in Behar and Gordon 6). Re-vision of dominant ideologies—of social, of political, and of cultural practices—is an act of survival for all women. La Chrisx's poetic metonymy—"Soy la comida en la mesa" (I'm the food on the table)—is a re-vision that works against the social construction of a woman's place. While it acknowledges the existence of the kitchen as the woman's place, this place does not necessarily constrain a woman's agency, as her poem illustrates—and as comments in the *charlas culinarias* demonstrate.

La Chrisx's third culinary metonymy, "soy la que calienta los TV dinners," also works within and against dominant, conceived notions of a woman's place. The representations of self, of a woman's identity, embedded in the reference "TV dinners" offer multiple levels of a woman's connection to the fabric of social and cultural life. One of these levels challenges the myth of a woman's place by demystifying the patriarchal order of the nuclear family previously adhered to within this poem. Simply heating TV dinners is not the traditional and cultural image of the wife-mother nurturer. Another challenge to the idea of the nuclear family is that if heating TV dinners is an act of necessity, the woman doing this action might be the breadwinner. Not the man. "TV dinners" can also refer to the woman who does not like to cook (as in my sister's case). Furthermore, heating TV dinners, can be a discursive device to critique the potential essentialization of traditional and cultural practices by embracing modernization and its practicalities.

The significance of this critique is that it challenges the notion that cultural practices once conceived as authentic must not change. If modifications have occurred in the process of a cultural practice, a suspicion of its validity, of its credibility, is often raised. What I mean by *cultural authenticity* is that culture often is seen as whole and coherent, which also means it must be unchangeable and fixed (Hall 233). The danger of this notion is that it limits the variations of narrative composition found in the process of cooking. Culture is not found within unchanging paradigms. Angela McRobbie defines culture as "how people see themselves, not as class subjects, not as psychoanalytical subjects, not as subjects of ideology, not as textual subjects, but as active agents whose sense of self is projected onto and expressed in an expansive range of cultural practices, including text, [and] images" (58). Here McRobbie illustrates why cultural practices are always in transition or crossing borders. The writers as cooks and the cooks as writers— active agents—are constantly refashioning and re-creating their recipes as they negotiate and articulate their sense of self according to the changes surrounding their lives.

During the *charlas culinarias,* all the women speak of the implications of modernization and how technology can, does, and must alter cultural and traditional practices. They speak conscientiously and critically of how such modifications affect the understanding of their own social, cultural, and economic positions. In the *charlas culinarias,* Mexican traditions and cultural practices are spoken of as culture-in-transition. One reference to modernization, to culture-in-transition, is the use of microwaves or toaster ovens in the process of making *enchiladas*.

Me: "And when do you eat?"

Alma: "When everyone is done, I prepare mine. Or I try to make them fast so that there might still be one person eating who would eat with me."

Mom: "And in the 'micro,' *mi'ja*. Maybe in the 'micro' could work."

Alma: "No, where it would work very well is in those little toaster ovens."[17]

In this segment of our *charla culinaria,* both my mother and sister believe in a certain methodological process of making *enchiladas* to achieve a perfect

personal taste, texture, and flavor. The example of culture-in-transition taking place at this temporal moment shows how modern techniques can be
incorporated into the methodology of making *enchiladas* without significantly altering for my sister and mother their own personal "perfect flavor"
of *enchiladas,* without sacrificing their own stories.

My mother and sister experience culture-in-transition not only in terms
of modern techniques but also through their different geo-economic and
social levels. The following dialogue between my mother's past and my sister's present best exemplifies such difference:

> *Alma:* "*Sopitos,* and all those things I like them but they are laborious.
> I'd rather buy them. That is the good thing about this country
> that I work, and I can buy whatever I want without the necessity
> of having to cook it."
>
> *Mom:* "That's the best thing about this place. But over there in the
> countryside, from where one comes—"
>
> *Alma:* "But the good thing is that I don't live in the countryside, Mom."
>
> *Mom:* "Over there in the countryside you don't have a choice. You have
> to do everything. The good thing about this place, if you don't
> cook or if you don't know, you can go and buy them. As long as
> you have a job. But over there in my countryside, from where I
> come. Either you learn, and you figure out ways of [cooking]—."
>
> *Alma:* "Or you die of hunger."
>
> *Mom:* "Or you die of hunger."[18]

Stuart Hall says that cultural practices "are deeply contradictory," and that
"they play on contradictions" (233). I do not agree that cultural practices
necessarily play on contradictions. What might seem a contradiction from
an outsider's perspective of a cultural practice, might be seen as adaptations
to new circumstances from the standpoint of those actively engaged in
given cultural practices, as my mother and sister's conversation reveals.

My disagreement with Hall's statement is articulated through my
ambivalent reading of Cordelia Candelaria's poem "Haciendo Tamales"
(Rebolledo and Rivero 115). Two lines from this poem, "Trabajo de amor
'pa enriquecer el saborcito" (labor of love to enrich the flavor) and "she
made her tamales from memory," turn my own gaze to the warm, safe,

comfortable embrace of my mother's cooking. Whenever anyone asks my mother for a recipe, her answer always has two parts. First she says, "El secreto es hacerlo con mucho amor" (the secret is to do it with lots of love). Then from her memorized "cookbook," she gives a recipe without ever saying how much of anything. From this familial perspective, I read "Haciendo Tamales" as a vivid cultural connection to my own life. But the air of authenticity suggested in making tamales in the following lines immediately fractures this connection:

> nomas handgrown y home-raised, todo
> Oregano had to be wildly grown
> in brown earth 'bajo la sombra
> Tamale wrappers had to be hojas
> dried from last year's corn.[19]

Even though my mother alludes to a similar procedure in the making of tortillas, her daily practice during an early period of her life was not an act of conserving her heritage. For my mother, making things from scratch was an act of necessity and not of keeping a "heritage":

> In Atlisco we arrived at Aunt Dora's house. And since she knew that
> I came from a small village, and she also had planted corn, she
> thought that I should make them *tortillas*. Therefore, I also had to
> prepare the *nixtamal* and to take it to the mill, and I had to make
> them *tortillas*. According to her, that work was easy for me. Don't
> think it wasn't a lot of work.[20]

My ambivalence with regard to Candelaria's poem is that while there is a similarity between her poetic description of making tamales with lots of love and from memory and my mother's expression of preparing a meal, there is also a great difference in terms of the reasons for preparing food from scratch. In Atlisco, making *tortillas* from scratch is for my mother a necessity owing to her dependent status in her Aunt Dora's house. My mother's comment about living in a village (*el pueblo*) before her relocation to Atlisco, a town, further emphasizes the concept of necessity rather than heritage. In her village or, as she calls it, her *cerro* (hill), buying ready-made *tortillas* was not a possibility. There were none to buy. For working-class people, doing things from scratch does not always represent an ideological, political, and cultural statement about heritage. Doing things from scratch is a process of gathering and reusing what they have access to.[21] Another question raised by the difference between Candelaria's poem and my mother's *charla culinaria* is the issue of audience. My mother is speaking to her daughter, but to whom is the poem speaking? The mixture of Spanish language without translation gives some indication of the intended readers. Those people with a similar cultural background to the poet's would be receptive to the ironic implication that there is not a unifying, pure heritage as the four lines of the poem suggest:

> cada sabor nuevo
> como el calor del Westinghouse where
> she cooked them with gas under G.E. lights—
> bien original to the max![22]

But is this a contradiction of cultural practice or is it really culture-in-transition? Does having no energy, no time, or cooking "under G.E. lights" compromise our heritage and make us cultureless? No. Our daily lives "are crisscrossed by border zones, pockets, and eruptions of all kinds" that transform our cultural practices (Rosaldo 207). The shifting of a culture's traditional practices and their meaning exists because culture is not a fixed category of daily practices but daily practices always in constant dialogue within the ever-changing social body.

The changes within the social body greatly affect the implications of kitchen politics. During the *charlas culinarias* with my family, politics within the realm of racial and ethnic issues are not broached, as they are in la Chrisx's poem "La Loca de la Raza Cósmica." This is not to say that no political self-awareness is expressed. If we view my mother's *charla culinaria* narrative as a continuum, her political consciousness is manifested through what Carol Hardy-Fanta defines as survival politics (46). The four basic principles of survival politics, according to Hardy-Fanta, are: (1) a class-linked concept—working class; (2) struggles outside political institutions; (3) individual, personal efforts that go on behind the scenes; (4) an informal, private, and individualistic process. None of these principles is difficult to illustrate within my mother's narrative of cooking practices. For my mother, her politics of survival take her from a dutiful, submissive wife to an independent and economically self-sufficient woman.

The first stage of her survival politics is in effect as she carves out a public space from within the privacy of her home.

> [Over there in Aguililla] when I already had many small children, you know that one needs to buy them clothes, underwear. I began to put my little selling stand right out there at the door of the house. I would make *morisqueta:* white rice and meat with chile. What else would I sell? *Tostadas* . . . I would make *pozole.*[23]

The "issue" in her political agenda, the selling of her food, is the literal necessity of dressing her many small children. Her *puestecito,* the table she located outside her door, does not constitute a conventional "political institution." The political struggle within this site represents an economic one. Also my mother's individual initiative, though not behind the scenes, is provoked by what she considers her only resources.

> *Me:* "But why did it occur to you to sell food?"
>
> *Mom:* "I thought of selling things there in the house, well, because I wanted to make some money; I wanted to have some money to buy something for my small children. And the only way was that I started selling right there at the door. Yes, I had customers. I don't know, supposedly, they liked my cooking. I didn't think my cooking was that good, but they liked it. Yes, yes, I would make a profit, because from the money I would make, I would buy more groceries, and I would still have money to buy little things for my small children, food, or clothes."[24]

This informal economic practice of selling food begins to represent for my mother independence and assertiveness. After the inauguration of her food-economic practice, her husband wants to move to another city. To such request, her initial response is

> After I already had my selling stand in Aguililla, [the] father of my children wanted us to move to Apatzingán. I would tell him that he should go, because from the selling of my food I was making enough money to feed the children. He still took me with him. But

later, when we were already in Apatzingán, your own father also started asking the workmen if they wanted to *asistirse* in a house to get their meals. Therefore, he started bringing me people from his work. And they gave me, I think, ten *pesos* daily for the meal. But I think that there were six or seven, so I would get seventy *pesos*. But with twenty, I would prepare the food. I would feed them, and I would still have fifty pesos left. And what is more, the food I would prepare was also enough to feed my children.[25]

At this point in my mother's life, home becomes the social body where her motherhood, wifehood, and businesshood are all simultaneously negotiated through her cooking practices. At this level of quotidian practice, of the mundane, my mother's actions illustrate how kitchen politics yield for her a level of self-esteem and self-belief about her capability of earning a living for herself and her children independent of her marriage to a "macho mexicano." My mother's own definition of a "macho mexicano" is "mujeriego, borracho y pegalón" (womanizer, drunken and abusive).

The Academic Cook

The language of everyday cooking is for me an attempt to articulate my own academic and intellectual quest. How can I build a bridge that connects the practice and language of nonacademic women with the practice and language of academic women? My interest is not to speak as a representative of nonacademic Chicana (Mexicana) women vis-à-vis an act of translation. My Catholic, Mexican guilt does not allow me to forget that I am the one sitting in front of a computer analyzing various culinary practices of cooks as writers and culinary images of writers as cooks while some women like my mother and sister are cleaning house or, in my aunt's case, running a boutique, coming home exhausted to face familial demands. What I am committed to is going through a process of reseasoning my own academic training so that I will not conceptualize and frame my subject of research within hierarchical and binary paradigms.

It *is* a privilege, a luxury, especially for someone who comes from a working-class background, to sit for endless hours writing and reading. But is it a better life choice or just a different one? My aunt, who acknowledges my privileged position during our *charla culinaria* when she asks me, "Y ¿qué tal, como la hice de contestadora?" (So how about it, how am I as an answerer?), also acknowledges the similarities in our lives toward the end of our *charla*. These are the words of a nonacademic, working-class Mexican theoretician, Esperanza Vélez:

> Aprendes con la vida. Como has aprendido tú, por necesidad. Son necesidades que tienes que llenar. Si tú para hacer una carrera tienes que estudiar, ¿verdad? Tienes que sacrificarte y tienes que echarle ganas. Y uno para ser ama de casa . . . tiene que aprender todas las labores del hogar. Entonces es una necesidad que tú adquieres. Es una necesidad que sepas aprender a comprar verduras, que sepas aprender a guisar. Son necesidades cotidianas. Son necesidades que la vida te exige y que tienes que aprender para cumplir con tus obligaciones. Porque en la vida tenemos obligaciones todos. Así lo veo yo, desde ese punto.[26]

I have presented a metaphorical portrait of the process of cooking in order to define an alternative form of expression and so avoid silencing the voices of women who speak, share, and assert themselves in ways other than writing. The language of cooking yields various narratives of self-representation. As we listen to this language, we must ask ourselves these questions: What do women say in their kitchen talk, not so much about their food per se, but about their relation to the social body as it is articulated through their cooking practices? How do these relations frame their awareness of their familial, social, cultural, and political identities? The language of everyday cooking requires that we academics develop an acute hearing ability to understand how women using this language narrate their own life stories.

With this academic research on culinary discourses, I am also fulfilling—in theory if not in practice—my childhood dream of one day becoming a professional chef. My interest in kitchens and cooking is not recent. I am a woman of the kitchen the kitchens of the restaurants where my mother worked when I was a child were my playgrounds. I have been cooking since I was five. In high school I read every single cookbook in the library. At seventeen I was an apprentice in my town's most famous gourmet restaurant. Now to ease the pace of academic life, I read *Bon Appétit*.

The stories shared in the *charlas culinarias* are the stories I grew up hearing. The cooks-as-writers' strength, knowledge, creativity, and conviction are what allow me to conclude this chapter by saying that while I am not a chef, I am an academic literary critic with a strong passion for others', and my own, culinary practices.

NOTES

[1] "When I got married, your father's sisters and his mother used to make really ugly tortillas. And when I saw they made some ugly tortillas, I no longer was embarrassed. I remember that I wanted to show them that I knew how to make tortillas better than them. They made really, really ugly tortillas. Uy—I would show off making my tortillas; I would put them in a little basket! Uy, my tortillas would come out so thin, puffed up so nicely! The ones I would make. I mean, yes, yes, I would beat them in making tortillas, over there. Yes, they would make some ugly, fat tortillas with holes in them." (All translations in this work are my own.) The culinary talks were conducted in Spanish, but for the benefit of non-Spanish readers I have incorporated the translations in the main text; however, the original expressions are in the notes so that these women's personal *chiste* is not lost in translation.

[2] "Clases de cocina nunca tomé. Lo que pasa es que a mí me gusta guisar. A mí sí me gusta guisar. No sé la gran cosa pero dicen que tengo buen sazón. Pero yo nunca tomé clases de cocina. La verdad a mí me gusta hacer un platillo y que lo disfrute mi familia. Es una forma de apapachar. O de agasajar a tu familia, ¿no? De dedicarles el tiempo en la cocina y prepararles algo sabroso y que digan. '¡Ay qué rico esta!' Me gusta cocinarle algo a la gente que quiero. A mis hijos, a mis sobrinas, a mis hermanas. A mi cuñado. Me gusta cocinarles cuando veo que disfrutan y yo disfruto verlos disfrutar lo que hice de comer."

[3] "Pues no sé. Nunca me ha gustado la cocina. Me llamaba la atención andar de vaga. Cocinar nunca me llamó la atención. Hay personas que desde chiquillas tienen nociones de cocinar y otras no. Y a mí nunca me llamó la atención cocinar y hasta la fecha no me gusta. Lo hago porque tengo que. De que me guste, de que diga 'Voy a meterme a la cocina.' No. No me gusta. Este, no sé mucho de cocina.

⁴ "Si tú haces una sopa de pasta seca, tienes que hacer una sopa ya sea de verdura o una sopa de crema. Para que combine, porque no puedes hacer sopa de pasta y sopa de pasta, ¿no? O sea, sopa aguada y sopa seca de pasta las dos. Son cosas que vas aprendiendo o través de la vida, ¿no?"

⁵ Paule Marshall describes the function of women's kitchen talk that took place in her childhood home: "The talk that filled the kitchen those afternoons was highly functional. It served as therapy, the cheapest kind available to my mother and her friends . . . It restored them to a sense of themselves and reaffirmed their self-worth . . . But more than therapy, the freewheeling, wideranging, exuberant talk functioned as an outlet for the tremendous creative energy they possessed" (6).

⁶ "Lo importante no es determinar si las mujeres debemos escribir con una estructura abierta o con una estructura cerrada, con un lenguaje poético o con un lenguaje obsceno, con la cabeza o con el corazón. Lo importante es aplicar esa lección fundamental que aprendimos de nuestras madres, las primeras, después de todo, en enseñarnos a bregar con fuego: el secreto de la escritura, como el de la buena cocina, no tiene nada que ver con el sexo, sino con la sabiduría con la que se combinan los ingredientes."

⁷ "I'm as simple as bread pudding / . . . I'm the meal on the table when they come / from work / I'm the one who heats TV dinners / I'm tamales at Christmas time / I'm Coconut."

⁸ The connection of *la capirotada* and the body is established by the fact that *la capirotada* is a dish made primarily of bread. The signifier of bread as the body in theological terms is that Jesus Christ says, "I am the bread of life . . . This is the living bread . . . the bread that I will give is my flesh, which I will give for the world" (John 6:48).

⁹ Louis Marin argues that the theoretical possibility for such connection is through the praxis of trans-significance, the process of a metaphor's becoming a metamorphosis. Martin also argues that with no "desire to be provocative, one might say that every culinary sign is eucharistic in some sense and to some extent; or, to pursue this vein of thought one step further, one might say that all cookery involves a theological, ideological, political, and economic operation by the means of which a nonsignified edible food stuff is transformed into a sign/body that is eaten."

[10] "I am the lover of my main man . . . I am the incarnation of the Virgin Mary . . . I am the Revolutionary . . . I am the Chicana at conferences . . . I am achieving higher status in the struggle of woman."

[11] The third space refers to an alternative space where the voices of those people traditionally located at the margins find a temporal location from which they can represent themselves ("The Third Space").

[12] "Es una forma de apapachar. Yo al menos así lo siento. Y siento que tú también lo ves desde ese punto de vista. Y a ti te gusta la cocina. Y yo creo que tú me comprendes porque a ti también—yo he visto que cuando yo llego te pones a cocinar o llega alguien que tú quieres, tú cocinas. Porque a ti también te gusta la cocina . . . Lo disfrutamos."

[13] *Alma:* "Okey, la mayoría de las personas meten las tortillas en el aceite primero. Y luego en chile. Luego ya le ponen el queso en medio y la enuelven. Y es como las hacen Yo así las hice y no me gustaron. Sabían a tortilla remojada con chile. Yo lo qué hago, la meto la tortilla al chile primero y luego la doro en aceite. Es más mugrero O sea te queda todo sucio. Otra cosa. Mucha gente, por ejemplo, van a cenar todos entonces hacen muchas enchiladas. Las meten al horno y luego ponen todo y todos se sirven. A mí no me gusta así. A mí me gusta hacerlas pa' las personas que van comiendo."

Yo:　　　"Pero de la otra manera se sientan todos a comer al mismo tiempo."

Mamá:　　"Pues nomás porque es más trabajo estar haciéndolas. Pero el saborcito, saborcito calientito."

[14] "Yo una vez hice una salsa de molcajete con orégano [y] se me ocurrió ponerla en medio antes de ponerle el queso y envolverla. Una vez se me ocurrió y supo rico, y es como le hago. O sea yo ya cambié mi receta. A unas personas yo les digo y dicen 'Ay, eso no son enchiladas.' Yo sé como a mí me gustan y es como yo las hago."

[15] "Yo nunca apunto medidas. Tú también haces las cosas al tanteo. ¿O tú sí usas medidas? No creo que vayas a la receta. [Yo] no me baso al libro y estar viendo lo que va [en la receta]."

[16] I am using *machismo* and *marianismo* in a rather general way. Within a Mexican context, *machismo* refers to the male law that governs a household, and *marianismo* is a term to describe a woman's spiritual and moral superiority through absolute submission of her will and invisibility of her self. In Chicana literature,

women, wives, who are physically, emotionally, or sexually abused are, none-theless, sometimes viewed as *marianistas*.

[17] *Yo:*   "¿Y a qué horas comes tú?"

    Alma: "Cuando terminan todos, preparo las mías. O trato rápido para que quede una de las personas a comer conmigo—"

    Mamá: "Y en el micro, mi'ja. A lo mejor en el micro, sí."

    Alma: "No, donde funcionaría muy bien es en los hornitos chiquitos."

[18] *Alma:* "Sopitos y todas esas cosas, me gustan pero son laboriosas. Yo mejor las compro. O sea, es lo bueno de este país que trabajo y me puedo comprar lo que yo quiera sin necesidad de ponerme a coci-narlo. Si no, lo cocinas o no comes."

    Mamá: "Eso es lo mejor de aquí. Pero allá en el cerro de donde uno viene—"

    Alma: "Pero lo bueno es que yo no me crié en el cerro 'ama."

    Mamá: "Allá en el cerro tienes que a fuerzas hacer las cosas. Lo bueno de aquí, si no cocinas o si no sabes, vas y compras. No más con que tengas trabajo. Pero allá en mi cerro, de allá de donde yo vengo, o te enseñas y le buscas la forma de hacerle—"

    Alma: "O te mueres de hambre"

    Mamá: "O te mueres de hambre . . ."

[19] "only handgrown and home-raised, everything. / beneath the shade / . . . leaves."

[20] "En Atlisco llegamos a la casa de la tía Dora. Y como sabía que venía del pueblo y ella también tenía maíz, se le ocurrió que me pusiera a hacerles tor-tillas. Así que también me puse a poner el nixtamal y a llevarlo al molino y a echarles tortillas. Según ella eso era fácil para mí. No te creas que era tan po-quito quihacer."

[21] See Tawadro; hooks. Even though their explanation of gathering and reusing material available in the homesite of women (particularly poor women) focuses on the source of material for the creation of art and the inscriptions of their lives into their art, gathering and reusing is also a practice of simple ne-cessity and survival.

[22] "each new flavor / from the heat of the Westinghouse . . . / really origi-nal to the max."

[23] "[Allá en Aguililla] cuando ya tenía muchos chiquillos, ya cuando tenía muchas criaturas, tú sabes que se necesita para comprarles ropita, calzoncitos, y

empecé yo a sacar mi puestecito, ahí en la puerta de la casa. Hacía que moris-
queta. arroz blanco y carne con chile. ¿Qué otra cosa vendí yo? Tostadas . . .
hacía pozole."

²⁴ *Yo:*   "¿Por qué se te ocurrió vender comida?"

Mamá: "Se me ocurrió vender cosas ahí en la casa, pos, porque quería ganar
un cinco, quería tener dinerito para comprarles algo a mis chiquillos.
Y de la única manera era eso. Empezar a vender ahí en la puerta. Sí
tenía clientela. No sé, que les gustaba mi sazón. Malaya pa' el sazón
que haya tenido yo, pero sí les gustaba. Sí, pues sí le sacaba dinero de
ganancia porque como quiera, ya de allí volvía a surtir y me quedaba
para comprarles cositas a los chiquillos, comida o ropita."

²⁵ "Después de que yo ya tenía mi vendimia en Aguililla, [el] papá de mis hijos que quería que nos fuéramos a Apatzingán. Le decía yo que se fuera, que al
cabo yo de allí yo ya estaba sacando para darles de comer a los niños. Y como
quiera me quizo llevar. Pero luego cuando ya nos fuimos a Apatzingán, también tu mismo papá empezó a decirles en el trabajo y que si querían—allá les
dicen 'asistirse' en una casa para que les den la alimentación." Así que me empezó a llevar gente de los trabajadores. Y me daban creo que diez pesos por día
pa' la comida. Pero creo que eran seis o siete, así que eran como setenta pesos,
pero yo con veinte hacía la comida. Les daba de comer y me quedaban cin-
cuenta y es más, la comida alcanzaba pa' mis hijos también."

²⁶ "Life teaches you. Like you have to learn due to necessity. These are necessities that you must fulfill. For you, in order to have a career you have to
study, right? You have to sacrifice yourself, and you have to put energy into your
career. For us, to be a housewife . . . we have learn to do all the household tasks.
Therefore, it is a necessity that you acquire. It is a necessity for you to learn to
know how to buy vegetables, which you learn to know how to cook. These
are quotidian necessities. These are necessities that life demands of you . . . You
must learn to fulfill your obligations. Because in life, obligations we all have.
This is how I see it, from this point of view."

WORKS CITED

Behar, Ruth, and Deborah A. Gordon. *Women Writing Culture.* Berkeley: U of
California P, 1995.

Castillo, Debora. *Talking Back*. Ithaca: Cornell UP, 1992.

Cixous, Hélène. "The Laugh of the Medusa." *SIGNS* 1/4 (1976): 875–93.

de Valdés, María Elena. "Verbal and Visual Representation of Women: *Como agua para chocolate/Like Water for Chocolate*." *World Literature Today*. 80 (1993): 78–82.

Douglass, Mary. "Deciphering a Meal." *Implicit Meanings: Essays in Anthropology*. London: Routledge and Kegan Paul, 1979. 249–75.

Ferré, Rosario. "La cocina de la escritura." *La sartén por el mango*. Ed. Patricia González and Eliana Ortega. Rio Piedras: Ediciones de Huracán, 1984.

Goldman, Anne. "'I Yam What I Yam': Cooking, Culture, and Colonialism." *De/Colonizing the Subject: The Politics of Gender in Women's Autobiography*. Ed. Sidonie Smith and Julia Watson. Minneapolis: U of Minnesota P, 1992.

Hall, Stuart. "Notes on Deconstructing the Popular." *People's History and Socialist Theory*. Ed. Rapheal Sammuel. London: Routledge and Kegan Paul, 1981. 227–339.

Hardy-Fanta, Carol. *Latina Politics/Latino Politics*. Philadelphia: Temple UP, 1993.

hooks, bell. "Aesthetic Inheritances." *Yearning: Race, Gender, and Cultural Politics*. Boston: South End, 1990. 115–22.

la Chrisx. "La Loca de la Raza Cósmica." *Infinite Divisions: An Anthology of Chicana Literature*. Ed. Tey Diana Rebolledo and Elena Rivera. Tucson: U of Arizona P, 1993. 84–88.

Lawless, Cecilia. "Experimental Cooking in *Como agua para chocolate*." *Monographic Review* 8 (1992): 269–72.

Leonardi, Susan. "Recipes for Reading: Summer Pasta, Lobster à la Risholme, and Key Lime Pie." *PMLA* 104 (1989): 340–47.

Marin, Louis. *Food for Thought*. Trans. Mette Hiort. Baltimore: Johns Hopkins UP, 1989.

Marshall, Paule. "From the Poets in the Kitchen." *Merle a Novella and Other Stories*. New York: Virago, 1983.

McRobbie, Angela. *Postmodernism and Popular Culture*. New York: Routledge, 1994.

Perez, Emma. "Sexuality and Discourse: Notes From a Chicana Survivor." *Building with Our Hands: New Directions in Chicana Studies*. Ed. Adela de la Torre and Beatríz M. Pesquera. Berkeley: U of California P, 1993. 57–71.

Rebolledo, Tey Diana. *Women Singing in the Snow: A Cultural Analysis of Chicana Literature*. Tucson: U of Arizona P, 1995.

———, and Eliana S. Rivero, comps. *Infinite Divisions: An Anthology of Chicana Literature*. Tucson: U of Arizona P, 1993.

Rodrique, Aron. "Difference and Tolerance in the Ottoman Empire: Interview by Nancy Reynolds." Contested Politics issue. *Stanford Humanities Review* 5/1 (1995): 81–90.

Rosaldo, Renato. *Culture and Truth*. Boston: Beacon, 1989.

Rutherford, Jonathan. "The Third Space: Interview with Homi Bhabha." *Identity: Community, Culture, Difference*. Ed. Jonathan Rutherford. London: Lawrence and Wisart, 1990. 207–21.

Tawadro, Gilane. "Beyond the Boundary: The Work of Three Black Women Artists in Britain." *Third Text* 8/9 (1989): 121–50.

Tsing, L. Anna. *In the Realm of the Diamond Queen*. Princeton, N.J.: Princeton UP, 1993.

Viramontes, Helena María. "Nopalitos: The Making of Fiction." *Making Face, Making Soul: Haciendo Caras*. Ed. Gloria Anzaldúa. San Francisco: Aunt Lute Foundation Book, 1990.

Yarbo-Bejarano, Yvonne. "Chicana Literature From a Chicana Feminist Perspective." *Chicana Creativity and Criticism*. Ed. María Herrera-Sobek and Helena María Viramontes. Abuquerque: U of New Mexico U, 1996. 213–18.

CHAPTER EIGHT

"In the Kitchen Family Bread Is Always Rising!"
Women's Culture and the Politics of Food
Benay Blend

Women's search for personal identities has probably never been pursued so actively in the United States as during the past thirty years of the women's movement. At the same time, Alex Haley's *Roots* was inspiring many people to take pride in their ancestral cultures and genetic origins. According to Donna Gabaccia, food became an important part of an effort initiated by various ethnicities to reclaim a history of culture, community, and identity that had been lost through several generations of assimilation into the mainstream. This chapter explores how contemporary women of diverse cultures have used writing about foodways to reclaim a female identity within a specific ethnic heritage. Because recipes, like culture, are handed down from generation to generation by oral history, culinary literature conveys a sense of how food sharing creates solidarity but also allows women to speak across cultures. As public women, the Native American and Chicana writers covered in this chapter are committed to the struggle for social justice and personal recovery. But at the same time, they are submerged in the mundane, and so invest daily life with the significance typically accorded to official history. The activity of almost all underscores a public call for legitimation of a space traditionally associated with and devalued as female. Their critical reconsideration of hierarchical oppositions involves reappropriating household metaphors to revalorize them for serious critical purposes. Nevertheless, while a woman might look to her foremother's labor of feeding a family as skilled practice, she often finds that the kitchen has been the locus of oppression, thereby privatizing and marginalizing the experiences of many women. To choose to live as a writer means confronting directly the conflicts between self-affirmation and domesticity inherent in female lives. Therefore, this chapter also explores how some women rebel against prevailing codes that define caring for others as a woman's natural role, but still honor their mothers' culinary labor as valuable and important work.

Recently, critics of literature have begun to look at how the exchange of recipes in texts expresses an identity politics in which the idea of cooking and authorship are connected. According to Diana Rebolledo, writing about food provides "an agency central to identity" (144). By recognizing that Chicanas can formulate a cultural polemic through their domestic practices, Rebolledo challenges the private/public dichotomy, including by association distinctions between mental and manual labor, theoretical and practical work. In *Food and the Making of Mexican Identity,* Jeffrey Pilcher examines the importance of women and domestic culture in forging a national community. For Mexicanas who "began to imagine their own national community in the familiar terms of the kitchen," Pilcher contends that domesticity "offered as valid a means for building communities as did politics" (66). In a similar vein, Donna R. Gabaccia charts how recurring human migrations have interacted with changes in the production and marketing of food, in her book *We Are What We Eat.* My work grounds culinary literature against a historical backdrop, reading it as political commentary in the writing of women who, excluded from access to high art, redefine culinary labor as a means to resist commodification of their culture. The following study draws on a broad variety of texts—fiction, poetry, culinary autobiography, and cookbooks. Because this chapter crosses so many conceptual frontiers, it also highlights the limits of academic disciplinary boundaries.

Equated with achieving consciousness, the art of cooking, according to Diana Rebolledo, has also been linked to women's ways of knowing (130). Many of the writers discussed here are concerned with the problems faced by women and the conditions that affect their future. Children and mothers form the central texts of many of these women's lives, and so inform their writing. All write from and about the margins, licensing them not only to speak of issues relating to the preparation of meals, the raising of children, and political activism in solidarity with other women, but also to ally with other groups on the peripheries of culture. By valuing the culinary experiences of marginalized persons, the authors also highlight how society marginalizes experiences of dominant persons, specifically those aspects of daily life that are not defined as public, masculine, and universal. Thinking about food as a concept of personal identity raises questions about the self as a discrete, disembodied ego. By claiming food as a serious literary subject, some writers discussed in this chapter also explore the ways that it validates a relational understanding of the self. For them, cooking involves a creative blending of the mental and physical, of theory and practice, activities that define theorizing/food making as a community activity.

In this chapter I compare how such writers as Pat Mora, Louise Ehrdrich, and Gloria Anzaldúa, among others, use cooking as a metaphor for writing about and breaking tradition. I explore how culinary cultures are used in a variety of ways. An overarching theme is the struggle that self-assertion demands, a struggle that is as much the task of family and community as of the writer herself. Using the metaphor of culinary labor to develop ethnic identity thus brings together endeavors in the cultural sphere with struggles in the political domain. In the sense that it replays political conflict as a struggle for cultural ownership, the culinary discourse of Chicana and Native American women writers could also be described as auto-ethnographic writing. These writers, then, pass down recipes as a means to preserve once-colonized histories; others view cooking as sources of creativity and sensuality. Taking culinary labor as an illuminating source, each formulates a food-centered, relational philosophy of human identity. In one form or another, these are texts that defy boundaries, inviting the reader to a place just beginning to be explored by those who consider food and its connection to women's culture a legitimate field of inquiry (see Scapp and Seitz; Counihan and Van Esterik; Curtin and Heldke).

Particularly for ethnic women writers, reproducing a recipe, like retelling a story, requires that they maneuver between personal and collective texts, between an autobiographical "I" and various forms of a political/cultural "we." This work addresses how each author claims or reclaims culinary rituals, transforming them or creating new ones out of personal and collective histories. Such explorations illuminate how women reproduce or resist and rebel against prevailing stereotypes of their own or the dominant culture. For many of the women considered in this essay, the cultural "we" of community and family relations always stands in relation to their own self-distinction. "I am an act of kneading," writes Anzaldúa, calling attention not only to her *mestizo* heritage but also to the autobiographical "I" that reproduces the values of her community. Her theorizing is not the one-sided activity of a detached subject, but rather assumes the reciprocal motions of mixing, kneading, and baking dough for bread. Transforming herself literally into "an act of writing and joining," she claims to be "not only . . . a creature of darkness and a creature of light, but also a creature that questions the definitions of light and dark and gives them new meanings" (*Borderlands* 81). Preparing food encourages Anzaldúa to blur the separation between herself and what she eats so that she enters into a kind of relationship with the ingredients. In the realm of theory, Anzaldúa's food-making activities thus challenge the subject/object dichotomy that characterizes traditional inquiry and that serves to separate her mental work from the manual work of daily living.

In commenting on and repeating recipes, such authors convey a sense of comfort in familiar ingredients ("To live in the Borderlands means to / put *chili* in the borscht / eat whole wheat *tortillas*") as well as the mutability of ethnic forms. As Jeffrey Pilcher notes, postrevolutionary Mexico saw, after 1920, not only violent struggle in the public realm but the "dinner table also became a battlefield as wheat bread of Spanish bakers challenged the corn tamales of Native women for inclusion in the Mexican national cuisine" (1). If Anzaldúa's culinary reference reproduces an ethnic identity that may be constant, its forms are constantly changing due to a number of other factors. In addition, she opens up a sense of difference between cultures ("To live in the Borderlands [also] means to . . . be stopped by *la migra* at the border checkpoint" [*Borderlands* 194]), focusing on the boundaries of her affiliation and exhorting readers to ponder the relation between the community created on a textual level and the community of readers outside it.

Negotiating Authority: Cooking as Identity Politics

Currently, critics of literature are looking at the ways in which the exchange of recipes offers one way of talking back. Debra Castillo's *Talking Back* offers a theory to explain how sharing recipes "serves as a model for a certain kind of feminine discourse that works through the manipulation of metaphors drawn from the domestic sphere" (xv). It suggests a common language among women, an idea shared by Susan Leonardi's "Recipes for Reading," which analyzes recipes as "highly embedded discourse akin to literary discourse" (340), identifying further this language use as gender-laden.

"Why do I crave recipes, seek to know how people who are part of me measure and combine ingredients in this life?" Pat Mora asks in her memoir (*House of Houses* 78). Mora acknowledges here, as do others elsewhere, that recipes have an underlying meaning. Charting the development of the self, Mora describes in the process the communal traditions and cultural practices upon which identity is grounded. In an essay, "Layers of Pleasure," Mora explains how recipes present an opportunity to experiment with composing as well as cooking. "Books, like children," she observes, "bring wrinkles and gifts, and a gift of my memoir is that I am able to braid together the threads of my life—gardening, cooking, writing" (150). Mora's identification with a long line of female ancestors connects her to a cultural construction of identity. Recollecting family lore, she evokes a sense of full family life, of the close bonds that in turn produce the narrator herself. She discovers that from the kitchen emanates not only food making but also ritual, tradition, and family history.

As the "knower," who remembers the recipes, who knows how to record them, Mora also represents the oral tradition that, she fears, is being lost. She insists on a proprietary interest in the reproduction of tradition while using the essay as an opening for personal recollection and renewal. "We need to get the recipes while we can," she warns, "absorb *el pasado,* the past," for, as "nourishment and delight for the body, for the soul" (151), food becomes more than sustenance; the cultural production of it poses answers to the dilemma, as the poet Margaret Randall puts it, of "men telling the stories / we must counter with our own" (*Hunger's Table* 85). In her imagined refuge, where generations of her family, living and dead, return to this *House of Houses* for just one year, Mora creates a "world that we can call our own, this family space through which generations move, each bringing its gifts, handing down languages and stories, recipes for living" (7). Emphasizing the labor involved in reproduction of cultural practices,

Mora strives on a textual level against the forces of assimilation, insisting on a familial, grounded sense of cultural specificity and preserving an ethnic difference that in turn provides her with the authority to pass down knowledge. For Mora, this sensitivity to the pressures of acculturation takes the form not of overt political rhetoric but, rather, of composing a composite genre: a combination of familial reminiscence and personal narrative, of description of custom, history, food, and folklore. Eating habits both symbolize and mark the boundaries of her culture.

As Mora shows, a good recipe encodes a cultural context, evidenced here in ancestral surroundings that span many generations. Critical responses to acculturation also mark the writing of Native American women; their strategies of self-assertion speak to and out of similar concerns and contexts. Both literatures—Chicana and Native American—are engaged in maintaining a culture changed but nevertheless experienced on its home ground. In *Dwellings,* Linda Hogan explains how, while "grind[ing] corn . . . on an ancient and sloping *metate,*" she saw the history of Chickasaw people "in that yield, a deep knowing of where our lives came from" (61), both collectively and personally. The invocation of specific food conceptualizes ethnicity as informed by a whole range of social, historical, and cultural circumstances within which the subject locates herself. Moreover, watching the corn defined a community that was expressly a woman's sphere. But because growing and harvesting the crops was essential to survival of the community, "woman's work" held a correspondingly higher status than in contemporary American society.

For Lucy Tapahonso, mutton, long a staple of Dine life, has the same appeal. "[It] is a literal reminder of the many meals at home," she writes, "celebrations and events of all types, fairs and ceremonies" (*Blue Horses* 37). Looking closely at the food habits of their people, both writers recall attitudes and customs that reveal historical and individual truths; in this way, each author defines an engaged subjectivity, an autobiographical presence that is defined geographically, culturally, and socially. "When we taste mutton, we are reminded of the mountains, the air, the laughter and humor surrounding a meal" (*Blue Horses* 37), Tapahonso writes, reiterating that food is more than sustenance; it has the power to bring her home. What makes mutton "ethnic" is its deep connections to spiritual, cultural, and economic contexts. Sharing particular foods with families and with friends, passing on food lore, and creating stories and myths about food's meaning, Tapahonso and Hogan regard eating habits as concrete symbols of their cultural and personal identity.

In the process of formulating an identity that is always female and often ethnic, some women have chosen to equate the writer with the cook. In an essay, "The Writes Ofrenda," for example, by Helen María Viramontes, ingredients are symbolic substances that make up ethnic identity ("From a small mound of flour dough, the rhythmic roll of the rolling pin, the symbols appear before me like my mother's perfect tortillas" [127]). Developing her identity as a Chicana writer within a familial, communal, and historical context, she draws connections between cuisine and identity that, according to Pilcher, reach deep into Mexican history. "Because tortilla making demanded so much time and effort," he records, "the activity acquired a corresponding significance in her [the Mexican woman's] personal and family history. Men complimented women by praising their tortillas, and some even claimed to identify the unique taste and texture of their wives' corn grinding and tortilla making" (106). In addition to her affiliation with an ethnic community and female network, however, Viramontes balances ethnographic impulses by retrieving an autobiographical presence ("They begin to take on a shape that is beyond me, but one that is directly connected to my hand" [129]), delineating an "I" in affiliation with a long line of women who expressed affection through their role in feeding the family. In her culinary metaphor, ingredients are symbolic substances that make up ethnic identity, but as author/cook she controls the words and ingredients that reinstate distinction, assuring that "no two [tortillas] are alike, and yet," at the same time, "they're all the same" (129) part of a "we" that is associated with a collective culture.

While Viramontes urges that contemporary Chicanas should honor their foremothers' history of service to their families, others caution against the ideological construction of such service as women's only role. Naomi Quiñónez, who refers to members of a poetry workshop she once led as "Molcajete Mamas," celebrates the self in relation to a collective history of Mexican women that likewise illustrates a blend of continuity and change. Quiñónez compares development of ethnic identity with the metaphor of an "ancient woman's tool," because, she says, it "holds as well as a symbol for modern Chicanas" (175). In the same way, however, that Mexican women have reevaluated these domestic symbols, whose association with purity and self-sacrifice once gained them entry into the public sphere, so Quiñónez honors her ethnic heritage without sacrificing subjectivity that emphasizes the unique qualities of the self. Just as kitchens are filled with women mixing ingredients and making meals, Quiñónez, through the writing of poetry, "break[s] apart and grind[s] the lines we have been given to create a new food" (175). Here she recasts a commonly held division of labor in which men strive, compete, and achieve in the public sphere while women are theoretically most gratified by feeding and nourishing others rather than themselves. Although Quiñónez's cook/poet is imaged as a nourisher, it is "our inner selves," she says, who benefit, not others. "Words are what is transformed" in her kitchen/workshop, "identity is what is being created" (175). By seizing authority in this nourishing space to control construction of her identity, Quiñónez converts the triad (woman-food-man) into a dyad (woman-food) that provides for her own pleasure and independence.

Eating is also related to self-creation in the writing of Louise Ehrdrich. In addition, she ponders the following question. Can culturally diverse cuisines be gracefully fused? It seems so in *The Antelope's Wife,* Ehrdrich's generational novel of an Ojibwa family set in contemporary Minneapolis, where food serves as a vehicle for memories. Just as the Native American baker Frank Shawano strives to re-create a perfect German cake remembered from a taste decades earlier, Ehrdrich's plot brings together many bloodlines and ethnicities into new recipes and patterns. On the day of Frank's wedding to Rozina, "professional, high-achieving" women of many "bloods—French, German, Ojibwa, surely a little Cree," and men, too, "moved in an aura of decision and risk" (157), making the kitchen a place where self-image, creativity, and nourishment take place. Along with the overarching imagery of the grandmother's beadwork, cooks, too, are here putting ingredients/beads "back together in new patterns, new strings" (220). Elsewhere, Gloria Anzaldúa describes this as an "ability of story (prose and poetry) to transform the storyteller and the listener into something or someone else," an art she calls "shamanistic. The writer as shape-changer, is a *nauhuatl*" (*Borderlands* 66) a shaman, as are the characters in Ehrdrich's work. At the closing, when all the family members gather at Rozina's for Christmas day, it is the grandmothers, in particular, who "prefer the burnt heart of the turkey to the white breast meat" and "bring out the worst in everyone" with "their wicked stories" (194), that transform "loss, darkness" (197) into "surprisingly . . . graciousness and hope" (194). Like Frank's dough, bloodlines in this novel are compressed and blended together, then rise in new "family stories [that] repeat themselves in patterns and waves generation to generation, across bloods and time" (200).

As "colliding histories and destinies" (197) inform the core of Ehrdrich's novel, in which her central "truth is that . . . there are may truths" (158), so Gloria Anzaldúa's truth lies in "shifting perspectives," in her "capacity to shift, in [her] 'seeing through' the membrane of the past superimposed on the present, in looking at [her] shadows and dealing with them" (*Making Face, Making Soul,* xxii). Often it is images of food that compel her back into those dimensions, so that she becomes both the one who "kneads and molds the dough, pats the round balls into tortillas," and the tools—stone *metate,* rolling pin, *comal*—that grind and cook the food. Becoming, then, not only cook/instrument/writer, but also ingredient/culture—"kernels [that] cling to the cob," *chili colorado,* that "cracks the rock," and *la masa harina* (tortilla flour)—Anzaldúa, as a *mestiza,* who is "indigenous like corn," knows that she is "a product of crossbreeding, designed for preservation under a variety of conditions." A shape-shifter, she becomes literally the ingredients of her birthplace, where, as a *mestiza,* she becomes "tenacious, tightly wrapped in the husks of her culture" (*Borderlands* 81), like an ear of corn. In Anzaldúa's work, eating practices bring to light philosophical concerns, including the puzzling divisions between culture and nature as well as those between appearance and reality.

Food, Sensuality, and Desire

Food's unusual ability to convey meaning as well as nourish bodies informs the work of other women writers. For example, Pat Mora has said that she thinks of food as performing almost like a language, and she explores this understanding in her work. In her essay, "Layers of Pleasure," she explores how cooking becomes a vehicle for artistic expression and an opportunity for resistance and sometimes even power. "The kitchen became one way I created my place in our family," she recalls, and it was a role made easier because, atypically, neither her grandmother nor "mother were tamale-making or tortilla-rolling women" (148). For Mora, food work became communal, creative, and comforting; "the kitchen became Pat's place, the special room in which I succeeded in bringing myself and others pleasure" (148). Long after writing replaced time spent in her garden and in the kitchen, Mora's interest in food remained, assuming a central place in her family memoir. Continuing to associate cooking with intimate connections of self to others, she notes that the "various recipes I've read include quite an array of possibilities for the creative cook, layers of nourishment," which she equates with "choices, options, like shaping a garden or an essay" (152), all food for thought about her family history, her current shifting contexts, and agendas for the future.

In *House of Houses,* Mora uses food as a token of exchange, connecting people to one another and to the fertility of the landscape. "All know," she writes, "I'm after stories, brewed in the bone. It's the older voices and bodies who have the patience to talk and remember" (7). This passage establishes a matrix of food, comfort, celebration, and human community that sustains Mora's writing. Her imagined world is centered on the consciousness of women whose existence is defined in harmony with the landscape and "feminine" rituals that are celebrated by food. Reminders of death are part of a cycle, as Mora states. "In my dream house, as in my dreams, we are together, the family spirits, the soul of this adobe" (43). To eat is to feed off of death, to be part of a cycle that includes reproduction, growth, decay, and regeneration.

House of Houses affirms a domestic world centered on women "whose hands like their mothers' know kitchen secrets" (78), comfort foods that she associates with women as food preparers and organizers of the family's emotional life. With their stories she also explores the ways in which human lives are woven together with a landscape "as familiar to me as my body" (4). "Within each of our bodies," she concludes, there is a paradox, "like the house that's green yet in the desert . . . private yet communal" (288). Although Mora sometimes privileges her role as individual, as writer, here she immerses herself harmoniously with past generations that, in turn, have become part of nature's cycle.

For Mora, to eat is also to participate in a living part of family history, the recipes having been passed down through generations. Far more than simply reflecting on the delights of family gatherings, however, female rituals of food commingle "sexual loves, poetry and song" (159), all elements, Mora says, of the meals women serve the family. Reflecting on the "sensuality of gardeners and cooks," Mora describes female relatives who normally "button their blouses to the neck, avert their eyes at bare curves and cleavage." In the kitchen, though, they succumb to a sensuous world of the body. "Such women," she says, "release their senses to play. With firm hands they knead bread dough and smell the drunk steam from cranberries simmering in port" (158). Her symbolic language of food also connects human sexuality with the landscape and calls attention to her connection of food to the fruitful garden. As elsewhere, human bodies are sensually linked to food and the fertile landscape.

"Why, in my fifties did I decide to explore this house and garden?" Mora asks in closing. By defining her relationship to a particular house and garden, with its "water song," she can imagine "a place to put the stories and the voices" before they vanish. It is a space, she says, "like all spaces, as real as we choose to make it," part of an endless flow of reshaping and renewal, like the cyclical alternations of repeating seasons that shape the sections of her book. In this state where, she says, the "universe is more than matter," Mora destabilizes dominant traditions of seeing oneself outside of and superior to nature (272).

In *House of Houses,* Mora fills her kitchen with female relatives mixing ingredients and making meals. According to Anne Goldman, "reproducing a recipe, like telling a story, may be at once cultural practice and autobiographical assertion" ("'I Yam What I Yam'" 172); therefore, self-articulation takes place always within a familial space. There, as Mora says, "family bread is always rising" (*Neplanta* 3), along with stories. In *Solar Storms,* Linda Hogan's novel of a tribal woman's search for identity in northern Minnesota, the protagonist, Angel Iron, uses bread making as a metaphor for constructing an image of cultural tradition while writing herself into the narrative. "Together," Angel thinks, "as I listen to [the grandmothers] talking outside at night, they formed the one woman I wanted to be someday, with a large portion of Dora-Rouge added to the recipe like flour or leavening." Like Mora's community of women, this elder relative, for Angel, would be, as the most important ingredient in the mixture, "the thing that held it all together" (234).

A Woman's Place?

As in Hogan's writing where food becomes a metonym for culture, the edible in Viramontes's writing is used to reconstruct cultural history, to ground familial memory, and to formulate individual authority. In Viramontes's *"Nopalitos,"* food and women's bodies, writing, and cooking, are incorporated into auto-ethnographic discourse built on a maternal authority. Memories of her mother's cooking establish Viramontes's presence, placing her in a culinary family line. Her childhood memories gender culinary and cultural traditions. "Love of stories and love of my mother, or all that seemed female in our household," Viramontes writes, have "influenced part of me," particularly her "capacity for invention" (292). Viramontes dignifies her mother's labor by recognizing its potential as expressive art. Gender definitions most likely placed her mother in the kitchen, but she converted what might have been a demand into a desire, a responsibility into a delight, a chore into a talent. For Viramontes, food making is valuable because it revalorizes women's work as a more creative form of labor within the home.

Cooking is something that continues to be imposed on women, but Viramontes sees it as an imaginative part of her mother's daily life. Just as Alice Walker, among others, has looked at the domestic arts crafted by African American foremothers as both the result of enforced labor and the creations of skillful craftswomen who are also often artists, so Viramontes looks to her mother for inspiration. "I have never been able to match her *nopales,"* she admits, but she has nevertheless learned to "invent time by first conjuring up the voices and spirits of the women living under brutal repressive regimes." If she waits for a room of her own, she might never write, but, "because I want to do justice to their voices," she finds that her "space on the kitchen table . . . long after midnight and before the start of the children's hectic morning [is] more of an inconvenience than a sacrifice" of time (292). Viramontes suggests that her sense of ethnic affiliation is a product of conscious maternal labor, the result of her mother's pride in feeding her family. The maintenance of a culture also requires work, she implies, and this responsibility is often a woman's duty.

When cooking discourses are embedded in creative texts, they often become a gendered series of linguistic maneuvers that are neither simple nor straightforward. What they do share, according to Anne Goldman, is affirmation that allows the writers to claim authority found in recipes of their foremothers (190). In Mora's words, "We, and all women, need and desire our past. We can value the resourcefulness of our mothers and the homes they created," she says, and in the "space they shaped for us" (*Neplanta* 3) she finds a metaphor for life. This sense of connection to tradition along with the spiritual sustenance necessary for work is echoed in the sentiment of Gloria Bird: "My mother is the link to our past, and without her knowledge I would not be able to pass this on to my children" (39).

Aurora Levins Morales, born in Puerto Rico of Jewish and Puerto Rican parents, nurtured on plantains and blintzes, also writes of how the essence of her culture has been handed down through oral history, generation after generation, through the selection and preparation of traditional food. Her maternal links return when she cooks traditional black bean dishes in her Berkeley kitchen. Although her daily cuisine is California fare, bottled spring water and yogurt in plastic pints, certain aromas bring back memories that she places within a cultural context. "It's a magic, a power, a ritual of love and work" that, she asserts, "rises in [her] kitchen" ("Kitchens" 297), reminding her of women who performed the same tasks of cultural translation through foodways back in her childhood home.

Destabilizing Images

Not all women writers feel nostalgic for tradition. In fact, changing the recipe can be a formula for the construction of a creative space in which to defy those limits imposed by society on women writers. The very notion of such autonomy connotes individual identity, yet, as Mora notes, "often we participate in our communities and are solitary writers, a tension" (*Neplanta* 133). Following in the mode of Gloria Anzaldúa's *Borderlands/LaFrontera,* which first articulated these shiftings as a positive means for Chicanas to choose whatever strategy would serve, Mora affirms that "we are psychologically comforted by being part of a continuum—diminished isolation, if you will" (*Neplanta* 43). Mora, along with others, has struggled with the dilemma of the relationship between individual and collective representation, "sometimes it's tug / -of-war that started in the womb," she says, of the "Mothers and Daughters" struggle. "Sometimes they feed on one another," she continues, in her poem of that same title, "memories sweet as hot bread / and lemon tea." But, "sometimes it's mother-stories / the young one can't remember." "The fight for space" (*Communion* 79) causes tension. But Mora has been able, because of her consciousness of gender as well as identity politics, to caution others to "carry the positive aspects of our culture with them for substance, but also to question and ponder what values and customs we wish to incorporate into our lives" (*Neplanta* 53). Faced with a rapidly changing family life, Mora elsewhere expresses concern about the present by recalling comfort foods linked to maternal love in a more comfortable, close-knit familial world. Yet while she values traditions that define membership within a culture, passed down from one generation to the next, she also reserves the right to change the defining ingredients through which one becomes a person.

"The recipes / hints for feeding / more with less" (*Communion* 79), become in Mora's poem, a blueprint for writing with a framework deeply rooted in ethnic beliefs and practices. "Personal archeology," she calls it elsewhere, "uncovering forgotten, / Broken pieces, sifting even in our dreams until we fit the jagged edges into round wholes / we cherish privately" (*Communion* 81). In the poem, "Cissy in a Bonnet," written for her daughter, Mora cautions, though, that "occasionally we / break the code, with our fingers read our early / symbols, reunite with the rare spirits we house" (*Communion* 81).

Viramontes agrees. In *"Nopalitos,"* an essay that looks back to her mother's culinary skills as a source of her own literary power, Viramontes explores the underside of "fierce family ties" that she believes can be oppressive at the same time that they offer solace. Although communal values can be a source of resistance against "a dominant culture that . . . labels us illegal alien," she understands that a relational model of self often implies that the interests of others should come before one's own. By asking her family to respect "my time, my words, myself," she draws attention to an individual woman's need for "respectability" within the larger culture's quest for social justice (293).

To have access to speech, to recipe sharing, assumes that women must feed others, thus cooking might become an obstacle to women's writing. Viramontes understands that those who honor the importance of a man's intellectual enterprise do not always grant a woman's work equal dignity. In the same way as quilts are considered crafts rather than fine arts, women's writing is often described as introspective and recreational, "a hobby," in Viramontes's words, something "we do after our responsibilities are fulfilled" (293). Putting another in front of oneself, as Viramontes knows, creates a situation in which there is potential for vulnerability and abuse.

Denial of the self and the feeding of others are enmeshed in this construction of an ideal woman that Viramontes challenges in her writing. When Mora asserts her right to pursue her own projects against the family claim, she also discovers the force of cultural expectation. In her poem "Old Crone," the work of caring has a darker side, as she challenges a powerful consensual understanding of womanly character by suggesting that women's care for others involves effort as well as love. In the process, she awakens what she says is an inner voice that is really her own guilt. Described as an old woman who "muttered her days away / inside" her, this "ideal" double equates food with maternal and wifely love. Asking Mora to privilege the reality of "baking fresh bread" and other time-consuming tasks, this inner self is passionate about giving food, not writing about it, as Mora does herself. When Mora holds fast to her autonomy, her inner voice "grew weary," allowing her to "see how small she was" to deprive her of time for writing. "Now," the poet sighs, "she sleeps for months at a time" (*Communion* 82), and so provides respite for the poet/cook's self-nourishment in place of the giving of that self to appease another's hunger. However, Mora still must calculate how much time to claim as hers, for she implies that her guilt might awaken at any time to label any exercise of her rights as "selfish."

In other ways the invocation of food signifies change and difference. Ana Castillo, a writer who strongly identifies her work as ethnography, addresses the issue of operating from a relational understanding of self in a patriarchal culture. Writing as an American Latina in a predominantly white, Anglo culture, Castillo stresses a particular feature of the outsider's existence. In her short story "Subtitles," she tells of a woman who claims to be "living in a foreign film"—"Fassbinderish," the protagonist thinks, for she is forced to "invent and reinvent" (176) new roles for the sake of others' entertainment. As an outsider, however, she acquires flexibility in shifting from the mainstream construction of life, where she is constructed as an outsider, to other constructions of life, where she has more control. In this way, she addresses the problem of affirming culture, without being typecast as its one-dimensional emissary, by presenting two alternative selves. Linking her identity to "Coalicue" (174), a pre-Columbian deity who represents duality, she employs role-playing to insist on identity as multiple and contingent upon circumstance. On the one hand, she performs "grand-mother-learned recipes very well" (179), while playing a role that is expected of her. On the other, the narrator uses her eccentric self-imaging to affirm that "a star can be anything she wants" (167). Thus, while using the trope of culinary family tree to suggest an ethnic type, she also indulges in crossover cooking by using a *metate* to grind ingredients for an Italian pesto. Claiming that "this is *very* American, you know" (179), Castillo constructs a plurality of selves that move easily between marginal to dominant culture. Just as Donna Gabaccia observes that various groups have crossed over culinary boundaries in large numbers during the latter twentieth century, so Castillo uses food making to signify that a lack of any one construction of the self as *the* correct construction is a kind of power.

Constructing an ethnic identity is a difficult maneuver in Castillo's text, it requires that her narrator "look like any of them, but . . . not any of them" as well, negotiating between the desire for cultural affirmation on the one hand and the requirements of being "a self-made star" on the other. As "Maria Sabina, Oaxacan Shamaness," (168), she is Other, with respect to her audience but also to her readers. "Miscast during what may have been the bloom of [her] womanhood," she compensates by posturing as a "renegade [who] does not bloom as much as explode" (167) the myths of racist typecasting.

Woman's Space as Public Space

One of the major contributions of these writers is an alliance of their private and public spaces, where there are no hierarchies to separate those who focus on domestic matters from those who write about intellectual concerns. In *Remedios,* Aurora Levins Morales draws from history, anthropology, poetry, herbal lore, and myth to reclaim the forgotten stories of women and cultures who have contributed to the history of Puerto Rico. A modern Jewish Latina *curandera* (healer), Morales's diverse legacies inspired her interest in what is often not recognized as important, such as the oral tradition and voices of the underclass, thus reiterating many of the dynamics described in this essay. For example, in *Take My Word,* Anne Goldman explores how culinary narratives confound the boundaries drawn between autobiography proper, where the subject emerges as unique, and ethnography, whose postcolonial roots have constructed the subject as representative of a culture, which is often a "dying breed" (30). As in many of the texts above, which conform to Goldman's notion that such autoethnographic writing "makes ethnicity concrete" (30), Morales bears witness to "the collective wounds of Puerto Rican women's oppression" while writing her own "buried memories of brutality" (xxv) into the narrative. She places herself within a history of those who are missing from official texts by "writ[ing] words to break both silences" (55), that of wounded nation and wounded individual, and so resists those literary traditions that have been canonized from the dominant point of view. By constructing an empowering image of cultural tradition out of her own healing power, based on medicinal knowledge of food and certain herbs, she notes how the individual "shape we grow into" depends on "long gone places, residues of ash or blood or iron, broken shards, the print of a foot, a kernel of corn" (xiii), all part of her own story of pain and healing through the restorative power of memory.

Replete with explanations of the healing properties of food and herbal lore, *Remedios* places women within an earth-centered sphere in order to destabilize certain predominate values. By denying that "all histories are written in books" (128), Morales reclaims practitioners of an oral tradition that have created art within a woman's space that sometimes is the kitchen. "Sometimes memory is a smooth river stone," she writes, or perhaps an artifact claimed by "a people's historian," (55), like herself, who "[has her] own stories" (108). Her other sources, too, are unconventional, as she extends the culinary metaphor to describe her bibliography. In *La Botanica,* where she keeps each "spice" that adds flavor to a particular story, Morales claims the authority of cook/author to control her own history/culinary concoction. But she also recognizes her place within a community by welcoming those who "want to put in a special order for additional names and dates" (209). As Castillo notes, describing a "feminist practice as housework or as a recipe," as Morales does, "enjoins a theoretical positioning," yet "that . . . job is never finished, because, like housework, it is by definition interminable" (305). In this way, Morales keeps her ending open. By eliciting suggestions from those who "want to track an especially juicy bit of historical gossip" to its source, followed by the exhortation "follow me" (209), she also counters communal cultural practices that in part construct the self by reinstating her own participation in collective history.

These writers, like female cooks, use various ingredients represented by the cultural work and history of their maternal predecessors. The activities of almost all underscore the building of a woman's culture by locating the self within a collective identity and reclaiming the common labors of the foremothers as a craft. Their use of an oral tradition to ally with and recuperate a sense of agency for the underclass becomes a metaphor for political and social struggle. Because it destabilizes certain predominant values that support the dominant culture, the culinary metaphor provides women writers with a discourse of resistance in which the self in relation to an ethnic group is empowered.

Along with the recipes there is a social context, such as folklore and cultural history, that embodies the writers' knowledge of a female legacy. Among recent writers who have looked to the rich and varied heritage of the West to find a regenerative and transforming sense of identity in the present is Anzaldúa, whose following words perhaps sum up best the themes I have explored here. "*Encrucijadas,* haunted by voices and images that violated us, bearing the pains of the past, we are slowly acquiring the tools to change the disabling images and memories, to replace them," she suggests, "with self-affirming ones, to recreate our pasts and alter them— for the past can be as malleable as the future" (*Making Face* xxvii). In this way, any recipe can be changed by the writer who makes the choice to tell another story.

WORKS CITED

Anzaldúa, Gloria. *Borderlands/LaFrontera*. San Francisco: Aunt Lute Books, 1987.

———, ed. *Making Face, Making Soul. Creative and Critical Perspectives by Feminists of Color*. San Francisco: Aunt Lute Books, 1990.

Bird, Gloria. "Breaking the Silence: Writing as 'Witness.'" *Speaking for the Generations: Native Writers on Writing*. Ed. Simon Ortiz. Tucson: U of Arizona P, 1998. 26–50.

Castillo, Ana. *Loverboys*. New York: Norton, 1996.

———. "Yes, dear critic, there really is an Alicia." *Mascaras*. Ed. Lucha Corpi. Berkeley: Third Woman, 1997. 153–63.

Castillo, Debra A. *Talking Back: Toward a Latin American Feminist Literary Criticism*. Ithaca: Cornell UP, 1992.

Counihan, Carole, and Penny Van Esterik, eds. *Food and Culture: A Reader*. New York: Routledge, 1997.

Curtin, Deane, and Lisa Heldke, eds. *Cooking, Eating, Thinking: Transformative Philosophies of Food*. Bloomington: Indiana UP, 1992.

Ehrdrich, Louise. *The Antelope's Wife*. New York: Harper Collins, 1998.

Gabaccia, Donna R. *We Are What We Eat Ethnic Food and the Making of Americans*. Cambridge: Harvard UP, 1998.

Goldman, Anne. "'I Yam What I Yam': Cooking, Culture, and Colonialism." *De/Colonizing the Subject: The Politics of Gender in Women's Autobiography*. Ed. Sidonie Smith and Julia Watson. Minneapolis: U of Minnesota P, 1992. 169–96.

———. *Take My Word: Autobiographical Innovations of Ethnic American Working Women*. Berkeley: U of California P, 1996.

Hogan, Linda. *Dwellings: A Spiritual History of the Living World* New York: Norton, 1995.

———. *Solar Storms*. New York: Simon and Schuster, 1995.

Howard, Josefina. *Rosa Mexicana: A Culinary Autobiography with 6y Recipes*. Introduction by Laura Esquivel. New York: Viking, 1998.

Leonardi, Susan. "Recipes for Reading: Summer Pasta, Lobster à la Riseholme, and Key Lime Pie." *PMLA* 104 (1989): 340–47.

Mora, Pat. *Communion*. Houston: Art Publico, 1997.

———. *House of Houses*. Boston: Beacon, 1997.

———. "Layers of Pleasure: Capirotada." *Through the Kitchen Window: Women Writers Explore the Intimate Meaning of Food and Cooking*. Ed. Arlene Voski Avakian. Boston: Beacon, 1997. 148–55.

———. *Neplanta: Essays from the Land in the Middle*. Albuquerque: U of New Mexico P, 1993.

Morales, Aurora Levins. "Kitchens." *Through the Kitchen Window: Women Writers Explore the Intimate Meanings of Food and Cooking*. Ed. Arlene Voski Avakian. Boston: Beacon, 1997. 296–99.

———. *Remedios: Stories of Earth and Iron from the History of Puertorriquenas*. Boston: Beacon, 1988.

Pilcher, Jeffrey M. *Que Vivan los Tamales!: Food and the Making of Mexican Identity*. Albuquerque: U of New Mexico P, 1998.

Quiñónez, Naomi. "Molcahete Mamas and Feathered Pens." *Mascaras*. Ed. Lucha Corpi. Berkeley: Third Woman, 1997. 169–70.

Randall, Margaret. *Hunger's Table: Women, Food and Politics*. Watsonville: Papier-Mache, 1997.

Rebolledo, Tey Diana. *Women Singing in the Snow: A Cultural Analysis of Chicana Literature*. Tucson: U of Arizona P, 1995.

Scapp, Ron, and Brian Seitz, eds. *Eating Culture*. Albany: SUNYP, 1998.

Tapahonso, Lucy. *Blue Horses*. Tucson: U of Arizona P, 1997.

Villaneuva, Alma Luz. "Abundance." *Mascaras*. Ed. Lucha Corpi. Berkeley: Third Woman, 1997. 37–57.

Viramontes, Helen María. "*Nopalitos:* The Making of Fiction." *Making Face, Making Soul: Creative Perspectives by Feminists of Color*. Ed. Gloria Anzaldúa. San Francisco: Aunt Lute Books, 1990. 293–97.

———. "The Writes Ofrenda." *Mascaras*. Ed. Lucha Corpi. Berkeley: Third Woman, 1997. 125–33.

CHAPTER NINE

Chapulines, *Mole, and* Pozole
Mexican Cuisines and the *Gringa* Imagination
Doris Friedensohn

Several years ago I began writing personal essays for a book to be titled "Delicious Acts of Defiance: Tales of Eating and Everyday Life." It's the autobiography of an eater, I tell people in a tone that is unabashedly gleeful. What food maven wouldn't be gleeful? The project allows me to turn each meal, restaurant visit, food shopping expedition, and trip abroad into a pleasurable, gluttonous, tax-deductible "research" opportunity.

Like most food mavens, I am passionate about what and where and how well I eat. But so are 97 percent of my friends, and my passion, though essential to the venture, is hardly a scholarly justification. Let's say that as an Americanist, I am interested in food as a yardstick of consciousness a reflection of the tensions between identities we are given by family, biology, birthplace, and a historic moment and identities we construct as sojourners in a multicultural and increasingly transnational world. In addition I am intrigued by the play of all those identifiers that constitute my "identity"—American, woman, middle-aged, middle-class, tenured professor, and traveler, to name a few—in defining my palate, orchestrating my menus, and lining my stomach.

"Food as a yardstick of consciousness" opens up a wide range of substantive concerns. Obviously the foods we eat tell much about where we have lived and where we have traveled, how much we earn, what we read, and whom we know. They indicate global markets and the demographics of worldwide migration on the one hand; and they reflect cultural aspirations, notions about health, political commitments, and religious beliefs (whether inherited or freely chosen), on the other. In this contemporary American culture of plenty, we are what we choose to eat—unless "we" happen to be poor or young, sick or incarcerated.

A globetrotter and border crosser, I move restlessly between the familiar and the foreign, and I flirt anxiously with the very far-out. In this essay I write not as a specialist on Mexican foodways but as an observer of my American and feminist food-loving but never food-neutral self in action and in reflection—in Mexico.

Writing about food is primal and confrontational—like looking in the mirror or arguing with a lover. Writing about food as a tourist is even more so. The condition of the tourist is, by definition, contradictory and rich in embarrassments. As a tourist, I crave new knowledge and intense experiences—up to a certain point. I want to expand my boundaries without losing them. I want adventure and safety, too. At middle age, I am willing to put my waistline at risk for unusual foods and culinary happenings, but I am cranky about infection, digestion, and bowels. It's one thing to buy an "alien" object as a souvenir, another to ingest it.

Chapulines

On a blistering hot afternoon in Oaxaca, my friend Nancy and I stroll north from the Zocalo in search of a restaurant called las Quince Letras. The guidebook warns that las Quince Letras is easy to miss—just an unremarkable purple entryway and a sign saying *restaurante*. We fail to spot it on the first pass, peering foolishly at rows of unmarked doorways for the address, Abasolo 300. The street is deserted, soundless. We feel disoriented. Behind the ubiquitous closed shutters, are local residents eating their *comida* in silence? Or, having finished the midday meal, are they grabbing a siesta before the second half of a long working day? Although we have been in Mexico for almost two weeks and feel no jet lag, our clocks won't run on local time.

It's shortly after 3:00 P.M. when *el restaurante* snaps into view. *Finalmente! Gracias a dios,* I catch myself thinking, a phrase I never use in English, but one that falls naturally from my lips in Spanish. The proprietor of las Quince Letras greets us with polite restraint. But when I ask quickly *si podemos comer,* hoping that it is not too late, he flashes a smile and waves us in. We follow him through a cool, darkened room into a plant-filled courtyard where lunch will be served. To us, and to us alone.

Although las Quince Letras has been touted as "an outstanding small restaurant," more than just another *comida* is riding on this visit. I have come for the house specialty, *botana oaxaquena*—an array of twelve appetizers including raw vegetables, chorizos, chicarrones (fried pork skin), tacos, guacamole, quesadilla, and my nervous passion, *chapulines.*

Chapulines, fried grasshoppers, are distinctly Oaxacan. At daybreak during the summer months, the small bugs are harvested with fine nets in cornfields, killed in a bath of scalding water, fried in lard, seasoned, and carried to market. They are sold from straw baskets on the main streets of the city by dozens of women and girls, who nibble as they walk. The bright red, crunchy snack—to be munched like peanuts or pepitas—is seasoned with garlic, chile power, and lime juice. Nippy in the mouth, and for Oaxacans, addictive.

On my first trip to Oaxaca in 1966, the mere mention of *chapulines* unsettled my stomach. Tasting was out of the question. My head is different now: more attuned to the vagaries of human consumption, more avid for oddball edibles. My stomach is different too: educated—over the last three decades—in New York's ethnic eateries and in exotic venues, from Rio to Cairo and Kyoto to Kathmandu, to appreciate strong tastes and weird textures. I've also learned, on trips like this, to cushion my digestive system with a morning cocktail of Pepto-Bismol and to keep a stash of Gelusil in my sportsack along with Band-Aids, bug spray, and sunblock.

In the cool of the courtyard, Nancy and I drink Coronas and wolf down warm tortillas. When the *botanos* are spread out before us, I fixate on the dish of bright red *chapulines* catching the afternoon light. They glow. Our table, with its red, blue, and green striped cloth, gaily painted crockery, and yellow zinnias, also glows. The owner, Sr. Alberto, stands by, alert to our needs. His wife Susana, the cook, grins encouragingly at us from the doorway of the kitchen. Three preteen children sprawl on the floor near her, drawing contentedly. My tourist's anxieties fall away. This tranquil domestic setting offers more protection to a *gringa* than a squadron of police: protection from beggars and sellers of trinkets and lottery tickets, from the din of traffic and dirt on the streets, from an overactive imagination of disease.

I turn off the movie in my head of female vendors fondling *chapulines* with their well-licked fingers and reach for "our" *chapulines*. I sprinkle a few on a bit of tortilla slathered with guacamole and take a cautious bite. The bland tortilla, the smooth-cool guacamole, the wake-up call of citrus and spice, and the airy crunch of *chapulines* make music in my mouth—not Mozart or hard rock but jazz riffs, full of sudden twists and surprise. From there on in, it's my hand to the dish to my mouth, again and again and again. Nancy, a fearless traveler who has driven across Asia with a fifteen-month-old child in a VW van, watches in amazement as I devour the grasshoppers. She leaves the treat untouched.

Chapulines intrigue me because they are of Oaxaca, for Oaxacans: exotic, categorically Other, incorruptible, beyond the reach of global markets. Or are they? Several years ago, in Zabars on the Upper West Side of Manhattan, I spotted chocolate-covered grasshoppers—six ounces in a slick package costing more than some Oaxacan market women earn in a week. I remember fancying the "candy" as a reminder of a food frontier I could not cross. Now that I have crossed over, I consider buying the chocolate version to amuse my grandchildren when I spin out my tale of *gringa* triumph. But no. As good Buddhists—brought up not to kill insects—the little kids will be horrified that I am so proud of being so cruel.

Mole

Most tourists go to Teotitlan del Valle—a famous Zapotec weaving village about forty minutes from Oaxaca—to shop for rugs. Nancy is avid to see weaving in situ; she wants to engage with the weavers, make a connection, bargain hard, and buy when the terms are right. While I'm a willing accomplice in this ritual encounter between First World buyers and Third World sellers, I have my own separate, North American consumer's agenda; my destination is Tlamanalli, a restaurant hyped by food connoisseurs as *the* place for "authentic," expertly prepared, and beautifully served Oaxacan cuisine.

When our taxi turns off the main road from Oaxaca at a sign announcing "Teotitlan del Valle/Centro," I am bewildered. I remember my original pilgrimage here in the mid-1960s when the red clay of the unpaved road

Attacking my *mole negro* with amateur's abandon, I wonder—certainly not for the first or last time—about the relationship between knowing how a dish is made and how much labor is required, appreciating its nuances, and assessing its quality. I may know what I like, but surely what I like is conditioned by what I know. In eating, as in loving, ignorance is only momentarily bliss. Alas, even as I struggle to do justice to the multilayered sauce and subtle chicken, the odds are poor: I am already too full from the guacamole, the brilliant *sopa,* and the picture-perfect quesadilla.

But something else is also at work, interfering with my attention to the *mole negro.* It's the restaurant as an institution and construct that preoccupies me. On the one hand, there is the apparent authenticity of the Zapotec kitchen and cuisine: the impressive, labor-intensive display of chopping and scraping, soaking and toasting, roasting and frying, mixing, blending and pureeing, all by hand, by women on their knees, close to the earth. On the other hand, there is the creation that is Tlamanalli: a shrewdly conceptualized, appealing, and pricey mecca for tourists accustomed to mixing commerce and the art of collecting with serious eating.

Tlamanalli sits inside and outside of the Zapotec past. Time stops in the preparation of food, but there's nothing old-fashioned about the Mendoza family's understanding of the power of tourism to enrich their coffers while eroding their traditions. The preindustrial and the postmodern meet in Tlamanalli: for Abigail Mendoza and her sisters, there is the demanding and lucrative restaurant business as cultural preservation; and for worldly, First World-weary travelers, there is the "experience" of a seemingly timeless, still exotic cuisine in a well-lit, living museum.

Pozole

Manolo, the Mexican guitarist at Shisuke's birthday party, leans toward me, his bedroom eyes fixed on my blond head, and croons: "Mexican music celebrates the woman, *ay, si, la mujer, su belleza,* her eyes, her hair, her skin, her face." I paste a smile on my face. Then, catching the look of unconcealed disgust on Nancy's face, I wish I hadn't. Macho treacle goes down hard at the tail end of the twentieth century—in spite of everything I've been told about the serenade ritual as a demonstration of *la cortesia mexicana.*

In a moment of confused consciousness, I blame myself for giving Manolo the "opening." I initiated the conversation with him, *en espanol,* to be charming and to pass the time while waiting for the festivities to begin.

Reaching for a beer, I remind myself that Nancy and I are guests of the Instituto Dinamico in Guanajuato, where Shisuke, a corporate manager from Japan turned Spanish student, is being feted. The Instituto, a new, American-owned language school, occupies the second floor of a dilapidated building with a graceful center courtyard. Its freshly painted rooms, white with a snappy folkloric blue and yellow trim, merit an "A" for *ambiente.* However, the collection of card tables and unmatched folding chairs in the office and classrooms, the handmade signs, sparse library holdings, and phone on the floor all announce that the school is—to put it generously—a work in progress.

Shisuke's party is our second huge meal of the day at the Instituto. It's also our second *pozole,* one of the richest and heaviest (and sometimes spiciest) of Mexican stews—made of hominy and pork and garnished with fresh vegetables and tortillas. For those of us given to eating salads in summer or a piece of grilled salmon with a splash of lemon, *pozole* is more than a "challenge." It's a threat. My irritation with Manolo, it occurs to me, my unseemly humorlessness, may be related to how fat and uncomfortable I'm feeling from the excesses of the midday *comida.*

The first *pozole* colors the day. The event leading up to it is billed as a cooking demonstration. Beginning at 9:30 in the morning, Rosalinda, a local chef of some distinction, is teaching students and staff to make *pozole rojo,* the hominy and pork stew flavored with intense red chilies. Our friends, Jim and Jennie from Portland, Oregon, who are studying Spanish at the school, have invited us to come along and watch. They are making a video of the demonstration as a favor to Rosalinda and Mercedes, the school's director.

The kitchen of the Instituto has no *ambiente* but considerable "authenticity." It is a small, dark, corridor-shaped space, barely large enough for Rosalinda and Shisuke, who has been enlisted as sous-chef, dishwasher, and errand runner. Rosalinda presides over a two-burner propane stove stacked on top of a makeshift counter; Shisuke peels, cuts, and chops on a rickety card table, the kitchen's only work space. Crowding the stove is the sink, a chipped, narrow, porcelain relic that gives cold water only.

Jim, Jennie, Nancy, and I hover in the doorway of the kitchen; we kib-
itz quietly, jostling one another for a view of the action. Mercedes and her
secretary, Esmerelda, drift around behind us, torn between the demands of
the chef and the chores of the day. Rosalinda, worlds removed from Julia
Child, is a no-nonsense cook: no jokes, no smiles, no entertaining anec-
dotes, no camaraderie with the video crew, and no thank-you's to Shisuke,
whose eyes tear from onions for almost an hour.

But Rosalinda knows *pozole.* Like a surgeon in an operating room, she
barks instructions to her underlings while announcing each procedure
clearly in Spanish. For almost three hours we stand by as boiled kernels of
corn, the hominy, simmer slowly in water to which pieces of pork shoulder,
garlic, and salt have been added. We stand by as the chilies are grilled until
they blister, then soaked, drained, pureed by hand, and strained through a
sieve into the soup. We stand by as the garnishes of lettuce, radishes, onions,
and lime are cut into slices and wedges, and tortillas are crisp fried.

There's no glamor here, only knowledge of the craft, gritty labor, and attention to detail. By the time lunch is served, in cheap red clay bowls, we
are weary but well informed. I eat carefully, alert to the body's messages.
The heat and spice of *pozole rojo* will be bad for my digestion, the Coronas
I drink to cool the mouth and throat will be bad for my head. Even before
I do away with my portion of *pozole,* I long for Gelusil and an extended
siesta. I swear that I'll put nothing in my mouth for the rest of the day.

Scheduling a siesta proves easier than skipping a meal. In travel, even
more than at home, debts must be acknowledged and honored. Mercedes,
who welcomed Nancy and me to the cooking demonstration and incorporated us into the little family of the Instituto, requests our presence at a party
for Shisuke. We cannot refuse the invitation, nor can we resist the pressure
to eat. The evening's *pozole blanco,* made without red chilies, which Mercedes has prepared during the late afternoon, is unexpectedly delicate and
delicious. *Muy sabroso,* delicious, I tell Mercedes, hoping she won't notice
that I've barely touched my dish. In fact, she doesn't. Mercedes's attention is
focused on Shisuke, the shy guest of honor—and on Manolo, who seems
happier drinking beer than singing for his supper. Of course, I'm grateful for
Manolo's indolence since his guitar playing is as bad as his conversation.
However, when the hat is passed at the end of the evening, I contribute

generously. The food has been free, unforgettable—and *sabrosa*. The bounty, in pesos, is his.

Three months later, on a chilly fall day in New York, I study the menu at Gabriela's while waiting for Alice to appear. A Mexican restaurant with a folklorico-funky decor, Gabriela's is popular with Upper West Side artists and intellectuals. The food, cooked by Gabriela Hernandez and her relatives from Jalisco and served by her husband Miguel, is straightforward and lusty—"authentic" in its resistance to New York hybridities and New York chic. Portions are huge, and the price is better than right.

It's 2:00 in the afternoon, a fine hour for *comida mexicana*—especially if one relishes the illusion of a restaurant of one's own. Alice, who arrives as I'm sipping a Corona, waits for my enthusiasms to announce themselves. I order Yucatan-style barbecued chicken—a local favorite—flavored with intense ancho chilies, garlic, and oregano. But for Alice, I insist that only *pozole* will do. Her hominy and pork stew is presented in an enormous earth-colored soup bowl, accompanied by raw vegetables and *tostados* (little fried tortillas). Vapor from the bowl rises like a great mushroom cloud, releasing an awesome chile-garlic aroma. I immediately regret my chicken.

Alice, it is clear, would have welcomed the chicken. She plans to write later in the afternoon and has begun agonizing over the impact of *pozole* on scholarship. I sympathize, releasing her from the obligation to earn an "A" for adventurous eating. After all, when Alice and I get together, having a meal is only an excuse for talking. And so we do at Gabriela's, for almost two hours, slipping out of our manic New York rhythms into the softness of Mexican time. Then, when the late autumn sun drops beneath the high-rise canyons on Amsterdam Avenue, we ask for *la cuenta,* the reckoning.

A tourist's learning curve is slow, I remind myself. There are such deep and elaborate constructions of the self to confront, so many real and imagined barriers to overcome. A few weeks in a foreign place, and I've barely nicked the outermost rings of the onion. But I'm lucky. At home in metropolitan New York, *gracias a dios,* global economics and the geopolitics of immigration, my traveling continues. The next time at Gabriela's, I'll order a *pozole* of my own.

CHAPTER TEN

Let's Cook Thai
Recipes for Colonialism
Lisa Heldke

I think I've finally figured out why I like Thanksgiving dinner so much, why I enjoy having it at my house, cooking all the food myself, and eating it—sometimes for days afterward. It's because I never wonder what to fix. I prepare virtually the same meal every year. It's a ritual for me; turkey, stuffing, mashed potatoes, gravy, squash, and pumpkin and mince pie appear every year. I like it this way. It's comfortable. It's delicious. I do it only once a year. And my mom does it that way. And there, perhaps, lies the crux of the matter. I have been eating this meal one day a year for my entire life, and over the years, it has come to be virtually the only full meal that my mother and I cook in common.

When I went away to graduate school some fifteen years ago, I entered a world of experimental cooking and eating, a world heavily populated with academics and people with disposable incomes who like to travel. It's a world in which entire cuisines can go in and out of vogue in a calendar year. Where lists of "in" ingredients are published in the glamorous food magazines to which some of us subscribe. In which people whisper conspiratorially about this place that just opened serving Hmong cuisine. It's a wonderful world, full of tastes I never tasted growing up in Rice Lake, Wisconsin, textures I never experienced in the land of hot dish. I love cooking and eating in that world.

However, I never know what to cook when I invite people over for dinner. Sometimes I get paralyzed with indecision. The night before the event, the floor of my living room is covered with cookbooks bristling with book-marks. There are cookbooks by my bed and next to the bathtub, even some actually in the kitchen. I've sketched out five possible menus, each featuring foods of a different nationality, most of them consisting of several dishes I've never cooked before. My mom doesn't do this. When she invites guests for dinner, she selects a menu from among her standards, preparing foods she's prepared and enjoyed countless times before, knowing that once again they will turn out well and everyone will enjoy the meal. I miss that. I envy that—especially when I spend three hours trying to decide on a menu, or when I try a new dish for company and it turns out to be awful and everyone at the meal has to try to pretend they are enjoying it.

So why do I do it? Surely no one holds a freshly sharpened carving knife to my throat and says "cook Indonesian next week when those people you barely know come over for dinner!" What's my motivation, anyway? Excellent question. And, as it turns out, disturbing answer—an answer of which I've come to be deeply suspicious.

After years of adventurous eating in graduate school and now as a professor, I have come to be seriously uncomfortable about the easy acquisitiveness with which I approach a new kind of food, the tenacity with which I collect eating adventures—as one might collect ritual artifacts from another culture without thinking about the appropriateness of removing them from their cultural setting. Other eating experiences have made me reflect on the circumstances that conspired to bring such far-flung cuisines into my world. On my first visit to an Eritrean restaurant, for example, I found myself thinking about how disturbing and how complicated it was to be eating the food of people who were in the middle of yet another politically and militarily induced famine. On another occasion, an offhand remark in a murder mystery I was reading started me thinking about the reasons there were so many Vietnamese restaurants in Minneapolis/St. Paul, reasons directly connected to the U.S. war in Vietnam and the resultant dislocation of Vietnamese, Laotian, and Hmong people.[1]

Cultural Colonialism

Eventually, I put a name to my penchant for ethnic foods—particularly the foods of economically dominated cultures. The name I chose was "cultural food colonialism." I had come to see my adventure cooking and eating as strongly motivated by an attitude bearing deep connections to Western colonialism and imperialism. When I began to examine my tendency to go culture hopping in the kitchen, I found that the attitude with which I approached such activities bore an uncomfortable resemblance to the attitude of various nineteenth- and early twentieth-century European painters, anthropologists, and explorers who set out in search of ever "newer," ever more "remote" cultures they could co-opt, borrow from freely and out of context, and use as the raw materials for their own efforts at creation and discovery.[2]

Of course, my eating was not simply colonizing; it was also an effort to play and to learn about other cultures in ways that I intended to be respectful. But underneath, or alongside, or over and above these other reasons, I could not deny that I was motivated by a deep desire to have contact with—to somehow own an experience of—an exotic Other as a way of making myself more interesting. Food adventuring, I was coming to decide, made me a participant in cultural colonialism, just as surely as eating Mexican strawberries in January made me a participant in economic colonialism.

This chapter is part of a larger work, *Let's Eat Chinese,* which explores the nature of cultural food colonialism: What is it? What are its symptoms, its manifestations, its cures? Who does it? Where? Why? In that work, I consider a range of activities in which food adventurers participate—everything from dining out to cooking to food journalism—and how of these activities manifests and reproduces cultural food colonialism. Here I look specifically at ethnic cookbooks. Cookbooks, like restaurant reviews, and like dining in ethnic restaurants, manifest cultural food colonialism in two ways: first, they speak to the food adventurer's never-ending quest for novel eating experiences—where novelty is also read as exoticism, and second, they turn the ethnic Other into a resource for the food adventurer's own use.

Before plunging further into an exploration of these two features of cultural colonialism, I pause to situate my project within the field of feminist thought. I see it as a feminist project on at least two levels. At the first, most banal level, my field of inquiry—food and cooking—is something traditionally regarded as "women's arena." For at least several decades now, feminist theorists have been exploring those domains of human experience traditionally identified as "belonging" to women. Reproductive issues, childbirth, the work of mothering, sexuality, sex work, pornography, women's health, and any number of other features of human life have come to be examined by scholars because of the efforts of feminists who have seen these "women's issues" as relevant *theoretical* issues. Feminist theorists have now begun to turn serious attention to food and eating—for nearly the first time since that original food theorist Plato took it up.[3]

I also understand this as a feminist project because of my theoretical approach; my work attempts to take up challenges posed by various strands of feminist theory, most notably those strands developed by feminists of color and Third World feminists (for example, bell hooks, Trinh T. Min-ha, Joanna Kadi). One of most important lessons white feminists learned from the work of feminists of color in the 1980s was that oppression—women's oppression—always exists along multiple axes simultaneously. Feminists must therefore take racism and classism seriously as central features of *women's* oppression—not as add-ons that can be considered after the "real" challenges of "women's" oppression have been met.

In the 1990s that lesson further evolved to emphasize the importance of investigating one's own privilege within systems of oppression—consider, for example, Ruth Frankenburg's analyses of the nature of whiteness. My work takes up the feminist project of interrogating my own location in systems of privilege and oppression—systems that variously privilege and marginalize me.[4] I explore cultural food colonialism, in part, in an attempt to understand my racial/ethnic and class privilege.

Let's Cook Thai

Take a walk through the cookbook section of your local book supermarket and you will confront a gigantic subsection of books promising to teach their readers how to cook some ethnic cuisine. The shelves will hold several works that have become classics in the field, such as Claudia Roden's *A Book of Middle Eastern Food* and *An Invitation to Indian Cooking* by Madhur Jaffrey. It will also include a significant number of new arrivals—new both in the sense of their publication dates and in terms of the cuisine they tout. (In the past fifteen years, for example, mainstream America has "discovered" the cuisines of Southeast Asia—especially Thailand, Vietnam, and Indonesia—and, even more recently, the foods of both East and West Africa.) You will also find a number of books that are the culinary equivalent of *If This Is Tuesday, It Must Be Belgium*—cookbooks that give you a smattering of recipes from every region of the globe, along with a winsome anecdote or two about the people of that region. The ethnic cookbook market has exploded in the United States, as has the market for the equipment, ingredients, and spices to cook the foods of the world. How does this explosion of interest in ethnic cooking feed into the phenomenon of cultural food colonialism?

Consider one example, *The Original Thai Cookbook* by Jennifer Brennan. Brennan opens her book with these lines: "It is dusk in Bangkok and you are going out to dinner. The chauffeured Mercedes 280 sweeps you from your luxury hotel through streets lined with large, spreading trees and picturesque tile-roofed wooden shops and houses." Brennan goes on to describe "your" arrival at an elegant Thai home—where you are greeted by an "exquisite, delicately boned Thai woman, youthful but of indeterminate age"—and also your meal—a "parade of unfamiliar and exotic dishes" (3–4).

Renato Rosaldo has coined the phrase "imperialist nostalgia" to describe the longing of the colonizer for that which he perceives to be destroyed by imperialism. Brennan here evokes what might be called nostalgia *for* imperialism when she invites her readers to imagine themselves as wealthy and privileged visitors in a culture not their own, and in which they are treated with great deference and respect by some of the wealthiest, most important people in the culture.

Brennan invites her readers to *be* the protagonist of this colonialist story. Her descriptions invite those readers to luxuriate in a fantasy of wealth and also beauty; she suggests that her readers—who are primarily women—should see themselves as "tall and angular" (5), a description that manifests long-standing Euro-American standards of feminine beauty emphasizing long, thin limbs. Reading this description, I find myself seduced by the glamorous role she has assigned me, a middle-class Euro-American woman who has never even been in a Mercedes, let alone traveled to Thailand, and whose body, while fairly tall, would never be described as angular. Just throw in some high cheekbones and a tousled mop of thick, blond hair while you're at it, and I'll sign up for this fantasy tour.

Brennan's description also effectively reduces the identity of the imaginary Thai hostess to her relationship with her guests; Brennan has invented this woman expressly to provide us Western "dinner guests" with pleasure, both visual and gustatory. The "exotic woman" provides just the right touch of beauty, mystery, and servility to get us Western gals into the spirit of imagining ourselves as the heroines of this colonialist culinary tale.[5]

Although she eventually gets down to the business of telling her readers how to cook their own food (a detail that acknowledges that we do not in fact have a Thai cook of our own), Brennan never completely dismisses the colonialist fantasy she has created. Her introduction to this book is just one illustration of the ways that ethnic cookbooks manifest and foster cultural colonization—in this case, by perpetuating a view of the Other as existing to serve and please the reader, and by creating a vision of this Other culture as exotic and alluring.

The Quest for the Exotic

Modern Western colonizing societies have been characterized in part by an obsessive attraction to the new, the unique, the obscure, and the unknown, where "new" is understood in relation to the colonizing society. Desire for new territory, new goods, new trade routes, and new sources of slaves sent European colonizers out to capture and control the rest of the world. The desire to understand the essence of human nature sent European and American anthropologists on a quest to find new, primitive societies not yet exposed to (Western) culture. The desire for new, unadulterated inspiration prompted European painters to move to places far from home. And today, desires for new flavors, new textures, and new styles of dining send us adventuring eaters flipping through the Yellow Pages, scouring the ads in ethnic and alternative newspapers, and wandering down unfamiliar streets in our cities, looking for restaurants featuring cuisines we've not yet experienced—"exotic" cuisines. For the food adventurer, the allure and attraction of such cuisines often consists quite simply in their unfamiliarity and unusualness.

Why does the novel hold such fascination for the food adventurer in American culture? We adventurers come to demand a continual supply of novelty in our diets in part simply to remain entertained. We crave the new just because it is unusual, unexpected, different; differentness is something we have come to expect and require. Of course, it is in the nature of novelty that it is quickly exhausted; if what we crave is novelty per se, our quest will be never-ending. Food magazines often feature articles informing their readers (in all seriousness) about which cuisines and ingredients are now "out" and which have come "in." In a single article, the daily diet of the people of Thailand can be declared passe in the United States.

Novelty is also attractive to adventuring food colonizers because it marks the presence of the exotic, where exotic is understood to mean not only "not local" but also "excitingly unusual." The exotic, in turn, we read as an indication of authenticity. Exotic food is understood as authentic precisely *because* of its strangeness, its novelty. Because it is unfamiliar to me, I assume it must be a genuine or essential part of that other culture; it becomes the marker of what distinguishes my culture from another. Whatever is so evidently not a part of my own culture must truly be a part of this other one. So, in a three-step process, that which is novel to me ends up being exotic, and that which is exotic I end up defining as most authentic to a culture.

How does the quest for the novel-exotic-authentic show up in ethnic cookbooks? Ethnic cookbooks teach their readers how to make the strange familiar by teaching them how to replicate unknown dishes. But how can the cookbook writer achieve this goal without sacrificing the exoticism of the food, given that exoticism has its roots in novelty—in unfamiliarity?

One answer is that for the cook, casual familiarity with a cuisine still radically unfamiliar to most of "us" represents a relationship to the exotic that is itself worth considerable cultural capital, in Pierre Bourdieu's term. A person who achieves such familiarity in a sense becomes the exotic—or at least the exotic once removed. If I can make Indonesian dishes that other food adventurers can only eat in restaurants, I become a kind of exotic myself. Jennifer Brennan—the cookbook author who took us for a ride in Bangkok in her Mercedes—approaches novelty this way in her cookbook.

Jennifer Brennan: The Exotic as Familiar

In the preface to *The Original Thai Cookbook,* Brennan writes that although there are now "Oriental" and Thai markets in "nearly every town," they are filled with "a dazzling and, sometimes, baffling array of foodstuffs: native herbs and spices . . . unusual species of fish; unlabeled cuts of meat, vegetables you might consider weeding from your garden; assortments of strange canned foods and sauces—all with exotic names, sometimes foreign language labels—all purveyed by shopkeepers unfamiliar with English."[6] In other words, although ingredients for Thai food are readily available to non-Thai cooks, availability does not automatically spell familiarity. Brennan emphasizes that language is of little help to the cook here; things are unlabeled, or labeled in a "foreign language," and the people in the stores speak another language too.[7]

Recall Brennan's invitation to imagine yourself visiting an elegant Thai home and being served a banquet. Brennan's lengthy description of this imaginary event highlights the glamorous novelty of everything from the street scenes to the clothing to the way the foods are presented. Her "reassurance of exoticism" serves two related purposes. First, it assures the nervous home cook, perhaps preparing a meal with which to impress her coworkers, that she is not simply naive or ignorant or overly cautious. This food really *is* strange! You don't have to be embarrassed about finding it so, because it really is! Second, it may confirm for the cook that the food she will learn to make is, in some apparently objective sense, exotic, and even familiarity with it cannot alter that fact. Its exoticism means that a cook will definitely earn cultural capital if she serves it to her dinner guests, for whom home-cooked Thai food is still likely to be a novelty.

Another example illustrates both purposes. It comes from a cookbook published twenty years before Brennan's, titled *Japanese Food and Cooking.* In the foreword, author Stuart Griffin describes the respective experiences of "Mrs. American Housewife" and "Mr. American Husband," who have moved to Japan. Mr. American Husband's arrival predates that of his wife, so he has had time to explore Japanese cuisine and to determine that he "could leave a lot of Japanese food alone," specifically the "big, briny tubs of pickles, the fish stands where every species eyed him, and the small

Let's Cook Thai   183

stool-and-counter shops with the stomach-turning cooking-oil smells . . .
But he found lots of things that he wanted to eat and did like" (xii). When
Mrs. American Housewife arrives, her husband and her Japanese cook en-
ter into a conspiracy to get her to try Japanese dishes. By the end of the
foreword, Mrs. American Housewife is hosting dinner parties for her
(American) friends, featuring an "entirely Japanese" menu (xiv)—pre-
pared, of course, by her cook. In presenting such foods to her guests, Mrs.
A. becomes to her friends a kind of exotic herself.

When Brennan and Griffin describe food as "strange" and "stomach-
turning," to whom are they speaking? Brennan identifies her audience as
English-speaking people in the United States. (Notably, the gender refer-
ences have disappeared by the time Brennan published her cookbook; nevertheless, it is still safe to assume that the person wielding the cookbook in
a kitchen is a woman.) But in emphasizing the "unfamiliarity" of the foods,
Brennan actually specifies her audience much further. Presumably, Thai
Americans would find many of the ingredients in Thai food quite familiar.
The same would likely be true of many Vietnamese Americans, Chinese
Americans, Indian Americans, Malaysian Americans—any people whose
heritage foods have influenced and been influenced by Thai foods. The
ingredients Brennan describes would, in fact, be deeply unfamiliar only to
certain English speakers in the United States. But Brennan's description of
the Asian grocery recognizes no such distinctions; "you" will find things
strange in such a store, she notes. "Strange," like "exotic," comes to mean
strange in principle because strange to us.

Even authors who are insiders to the cuisines about which they write
come to use words evincing novelty and exoticism to describe their own
cuisines. Claudia Roden, for example, evokes notions of the exotic Middle
East when she variously describes certain salads as "rich and exotic" (59),
baba ghanoush as "exciting and vulgarly seductive" (46), and Turkish Delight as a food "no harem film scene could be without" (423). That such descriptions also often employ sexual imagery is, of course, no accident, as we
saw earlier in Brennan's description, linking food with sexuality or the sexual attractiveness of women is one way to emphasize the exoticism of a food.
Women reading this cookbook may feel as though we are being invited to
see ourselves as "vulgarly seductive" by extension, when we cook this food.

The Other as Resource

Middle-class members of a colonizing society such as the United States in-habit an atmosphere in which it becomes customary to regard members of a colonized culture as "resources," sources of materials to be extracted to enhance one's own life. In the case of cultural colonialism, the materials are cultural ones. It is no coincidence that the cultures most likely to undergo such treatment at the hands of food adventurers are those described as Third World or nonwhite. There is a tangled interconnection in Euro-American culture between those cultures defined as exotic and Other, and those iden-tified as Third World.

In the world of the ethnic cookbook, the cooking techniques of the Other become marvelous resources that can be scooped up, "developed," and sold to Us, without giving much attention or credit to the women ac-tually responsible for preserving and expanding this cuisine. Recipes be-come commodities we are entitled to possess when they are taken up into the Western cookbook industry; foods become "developed" when they can be prepared in the West.

In her book *Imperial Eyes,* Mary Louise Pratt suggests that to treat the Other as a resource for one's own use can take many forms—even ven-eration and admiration.[8] This observation is well worth keeping in mind when one examines ethnic cookbooks, because many of them exhibit ap-preciation for a food tradition even as they preserve an "essential colonized quality" (163) in the relationship between the cookbook writer and her cook/informant. The case of recipe collecting provides one excellent illus-tration of this.

Borrowing or Stealing?

Where do recipes come from? And when is it proper to say that a recipe was "stolen," or inadequately credited? When it comes to cookbooks in general, and "ethnic" cookbooks in particular, the definitions of these terms decidedly favor the interests of colonizers. A cookbook author is de-scribed as having "stolen" recipes only if they have previously appeared in *published* form—a form of communicating that privileges people on the basis of class and education as well as race, and often sex. Consider the following case: Ann Barr and Paul Levy in *The Foodie Handbook* praise Claudia Roden for her careful "anthropological" work to credit sources of her recipes in *A Book of Middle Eastern Food* (110). But although Roden is careful to identify the sources of the recipes she reproduces when those sources are cookbooks, she acknowledges unpublished sources by name only in the acknowledgments to her book—and then only in a brief, general list of those women to whom she is "particularly indebted."

Barr and Levy's praise for the integrity of "scholar cooks"[9] such as Roden rests on the unstated assumption that only published sources require crediting—an assumption validated by and codified in copyright laws and institutional policies regarding plagiarism. This assumption allows them to regard as highly principled Roden's practice of sometimes describing, but almost never naming, the Middle Eastern women cooks from whom she receives these previously unpublished recipes. But when coupled with her careful crediting of previously published recipes, her practices actually create cookbooks that reflect and reinforce the colonialist and classist societies into which they are received and from which they come. (By "societies from which they come," I mean primarily colonialist Western societies. Their work comes from these societies in a complex manner because Roden is an Egyptian Jew who was educated and has spent much of her adult life in Europe; she is a kind of "insider outsider" who, in part because of her class position, did not in fact learn to cook until she went to Europe.)

In Roden's cookbook, the unpublished women who contributed recipes become interchangeable parts, relevant only for the (universalizable) quality of their being "native cooks." She tells "colorful" stories about some of them in the body of the book, but the reader can match their names to their stories (or their recipes) in only a few cases—and then only with assiduous detective work. They need not be identified definitively, because they cannot be stolen from; they do not own their creations in any genuine (read: legally binding) sense of the word. On the other hand, the creations of cookbook authors, who have access to the machinery of publishing, must be respected and properly attributed.

Barr and Levy's praise of Roden is situated in the context of their discussion of a case of recipe plagiarism. For cookbook writers, the ethics of recipe "borrowing" versus "theft" seem to follow the rules governing plagiarism. According to these, borrowing only becomes theft if a recipe has already appeared in print and one fails explicitly to acknowledge it. Cookbook writers express shock, dismay, or anger when another writer reproduces one of their published recipes without citing its source. However, they waste no emotion over the writer who reproduces recipes gathered "in the field" from unpublished "sources" who go unnamed and uncredited.[10]

Taking up the legal issue, Barr and Levy argue that it is both "mad" and "unenforceable" to suggest that an individual ought to have the right to copyright the directions for an omelet or a traditional French casserole (108); how could any individual "own" the procedure for making dishes so ubiquitous? On the other hand, they favorably report that in a 1984 case Richard Olney successfully sued Richard Nelson for copyright infringement, claiming that Nelson had reproduced thirty-nine of Olney's published recipes in one of his own cookbooks. Thus, while they are uncomfortable with the idea of copyrighting some kinds of recipes, Barr and Levy suggest that justice was served in the Olney case, because Olney is an "originator" of recipes (110)—as opposed to an anthologist (like Nelson) or an anthropologist (like Roden). In support of their view, Barr and Levy quote passages of the relevant recipes to show that Nelson copied ingredients, procedures, even stylistic touches from Olney.

Olney "owned" his recipes in a way that no one can own the omelet recipe because he both "invented" and published them. The latter step apparently is necessary; Barr and Levy have no pity for the author who prints recipes on index cards and distributes them to her friends and then cries "thief."[11] But in the end, it doesn't matter; just because you receive in the mail an unsigned copy of *On the Road,* written in pencil on paper torn from a wide-ruled spiral notebook, you cannot publish Jack Kerouac's words under your own name.

But what of other cases, in which the recipes in question are not originals, but are the "ethnic" equivalents of the omelet? How are we to understand the "ownership rights" of an "anthropologist cook" who publishes the recipes she has "collected in the field," only to have someone else republish those recipes in their own book? Does the anthropologist have the right to complain about theft? Barr and Levy suggest that she does, in their sympathetic consideration of Claudia Roden, whose work has been the site of much borrowing by other cookbook authors. Barr and Levy report that Roden is pleased to see people using the recipes she gathered but not so pleased to see those recipes reappearing in print. In particular, she is "hurt and angry that Arto der Haroutunian, in his books . . . has a great many of the same recipes as hers (*some of which had never been in print before*), similarly described and including some of the mistakes . . . As a writer who gathered her material physically, Mrs. Roden feels 'He has stolen my shadow'" (112, emphasis added). Roden's anger here suggests that it is not only the originator of a recipe whose work can be stolen; you are also a victim of theft if the recipes you collect and publish are subsequently published by someone else.

That Roden is the victim of a theft of "original material" seems obvious on one level. In a context defined by copyright law, der Haroutunian's acts do constitute a kind of plagiarism of Roden's original work. But consider the matter again; what he stole were, for the most part, recipes she gathered from other women—along with published texts she excerpted and organized in a particular way. Publishing, in this context, comes to be its own kind of originality—or comes to mean originality.

Furthermore, publishing a thing seems to make it one's own, regardless of who "owned" it in the first place. Roden does not claim that she created the recipes; indeed she expressly describes them as belonging to the particular towns, villages, communities, countries in which she located them (Barr and Levy 112). Nevertheless, she says that *her* shadow has been stolen by der Haroutunian.

While I agree that some kind of harm has been done to Roden by those who have republished parts of her book, I want to redirect the discussion to the kinds of harm that her explanation obscures—namely, harm done to the Middle Eastern women at whose stoves Roden stood and from whom she learned the recipes she reproduced in her cookbook. This harm does not fall neatly under the category of theft, because the women cannot be regarded as the owners of recipes in the sense required. The language of property does not help us to understand such harm for at least two reasons: first, these cooks have not laid any claim to the recipes (say, by publishing them themselves or by cooking them in a restaurant for paying customers), nor will they likely do so, because, second, the recipes from which they cook are often as common to them as the omelet is to a French cook, and thus not the sort of thing they would be inclined to think could be owned. It is not appropriate to describe Claudia Roden as "stealing" recipes from the women with whom she studied. She could not rectify the harm done to them simply by documenting the "originators" of her recipes.

Roden erases or generalizes the identities of most of the women who give her recipes.[12] She does identify various of her relatives as the sources of recipes; she notes, for example, that "my mother discovered [this recipe] in the Sudan, and has made it ever since" (43). But in most cases, she mentions only the primary region in which a dish is served and says nothing about the particular woman or women from whom she got the recipe. (Recipes are peppered with phrases such as "A Greek favorite," and "Found in different versions in Tunisia and Morocco.") By contrast, she carefully notes the dishes she found in particular published cookbooks. (For example, with respect to a chicken recipe, she notes: "A splendid dish described to me by an aunt in Paris, the origin of which I was thrilled to discover in al-Baghdadi's medieval cooking manual" [184].) The effect of this differential treatment is to blur the "ordinary" women who contributed to this cookbook into a mass of interchangeable parts. She renders invisible the work done by members of this mass to create, modify, adapt, and compile recipes; it does not matter which individual was responsible for which modification. Only her own work on these tasks is visible in her text.

A critic could reasonably respond that, in fact, these recipes have no originators: "You have already pointed out that many of them are as ubiquitous in the Middle East as the omelet is in France. Are you advocating that Roden give credit to particular women for their contributions of a particular recipe? Why would that make sense, given their ubiquity?" My first answer would be that it makes as much sense to credit these conduits as it does to credit Roden herself; their participation in making these recipes available is certainly as relevant as hers. Her interaction with the publishing industry should not alone give her special, superior claims to ownership.

Furthermore, I do not advocate making particular women, or even their communities, the owners of recipes any more than I advocate allowing Roden to make that claim. The problem emerges from the fact that Roden and other anthropologist cooks transform "traditional" recipes into commodities. They treat the recipes they gather as resources—raw materials onto which they put their creative stamp—by surrounding the recipes with scholarly background information, a personal anecdote, or a relevant quotation from a work of poetry or literature. With this creative transformation, the recipes become property that can be stolen.

Roden has gathered the creative productions of various peoples to make her own cultural creation. Other women's (often other cultures') recipes are the raw materials she harvested and "refined" into a work of "genuine culture." In her case, this refinement involved situating the recipes alongside erudite quotations from Middle Eastern texts, stories she collected about the various dishes, or accounts of the processes by which she came into possession of the recipes. Because she regards her work as a genuine cultural product—not just a "natural outgrowth" of a culture, as is the case with the recipes she collects—she expresses outrage at its being plagiarized.

I want to look at the issue of recipe originality, borrowing, and theft in one final way before leaving it. Another factor contributing to the complexity of this issue is that everyday recipe creation has traditionally been women's work done in the home, whereas the harms that are identified and codified by law tend to be those that befall the creative work men have traditionally done in more public arenas.

Like other kinds of women's creative work, such as quilting and weaving, recipe creation tends to be social. By this I mean not only that the physical work may be done in groups, but also that the creation is frequently the result of many women's contributing their own ideas to the general plan, often over considerable spans of time. A recipe that passes from one cook to another may undergo slight modifications to accommodate differences in taste or unavailability of an ingredient, to streamline or complicate a process, or for unidentifiable reasons.[13] We might say that such a recipe is "original" to everyone and no one; its beginning is unknown, but the contributions of particular cooks may be read in it by someone who knows how to decipher such an "evolutionary" record. (I once heard a food expert analyze the Thanksgiving dinners of several families living in different parts of the United States. On the basis of the foods present in the meal, and the way that those foods were prepared, she was able to identify, with accuracy, the areas of the country in which that family had lived over the past generations.) Cooks who have contributed to the evolution of a recipe may well be pleased and proud when someone else takes up their modification—whether or not the other cook knows who is responsible for it.

The categories originality and plagiarism pertain to more individualistic art forms, such as novel writing and painting—which have been regarded as "high art" and have primarily been the purview of a privileged minority of men. These terms cannot be applied so aptly to other art forms, particularly collective and cumulative ones. However, they often are (awkwardly) applied to these forms, perhaps as an attempt to gain legitimacy for them. For example, women often have (in reality and in fiction) appealed to claims of originality and ownership, to accuse others of "stealing" their recipes. Of course, the women who have done so are often subjected to mockery. (My morning radio station regularly plays the song "Lime Jello, Marshmallow, Cottage Cheese Surprise," in which a woman discusses the dishes that have been brought to a "ladies'" potluck luncheon. The singer, who brought the title dish to the potluck, at one point exclaims, "I did not steal that recipe, it's lies, I tell you, lies!" The line is greeted with guffaws of laughter from the audience.) I suggest that such mockery reflects both the pervasive sense that an individual's recipes are not original to them and thus cannot be owned by them and the sense that, even if recipes could be stolen, their theft would be no crime since recipes simply aren't important enough to be the objects of moral concern.[14]

Recipes for Anticolonialism

When I began exploring cultural food colonialism, I naively believed that cooking was an unambiguously anticolonialist activity, one that could be employed by anyone who wished to develop a way of living in the world that resisted colonialism. Although I no longer think of cooking as magically resistant and am deeply critical of much that goes on in the pages of various ethnic cookbooks, I still believe that cooking has important potential as a site for anticolonialist activity. Food is a wonderful medium for this because culinary diversity is already so much a part of the daily life of many Americans—and because food in general is an essential part of everyone's daily life. Because we must eat, opportunities for becoming anticolonialist in the kitchen present themselves to us with tremendous frequency. Most of us don't go to art museums or concerts every day of the week—but we do eat dinner every night, and we often cook it ourselves.

The question for me is, How can one enact anticolonialist resistance in the kitchen, the grocery story, the cookbook? How can I transform my ethnic cooking into what bell hooks calls a critical intervention in the machinery of colonialism? We who would be anticolonialists must learn how to engage with cuisines, cooks, and eaters from cultures other than our own—not as resources but as conversation partners. We must also recognize that our privilege (racial, ethnic, class, gender) is something food adventurers cannot simply give up, that while I have the luxury of experimenting with other cuisines in the kitchen, my privilege—and my guilt about it—will not be banished simply by my forsaking this luxury.

Writing on the subject of white racism against blacks, bell hooks argues, "Subject to subject contact between white and black which signals the absence of domination . . . must emerge through mutual choice and negotiation . . . [S]imply by expressing their desire for 'intimate' contact with black people, white people do not eradicate the politics of racial domination" (28). Cookbook author Jennifer Brennan does not magically neutralize the colonialist dynamic between herself and her private cook simply by making herself at home in the kitchen and cozying up to the cook to ask sincere, well-meaning questions about whether the Thai really use ketchup in their *paad thai*. Such presumed intimacy can in fact reinforce the dynamic, because it highlights the unreciprocated ways Brennan has access to her cook.

What would mutual choice and negotiation require in such an interaction, what must happen in order to change this into a subject-to-subject exchange? At the very least, Brennan and her "changing parade of household cooks" (preface) would have to discuss the terms under which it would be justifiable for her to publish their work—to take their skills and recipes and market them under her own name. It would require that the cooks be able to make an informed choice about whether or not to participate in this cookbook-making enterprise in the first place—that they understand the larger, long-term consequences of participating in it. Would they still want to participate in the project if they knew how angry Claudia Roden was about Middle Eastern cuisine's unfortunate transformation in the pages of Euro-American cookbooks? They may; my point is that mutual choice would require that both parties making the choices have sufficient information on which to base their choices. Given that Brennan has the publishing power—and more access to information about how these recipes will be used in the United States—she has a particular obligation to exchange that information with her cooks.

"Mutual recognition of racism," hooks continues "its impact both on those who are dominated and those who dominate, is the only standpoint that makes possible an encounter between races that is not based on denial and fantasy" (28). Such a requirement would transform the way in which Euro-American cookbook writers such as Brennan collect their materials for ethnic cookbooks; it would also result in cookbooks with a very different format. Perhaps ethnic cookbooks written by outsiders to a cuisine could be constructed in ways that actually acknowledge and grapple with the fact of continued colonialist domination by Western cultures. Perhaps cookbooks could be written as genuine collaborations, as opposed to the de facto collaborations they so often are now. (It's worth noting, in this regard, that collaboration is already highly developed and appreciated in one arena—namely, the community fund-raising cookbook. In such cookbooks, one often finds multiple, nearly identical, copies of a recipe, each credited to a different cook. Such repetition may seem ridiculous to someone who just wants to know how to make a dish, but when it is considered as a record of how a community cooks, it becomes a valuable source of information.)

hooks's message, translated into the realm of food adventuring, is that our only hope for becoming anticolonialists lies in our placing the colonizing relationship squarely in the center of the dining table; only by addressing colonialism directly through our cooking and eating can we possibly transform them into activities that resist exploitation. If "eating ethnic" cannot remain pleasurable once we acknowledge how domination shapes our exchanges with the Other, then we must acknowledge that it is a pleasure well lost.[15]

The anticolonialist aims to disengage from an attitude and a way of life that exploit and oppress and to develop alternatives that subvert the colonizing order. We need to learn how to participate in anticolonialist exchanges of food. We need to find useful, anticolonialist ways to make dinner.

NOTES

[1] Sara Paretsky, in her 1985 novel *Killing Orders,* writes, "I stopped for a breakfast falafel sandwich at a storefront Lebanese restaurant. The decimation of Lebanon was showing up in Chicago as a series of restaurants and little shops, just as the destruction of Vietnam had been visible here a decade earlier. If you never read the news but ate out a lot you should be able to tell who was getting beaten up around the world" (36).

[2] Explorers Richard Burton and Henry Schoolcraft, for example, "discovered" the headwaters of the Nile and the Mississippi, respectively—with the help of local folks who already knew what Burton and Schoolcraft had come to discover. For an analysis of Burton's much-aided journey to the headwaters of the Nile, see Mary Louise Pratt, *Imperial Eyes.* For an analysis of Schoolcraft's use of Ojibwe experts to locate the headwaters of the Mississippi, see Gerald Vizenor, *The People Named the Chippewa.*

The painter Paul Gauguin went to Tahiti to "immerse [him]self in virgin nature, see no one but savages, live their life" so that he might make "simple, very simple art"—using their lives and art as his raw material (qtd. in Guerin 48).

[3] Plato makes such frequent use of food to illustrate his claims that one is forced to conclude that the references are anything but accidental. For two considerations of Plato's conceptions of food, see my "Foodmaking as a Thoughtful Practice" and "Do You Really Know How to Cook?"

[4] In what may seem an ironic turn, it is the centrality of feminist theory to my own way of doing theory—the centrality of challenges, questions, and critiques from feminists of color—that makes it sometimes appear as if my work "isn't about women at all." My work is *not* about women, when that phrase is understood to mean "about women by not being about men, about women by talking about women and gender exclusively." But it is precisely this notion of feminism—and of being "about women"—that I wish to undermine, following in the path of Third World feminist theorists. Such "aboutness" necessarily brackets or erases race, class, and other markers of difference, as not being central to "women's" identities.

[5] Trinh T. Min-ha notes: "Today, the unspoiled parts of Japan, the far-flung locations in the archipelago, are those that tourism officials actively promote for the more venturesome visitors. Similarly, the Third World representative the

modern sophisticated public ideally seeks is the *unspoiled* African, Asian, or Native American, who remains more preoccupied with her/his image of the *real* native—the *truly different*—than with the issues of hegemony, racism, feminism, and social change (which s/he lightly touches on in conformance to the reigning fashion of liberal discourse)" (88).

⁶ There is something more than a little odd about the name of this cookbook. What does it mean for a Westerner to lay a claim to the "territory" of Thai food, by describing as "original" a book that records a culture not her own? The book jacket explains the meaning *original* is to have in this context: this is the first Thai cookbook published in English in the United States. This explanation of the word *original* tends to invite the conclusion that something comes into existence only when it does so in the United States.

⁷ It is worth noting that the situation with respect to Thai foods has changed dramatically since Brennan published this book in 1981. Now, not only are there more Asian groceries in the United States, but also one can buy many of the ingredients for Thai foods in food cooperatives and upscale supermarkets. One can even buy various premixed "Thai spices" in foil packets and glass jars, with directions clearly labeled in idiomatically flawless American English. They are considerably more expensive and less accessible than the ubiquitous taco seasoning packets, but I have little doubt that these spice packets will one day be every bit as common, as Thai food becomes a part of the mainstream U.S. consumer economy.

⁸ Discussing Maria Graham Callcott's *Journal of a Residence in Chile during the Year 1822*—a section of the book in which Graham describes learning to make pottery—Pratt writes: "Rather than treating the artisanal pottery works as a deplorable instance of backwardness in need of correction, Graham presents it in this episode almost as a utopia, and a matriarchal one at that. The family-based, non-mechanized production is presided over by a female authority figure. Yet even as she affirms non-industrial and feminocentric values, Graham also affirms European privilege. In relation to her, the potters retain the essential colonized quality of *disponibilité* they unquestioningly accept Graham's intrusion and spontaneously take up the roles Graham wishes them to" (163). As Pratt suggests, to treat the Other as a resource for one's own use can take many forms, some of which even involve veneration and admiration. This observation is well worth keeping in mind when one examines ethnic cookbooks;

many of them exhibit appreciation for a food tradition, even as they preserve the "essential colonized quality" of the relationship between the cookbook writer and her cook/informant.

⁹ Levy describes Elizabeth David as the inspiration for—and the original example of—a group of people he names "scholar cooks" (31). Among the scholar cooks, presumably, the anthropologist cooks are just one subspecies. Other scholar cooks include diplomat-turned-fish-specialist Alan Davidson, and Jane Grigson.

¹⁰ If we consider cooking itself—rather than cookbook writing—we may locate another, similar definition of theft, one very much rooted in class and gender. Chefs can be thought of as stealing one another's dishes, particularly "signature dishes" they have invented, even if those dishes have never been published. (They cannot, so far as I know, sue for such theft, their primary recourse is probably ridicule.) Famous chefs, who get paid for their work, can most easily make this claim, because they can produce the most evidence for it. Unknown chefs—like unknown songwriters—will have more difficulty proving that they've been robbed of a culinary idea. And women who are not chefs for pay but simply cook at home for their families will have insurmountable difficulty; a recipe must become a commodity before it can be stolen. The thing to note is that with cooking, as with cookbooks, proving originality is important—but having the power to reinforce a claim to originality is crucial.

¹¹ Indeed, the prevalence of recipe-card exchanges serves to temper some of their outrage over the Olney-Nelson case; it seems that Nelson got his recipes not out of Olney's book but from a set of recipe cards he had received in the mail and used for years in his cooking class with no idea of their origin.

¹² Lutz and Collins, in *Reading National Geographic,* examine the similar ways that *National Geographic* transforms the individuals in its photographs into "types," nearly interchangeable members of the group known as Other (see esp. chap. 4).

¹³ Not all recipes change, of course, some foods are temperamental enough that cooks feel disinclined to change them, for fear that they will fail. Not all cooks feel comfortable modifying recipes either. In my own family, for example, my mother and I are much more likely to tinker with a recipe than are my two sisters. (Interestingly enough, both of them are trained as scientists.) For one philosophical discussion of the processes of recipe creation and exchange, see my "Recipes for Theory Making."

[14] I would contrast this to the respect, bordering on reverence, with which recipes used in restaurants are often treated, the deference with which a customer asks for the recipe for a particular dish and the gratitude they heap on the cook/chef willing to pass it along. In food magazines, this difference is sometimes manifested in the presence of two separate recipe columns. In one, readers ask other readers to share a recipe for some particular food ("I'm looking for a good recipe for pumpkin bread. Does anyone have one that uses orange juice?"). In the other, readers write in to ask for specific recipes they have tasted in restaurants (recipes they perhaps were too intimidated to request in person), and almost invariably, they couch their requests in the language of a supplicant: "Do you think you could ever possibly get them to release the recipe for this chicken dish I had?"

[15] Wendell Berry, in "The Pleasures of Eating," describes an extensive pleasure in one's food, which "does not depend on ignorance" of the conditions under which that food is grown, harvested, and brought to you. For him, this pleasure is not "merely aesthetic" but ethical, political, and environmental as well (378).

WORKS CITED

Barr, Ann, and Paul Levy. *The Official Foodie Handbook: Be Modern—Worship Food*. New York: Timber House, 1984.

Berry, Wendell. "The Pleasures of Eating." *Cooking, Eating, Thinking: Transformative Philosophies of Food*. Ed. Deane Curtin and Lisa Heldke. Bloomington: Indiana UP, 1992. 374–79.

Bourdieu, Pierre. *Distinction: A Social Critique of the Judgment of Taste*. Trans. Richard Nice. Cambridge: Harvard UP, 1984.

Brennan, Jennifer. *The Original Thai Cookbook*. New York: Perigee, 1981.

Frankenberg, Ruth. *White Women, Race Matters: The Social Construction of Whiteness*. Minneapolis: U of Minnesota P, 1993.

Griffin, Stuart. *Japanese Food and Cooking*. Rutland, Vt.: Charles E. Tuttle, 1959.

Guerin, Daniel, ed. *The Writings of a Savage Paul Gauguin*. Trans. Eleanor Levieux. New York: Viking, 1978.

Heldke, Lisa. "Do You Really Know How to Cook? A Discussion of Plato's Gorgias." Unpublished paper.

———. "Foodmaking as a Thoughtful Practice." *Cooking, Eating, Thinking: Transformative Philosophies of Food.* Ed. Deane Curtin and Lisa Heldke. Bloomington: Indiana UP, 1992.

———. "Recipes for Theory Making." *Hypatia* 3.2 (1988): 15–31.

hooks, bell. *Black Looks: Race and Representation.* Boston: South End, 1992.

Iyer, Pico. *Video Night in Kathmandu.* New York: Knopf, 1988.

Jaffrey, Madhur. *An Invitation to Indian Cooking.* New York: Vintage, 1973.

Kadi, Joanna. *Thinking Class.* Boston: South End, 1996.

Lutz, Catherine A., and Jane L. Collins. *Reading National Geographic.* Chicago: U of Chicago P, 1993.

Min-ha, Trinh T. *Woman Native Other: Writing Postcoloniality and Feminism.* Bloomington: Indiana UP, 1989.

Paretsky, Sara. *Killing Orders.* New York: Ballantine, 1985.

Pratt, Mary Louise. *Imperial Eyes: Travel Writing and Transculturation.* New York: Routledge, 1992.

Roden, Claudia. *A Book of Middle Eastern Food.* New York: Vintage, 1974.

Rosaldo, Renato. *Culture and Truth.* Boston: Beacon, 1989.

Vizenor, Gerald. *The People Named the Chippewa: Narrative Histories.* Minneapolis: U of Minnesota P, 1984.

CHAPTER ELEVEN

Gendered Feasts
A Feminist Reflects on Dining in New Orleans
Heather Schell

Have you ever seen an advertisement for chicken meat that features live chickens vying to be chosen for the slaughterhouse? Some of the chickens brag about how plump and tender they are, while others face the heartbreak of rejection and survival. Remember the 1970s ad campaign in which Charley, an ambitious tuna, strives in vain to get canned? I have always wondered why advertisers would select such a strategy. Who wants to eat talking chickens? Or, for that matter, who wants to eat a tuna fish with a name, or raisins or chili peppers or even bananas that sing and dance? Animals who are protagonists of their own little stories—whether Chicken Little, the Ugly Duckling, Miss Jemima Puddleduck, or the Purdue chicken—are not animals that I want to eat. I won't go so far as to claim that food commercials with anthropomorphized animals are responsible for driving me to vegetarianism, but even in my meat-eating youth I found these depictions unsettling.

As you read this chapter, you may wonder whether I am assuming that you are a vegetarian or a meat eater. You may also, at some points, wonder whether I mean to imply that all men are bad—or, for that matter, that all whites, Americans, eaters of anthropomorphized food, and so forth, are bad. Therefore, I'd like to start with a quick note on the word *we*. I am using *we* broadly to refer both to U.S. citizens (including myself) and to whoever is engaged in thinking about this topic with me. There will undoubtedly be many instances in which you would not include yourself as part of this "we." In fact, often I use the term in places where I do not believe that it applies to me: for example, I may write that "we" eat vast quantities of meat in this country. Furthermore, I may label something as a "male fantasy" without intending to imply that our male friends or fathers are obsessed with the idea. I am not accusing my readers of sexism, racism, or any other "ism." In each case, you are the best judge of whether or not my "we" applies to you or to people whom you know. My assumption is that if you are reading this essay in the first place, the "we" in many cases does not pertain to you.

In the early 1990s I visited New Orleans and was amazed by the city's full-scale campaign to market anthropomorphized food products. It has made me think about the ways in which we invest food with meaning, about our habit of believing that what we eat (and how we eat it) expresses something about the kind of people we are. Food is not only a means of displaying who we are but a substance that can transform us into who we want to be. Of course, this is not literally true, but the belief is meaningful. In this chapter, I explore the symbolic meaning of food. I believe that I have finally figured out what the anthropomorphized chicken means, but my provisional answers are unsettling: these depictions of animals invite us to play out unequal social power relationships through eating. Animated food targets our desire to feel power over others. In the United States, this powerful person has traditionally been a straight, wealthy, white male, but souvenirs are more egalitarian: anyone with enough money to visit New Orleans can buy an image of someone still lower on the social totem pole and enjoy the symbolic thrill of eating it. It is no surprise that almost all images of anthropomorphized food, in New Orleans as well as in the national media, represent creatures with low social status, such as women and ethnic minorities.

To begin, I explore how anthropomorphized food is crafted to address a white male audience by conjuring images of white masculine power and voluntary female or black subjugation. Next I investigate our ideas about ourselves as eaters in a zoological sense, particularly in terms of the prevalent fantasy that humans are the ultimate predators. Our culture increasingly privileges predatory behavior; furthermore, we rationalize our predatory aspirations as "natural" and "healthy" by willfully misreading the theory of natural selection. I close with a look at the gender dynamics of our beliefs about predatory behavior. This system of beliefs is central to our culture's gender roles, providing a "natural" illustration of what it means to be masculine or feminine. By critically examining these beliefs, we can see that they bolster a system of sexual dominance.

New Orleans is a city where people go for a hot time. Mardi Gras probably best exemplifies the city's licentious reputation, but Bourbon Street in the French Quarter remains active year-round, day and night. Public consumption of alcohol is legal, and age requirements are only casually enforced. Bars along Bourbon Street offer striptease shows for a variety of sexual inclinations; men, women, and men dressed like women remove their clothing nightly. Witchcraft is a regulated state religion, and licensed as well as unlicensed practitioners make their services available to tourists. And this naughty, racy self-representation constitutes a large part of New Orleans's appeal to tourists. I overheard a man asking advice from a local and then confidently informing his friend, "She says this one's the hottest." He was purchasing a bottle of pepper sauce.

When my partner was planning to attend a conference in the Big Easy in the early 1990s, I invited myself along. I had wanted to see New Orleans since my college days, when friends had taken road trips to Mardi Gras and returned home laden with brightly colored plastic beads, hurricane glasses, and the occasional sexually transmitted disease. For this trip, I ignored the conference and spent my days wandering around the French Quarter. I stopped to browse in every tourist trap. It doesn't take too many such stops to notice patterns in the local marketing strategies. In New Orleans, there are three main categories of souvenirs: voodoo, Mardi Gras, and food. In addition to various kinds of prepackaged food, the food souvenirs also include the same junk—toothpick holders, T-shirts, mugs—one sees in most American tourist spots, only remade with a food theme. These food souvenirs are usually "ethnic." For my purposes here, I use the term *ethnic food* to describe those cuisines designated by nation or ethnicity of origin, as distinguished from those described defined by ingredients or method of preparation, such as "seafood" or "kosher" or "barbecue" (even though many of these foods are also marked in terms of ethnicity and socioeconomic status).

The two most marketed ethnic food categories in New Orleans are Creole and Cajun. The city has a history of acknowledged interracial sex, and the descendants of such interactions, of mixed African American, French, Spanish, and Native American ancestry, are the group generally referred to under the designation *Creole*. Confusingly, the term *Creole* has also been applied to Europeans born in the West Indies; for example, Bertha Mason in *Jane Eyre* is Creole. A time line of Louisiana's ethnicity in Jean Lafitte Park merges its French and African American branches into a Creole branch, at which point the African American branch ends while the French branch continues. This suggests that all African Americans living in New Orleans today are Creole. Because depictions of Creole people aimed at tourists in New Orleans seem to agree with the time line's definition, that is the usage I adopt in this essay. The meaning of *Cajun* is less messy. According to the same time line, *Cajun* refers to the rural French who migrated first to Canada and then were forced to leave when they refused to swear allegiance to the British crown. They settled in the swampy, alligator-infested regions of Louisiana. If all this were not sufficiently complicated, Creole and Cajun also have specific meanings in reference to food. Crudely speaking, "Creole" in a cookbook title is invariably followed by the word "cuisine," while books with Cajun recipes usually refer self-consciously to "cookin'." Depictions of anthropomorphized crawfish often accompany foods designated as Creole; animated "'gators" indicate Cajun food, though Cajun "cookin'" does not appear to rely on alligators.

One of the souvenirs featured in almost every shop was a series of oversized postcard replicas of turn-of-the-century labels and advertisements for local food products. These labels frequently depicted caricatures of African American servants or slaves, "Aunts" or "Uncles," offering food either directly to us or to a white customer/master figure—for example, an early Tabasco sauce ad showing a dapper black man presenting the sauce on a tray to a white man seated at a table. These representations are obviously not unique to New Orleans—Uncle Ben's rice and Aunt Jemimah's syrup attest to their marketing power. However, these figures don't appear on New Orleans food souvenirs nowadays—except, of course, on these postcards and other items supposedly neutralized by their nature as historical replicas.[1] Thus, such racism is ostensibly contained within the past. We aren't seeing current racial stereotypes, only (beloved) depictions of past racial stereotypes.

Packaging that aims to be up-to-date does not use these offensive figures but, instead, serves up caricatures of anthropomorphized living food. Alligators and crawfish wearing aprons and chefs' hats appear on magnets, caps, mugs, postcards, cookbooks, and aprons, of which the two last mentioned are almost as ubiquitous as T-shirts in the New Orleans tourist stores. A shirt blazoned with a recipe for blackened redfish is illustrated with a picture of the recipe's other ingredients stuffing themselves down the fish's throat, poking the fish with forks, with tins of spices on tiny legs running toward the fish to dash themselves against it. Animate, anthropomorphized food is a common trope in U.S. advertising, as the phenomenal success of the Claymation California Raisins illustrates. In fact, including the ultimate white bread Pillsbury Dough Boy, one soon gets the distinct impression that these depictions are also marked by race and gender. Apparently, even among singing lobsters such categories still matter. I return to this point later with the New Orleans crawfish.

In addition to the disturbing implications of conscious food, many of these souvenirs further depict the food as inviting us to eat it, actively participating in its own consumption. An illustration on a soup mix shows the familiar 'gator in a chef's hat, this time immersed in a large cookpot, stirring itself with a spoon. Questions of compulsion and consent can scarcely be formulated when the food is an active participant in its own demise.

Some depictions have a blatant sexual message as well. One T-shirt has a picture of a Louisiana oyster with the caption "Eat me raw." Notice the gender ambivalence here—although the message clearly suggests oral sex, it's impossible to determine which specific genitalia are offered. Another, stranger example comes from a series of recipe postcards, most of which are decorated with a little watercolor of the prepared dish. The postcard for Cajun dirty rice features a striptease grain of rice, "Steemie la Grain," taking it all off in a show on Bourbon Street. She's dancing with a spoon, the implement with which we would eat her. A neon sign above her head flashes "Hot!" I am writing as though Steemie is unambiguously a female grain of rice, but she has no obvious sexual characteristics. She is removing a little bikini and sports a blond wig. When we consider the variety of sex shows on Bourbon Street, we could see Steemie as either a female or a female impersonator. This possibility makes the dirty rice even more tantalizing and naughty. These and similar images suggest that one's sex is less a concrete attribute than a particular position in a power relationship. For whatever the biological sex of Steemie and the raw oyster—if they can be said to possess biological sex—one thing is constant: the images cater to men as their imagined audience, their purchasers.

For example, while in theory anyone could buy the "Eat me raw" T-shirt, how many women would dare wear it? It would seem at the very least to be an open invitation to harassment. This merchandise promises a kind of lascivious egalitarianism that the reality of New Orleans contradicts. Similarly, these particular souvenirs erase the cost both of the animated food and of its human corollaries. Steemie will give herself to us for a price; so would the oysters, if we take the message literally: while every café, restaurant, and bistro offers shellfish, they aren't giving it away. One cannot ignore the power relationship involved in being for sale, both for women and for African Americans in a country with slavery in its past. By presenting the animated food as free, the souvenirs play on two fantasies: we tourists can have any desire fulfilled at no cost to ourselves, and the food itself is free to choose its fate. The food products have weighed their options and want to be consumed. Perhaps most people would have to pay, but for us, they would almost give themselves away for free. Among heterosexual males, this is a popular fantasy about female prostitutes, immortalized in films such as *Leaving Las Vegas* and *Pretty Woman*. It is also a fantasy about slavery, straight out of *Gone With the Wind:* Mammy will stay and take care of us, even after abolition, because she *wants* to be our Mammy.

We should think about the implications of purchasing this tourist paraphernalia—if "we" here means feminists, we should stop to think even longer. I had eaten raw oysters on several occasions before visiting New Orleans. They are purportedly very sexy things to eat, aphrodisiacs that slip sensuously down the throat, no teeth involved. I think I liked eating oysters primarily because they were salty and sophisticated, at least from the perspective of my rural upbringing. While in the Big Easy, therefore, I gorged myself on oysters. I swallowed a half dozen or even a dozen with every lunch and dinner, and on one occasion went straight from a snack of oysters to a dinner of oysters, with only the break of walking from the first café to a restaurant across the street. I made the Walrus and the Carpenter look abstemious. After my last meal of oysters, I suddenly stopped to think about when oysters on the half shell actually die. They have to be kept alive until the last minute, or else they spoil. In fact, no reputable restaurant would stick a blade into an oyster that had already died. The knife merely severs the ligaments that attach the shellfish to its shell. When does the oyster die, then? I finally realized that we eat oysters not merely raw, but alive. We don't chew oysters, so they must die in our stomach acid. New Orleans's anthropomorphized shellfish aside, I don't know that oysters are sentient like the trusting creatures in the Lewis Carroll poem. I don't think they feel betrayed to find themselves on a plate after being treated to cornmeal. On the other hand, I haven't eaten an oyster since. For me, what's most disturbing is the connection to the reputation of raw oysters as a sexy food—how much of the "sexiness" springs from the fact that we eat them alive? I had always though it was just something about the texture, but I no longer believe that. After all, the animated oyster T-shirt I mentioned earlier, as well as the other food souvenirs, is encouraging us to pretend that our food is not only alive but conscious. The marketers must think that we would like the idea of eating living, self-aware food, especially food that's just begging for it: "Eat me raw."

As you have probably noticed from my descriptions of the souvenirs, there seems to be some confusion, at least in the world of images, between a cuisine and the people associated with producing it. A Cajun dish becomes a Cajun person; a Cajun person becomes "hot" and "dirty" like a rice dish. I saw little toothpick holders shaped like Mammy figures, fat Creole chefs, and crawfish standing side by side on shelves. These were all clearly produced by the same manufacturer: they were the same size and relied on the same color scheme. The Mammy wears a red dress and white apron; the chef is decked out in a white chef's outfit and hat; the red crawfish sports both a white apron and a chef's hat. This crustacean synthesizes the two racial stereotypes into an anthropomorphized ingredient. Now it can cook itself. Most of the animated crawfish on tourist souvenirs wear this creolized outfit.

On a postcard for pralines, we can see a slightly different example of people slipping into food. The main interest of the picture, the aspect immediately apparent to a casual glance, is the group of three large Creole women wearing red dresses and white aprons and headdresses. On closer inspection of the postcard, one can see that the women are standing behind a counter, on the top of which fresh pralines are cooling. Any but the most recently arrived tourists could identify this scene from a praline shop on the tourist strip near the river, where a wall of glass lets passersby look into a room in which three similarly clad women make the store's "authentic" Creole pralines. Like the reproduction postcards, this activity is a somewhat historical reenactment, a supposedly neutral act. I was told that praline making and selling had been an industry dominated by free Creole women. In the praline shop today, a space of past freedom is acted out in a small room in which employees in costumes display their skills for tourists. This changes the meaning of the praline making, in my opinion. Maybe the store's owners are Creole—perhaps the women on display are the owners, amusing themselves by wearing Mammy costumes—but if not, it appears to be exploitation ironically disguised as a demonstration of (past) liberty. The caption on the back of the postcard reads simply: "Pralines." The little description that follows makes no reference to the pralines' makers.

There is a gap between the front and the back of the postcard, between the depiction of the pralines and the women who make them on the one side, and the disassociated Creole pralines in the description. This gap shows us how social meanings are mixed into the praline batter, how disturbingly racist images are replaced through a sleight of hand with "innocent" anthropomorphized food. In the picture, the women and the pralines are separate entities, chefs producing their specialties; in the description, the people and the pecan candy are merged to become Creole pralines. As such, they are animate subjects that we can consume without guilt. Racist imagery of black people veers toward the extremely scary or the comforting. The New Orleans tourist industry likes to emphasize the comforting imagery, of course, proffering familiar, unthreatening, servile types like Mammies and Uncle Toms. The anthropomorphized food does exactly the same thing. All the ambiguities of Creole ethnicity are simplified by the postcard, as clear as the glass through which we can see the costumed Creole women, as sweet as the pralines we can sample and take home.

Several interesting repercussions follow once people have been symbolically synthesized with food. First, ethnic food becomes a metonym for the people who originally created it, allowing the food to substitute for the people in any context. For example, many T-shirts with the caption "New Orleans Jazz" have images of saxophone-wielding crawfish or even animated hot sauce bottles that are clearly intended to represent African American musicians. Such use is common. Mexican food products and ads for Spanish-language classes often feature chili peppers wearing sombreros. I once noticed an interesting personal ad in *Potpourri*, a Palo Alto, California, free newspaper; the lovelorn author, in search of an SAF (single Asian female), headed the ad with the title, "Desperately Seeking Sushi."

The second implication is that eating ethnic food teaches us something about the culture in which it originated: Dirty rice is a Cajun woman or female impersonator, Cajun sexuality, New Orleans's nightlife and locale. Pralines are the historical truth of Creole free women, colorful costumes, and living southern tradition. Eating dirty rice is a metaphor for having a sexual encounter with a Cajun; eating a praline makes the eater part of a traditional Creole family. And the value of this cultural experience relies on the authenticity of the food. Authenticity could, in theory, refer to a dish's ingredients or the method of preparation; in practice, we usually evaluate authenticity based on whether or not people "of the community" eat it. In restaurants where the locals cook and eat, we believe that they somehow imbue the food with their ethnicity. It's their presence *in the food* that teaches us about the culture when we dine. We eat the food to ingest Creole or Cajun culture, as a substitute for Creoles or Cajuns.

This applies to ethnic food more generally. Among North Americans with aspirations to gentility, the ability to eat ethnic food signifies worldliness and cultural knowledge. And eating ethnic food *does* require ability: to interpret the menu well enough to avoid accidentally ordering tripe, pigs' feet, or some other personally tabooed food; to wield the foreign utensils correctly or eat with her hands without dropping everything into her lap or flinging food onto people at other tables; to fish out the morsel that has fallen off her skewer into the communal cooking pot; to swallow after she has suddenly, sickeningly realized that the texture in her mouth has passed acceptable limits of the unfamiliar (suspiciously chewy, slippery, gritty, or gummy); to continue eating when the chilies are too hot, or at the very least to resist gasping and gulping water. An American raised on pot roast and potatoes who can confidently pick up a piece of sushi with chopsticks and eat it before it falls apart has indeed learned something. Still, has such an eater learned as much as she thinks she has? (Incidentally, I have recently been informed by a non-Asian friend that no one in Japan would dream of eating sushi with chopsticks, so I have mastered a useless skill).

The educated, urban Americans with cultural aspirations about whom I am now generalizing cross race and gender boundaries to some extent. We share a belief that the ability to eat various ethnic food is extremely meaningful. We think such an ability says a lot about us, and we speak condescendingly about Americans who are not conversant with ethnic food. The Midwest, where I now live, is the usual target of our scorn; places that are recognized as ethnic regions themselves, such as New England or the South, are exempted and expected only to consume their own ethnic food (and nothing else, either—though we ourselves would appreciate finding a good Italian place in town when we visit). We try to force unenlightened relatives and acquaintances to try this food, and, if we succeed, we also make them submit to a lecture about the culture's food. This lecture lasts throughout the entire meal. I've seen many people at other tables enduring such lectures from their dinner companions . . . that is, I notice this when I'm not too busy lecturing my own companions, or being lectured myself.

Why in the world do we take this so seriously? I can wander quite comfortably through Chinatown in San Francisco without any knowledge of the Chinese language, without wearing a tunic and loose pants, or in any other way being informed about Chinese culture. Once I step into a Chinese restaurant, my personal standards change. I am reluctant to betray any kind of ignorance, even when this pretense is to my disadvantage. If the table is set with silverware, I request chopsticks. I shun chop suey and chow mein; similarly, I avoid places that offer a small "American" selection (usually featuring hot dogs or mashed potatoes or other embarrassing food): any Chinese restaurant more tolerant than I of unenlightened American diners must be awful. I take myself too seriously.

My desire simultaneously to convey and to receive some kind of ethnic knowledge through eating has repeatedly led me to make a fool of myself.

In an upscale Moroccan restaurant, a Moroccan friend once told me that couscous was traditionally eaten with one's fingers. I immediately set aside my spoon and demanded lessons. For the rest of the meal, while he enjoyed his chicken with lemon and olives, I tried in vain to eat the couscous in the tidy way he had demonstrated. I was undeterred by the tickle of small grains of wheat rolling down the inside of my right sleeve, frustrated but not stopped by the quantity of couscous collecting in my lap. My friend was sublimely unselfconscious during this spectacle. He waited until the end of the meal, when the waiter had removed our dishes, to say, "Of course, in Morocco no one would eat couscous with their fingers in a nice restaurant."

And, of course, no American friend would play this sort of trick on me. My American friends also have a sense of the ridiculous, but they would simply have been too embarrassed to be associated in any way with such a messy meal. They would have felt that my behavior was reflecting poorly on *their* knowledge of ethnic food. Similarly, I would not have fallen for this practical joke if I had been eating with an American friend. At worst, I would have finished the meal with a spoon while planning to make couscous at home, in order to practice eating it in privacy; later, I could take a different American friend to the restaurant and have the pleasure of demonstrating proper couscous consumption to her. In this case, however, I was in the company of a Moroccan friend, and my desire to appear sophisticated in an ethnic restaurant had temporarily been overridden by the compulsion to learn the "authentic" way to eat, from an expert (that is, anyone from that culture).

This belief among some Americans that we show our knowledge of a culture by our knowledge of its food is sincere but shaky. We have constantly to bolster our knowledge, to demonstrate it to others. When we feel driven to initiate others in the wonders of ethnic foods, and we try to educate them in proper technique, we have multiple interests. I think that our pleasure in the tasty food is an undeservedly small part of what motivates us. By teaching acquaintances the right way to eat ethnic food, we can show off our own abilities, not only to our companions but to the waiters! Furthermore, just as we accrue additional knowledge if we have the opportunity to eat ethnic with experienced diners (ideally someone from the appropriate country or region, or an American who has lived there, or an

American who has lived with someone from there), we also earn some more knowledge points when we sign up a new friend. Once in the restaurant, the novices have to learn to eat the right way as soon as possible, or their ineptitude will reflect poorly on us. We have to ensure that they order dishes we consider truly authentic, not mulligatawny stew or taco salad. You might protest that this would apply to any fancy restaurant or formal meal; concern about which fork to use is a cliché in etiquette books, after all. However, with ethnic food, anything fancier than take-out requires very much the same kind of careful anxiety as a first, formal meal with the family of one's new love.

This whole phenomenon strikes me as uniquely American. As the incident in the Moroccan restaurant illustrates, most people from other countries do not particularly seem offended by American ignorance about their food. I worked briefly for a Chinese architect in San Francisco who considered Chinese American restaurants hysterically entertaining and aspired eventually to have eaten at every single one in the Bay Area. My friends from other countries seem unconcerned about preserving cultural purity in their cooking and happily produce mashed potatoes for potlucks. They don't correct me if I eat the food in the wrong order, or use my dipping sauce as salad dressing, or otherwise demonstrate my ignorance. They only want me to try the different dishes; while they are polite about my tentative displays of food knowledge ("This is kimchee, right?"), this knowledge is not *meaningful* to them.

Such knowledge is extremely meaningful to Americans. An American woman in the rural Midwest has a special structure in her backyard in which she holds authentic Japanese tea ceremonies; she learned how to do this on the West Coast. I once met a man whose particular specialty was proper European-style dining, which he took so seriously that he would pop red wine into the microwave to get it to the correct "room" temperature. He had informed all his friends, and apparently believed himself, that his parents immigrated from Milan; instead, it turns out that his *grandparents* immigrated from the *south* of Italy. In case you are not a Europeanized sophisticate, cities in the north of Italy (like Milan) are much more prestigious homelands than those in the south—this carries a similar connotation to growing up in Manhattan versus Mississippi. The last time I saw one particular beloved aunt, who had recently become happily involved with an extremely charm-ing American-born Chinese man, she was very concerned about having rice and tea with every meal. When my mother, in a panic, realized that she had forgotten to prepare rice with dinner (eggplant parmesan, if I remem-ber correctly), he responded, "That's very bad. Chinese people die if they skip rice for one meal." Nothing he said successfully dissuaded my aunt from her attempts to protect his cultural heritage.

There are at least two sound, authoritative explanations already on the table, so to speak, for our behavior regarding food. I am about to simplify both of them drastically, but the point holds regardless. The first explana-tion springs from Pierre Bourdieu's idea of "cultural capital," the knowledge with which people from the upper classes would have been raised: middle-class people with aspirations toward grandeur get prestige by showing that they are also knowledgeable about "high" culture, such as opera, wine, painting, ballet, and Literature with a capital L. Similarly, our familiarity with food from other cultures suggests that we are well traveled and cos-mopolitan. For those of us who have acquired our cultural knowledge after childhood, it will never feel quite natural to us. Therefore, we will carefully try to guard it, double-check the pronunciation of that French sauce, read a guide to fine wines to ensure we behave appropriately when the waiter presents us with the cork. Just as we would wince if our companion at the symphony applauded loudly between movements, we would blush to dine with someone who mistook her bread for the napkin in an Ethiopian restaurant. It would have blown our cover. This explanation is quite per-suasive. It accounts for some of the inexplicable behavior from otherwise intelligent, sensible people.

The other explanation accounts for a question that "cultural capital" does not address: why ethnic food, exactly? Yes, in the past familiarity with eth-nic food would have testified to world travel; for example, in the nineteenth century, English military people who had spent time in India occasionally enjoyed serving curries back home. Now, however, no one would assume that I acquired my taste for soups with lemon grass and coconut milk while living in Thailand, as indeed I did not. To explain the ethnic component, we need to think about our white-bread, middle-American culture, which has been called "the culture of no culture." White American people often don't see our culture as a culture. It looks absolutely generic, the same ordinary, cultureless life that everyone shares with families on television sitcoms. Our corporations have done their best to infiltrate everywhere in the world with our cultureless products, so we cannot even go abroad to escape the ubiquitous McDonald's, Coca-Cola, and mugs shaped like Looney Tunes characters. Right now I am staying in the Mosel Valley, a wine-making region on the western side of Germany, and the local stores carry Gallo. Many scholars have persuasively argued that it is this disappointing situation that has made Americans passionate about trying to adopt other cultures. "All-American" seems to us like a perfect synonym for boring, generic, and bland. If we can identify any kind of ethnic heritage in our family's past, we want it back; we are as eager to recover the lost culture of our immigrant ancestors as they were to assimilate. We want to disassociate ourselves from the Rice-a-Roni and Jell-O we ate as children, we want to immerse ourselves in a world seasoned by cilantro, cardamom, and saffron.

I like both of these explanations. They were not conceived especially to explain our food habits, but they work quite nicely. Still, there's something missing. You might have noticed that in a chapter purportedly about women and food, neither interpretation I've just offered seems to have any kind of gender dynamic at all. Does it seem plausible that our strange food behavior is completely gender-neutral? Nothing else ever seems to be. Also, the animated food I discussed in the earlier part of the essay does not submit to either explanation.

The gender issues involved in the American obsession with ethnic food show nowhere more clearly than in the case of chili peppers, which have colonized American cuisine over the past decade. In lowbrow as well as highbrow settings, men intent on displaying masculinity are absolutely incorrigible around chili peppers. They have to eat hot food, and they add hot sauce if possible. They like jalapeños on pizza, deep-fried and stuffed with cheese, sprinkled in red flakes on their pasta dishes. Many women who grew up with bland middle-American diets also appreciate a good salsa, and some display a definite machismo when they do so; however, for some men hot sauce works like a red flag to their sense of masculinity. I must confess that I don't like hot food. My desire to avoid dishes with chili peppers has given me an unusual opportunity to witness the stakes involved with chili peppers. I have provoked overt hostility from men whom I scarcely know, friends' acquaintances who have occasionally joined us for dinner. I have been accused of willful cultural ignorance, of revealing myself as an ugly American. I have been questioned suspiciously about my motives, though apparently their desire to eat hot food is so instinctive and true that it needs no explanation. No kind of reasoning will assuage their anger. Several times, after we have reached an agreement about ordering one or two mild dishes, one of them jockeyed for the opportunity to order for the table and then "forgot" to ask for some of the dishes mild. I soon learned that I needed to win the competition to order; in response, they would sulk and continue to obsess about my psychological flaws throughout the meal. I could never convince them that whether or not I eat hot food is meaningless. It is definitely not meaningless, not to them. Lying is the only way of avoiding this problem. "I have spastic colitis," I now say, or "I have an ulcer." (Incidentally, this has given me new insight into the implausible food allergies that some of my women friends have.) No one is ever offended by unsavory medical problems, but I am in for an argument if I ever foolishly try to explain that I don't like to eat spicy food because it hurts my mouth. "You'll get used to it," they tell me contemptuously.

They are right. Chili peppers are hot because of the chemical capsaicin. When people eat chili peppers regularly, the capsaicin damages the nerve endings in their mouths (Barber D5). One has to learn to eat chilies, and North Americans who have developed a taste for heat over the past ten years have had to be willing to endure some burning pain. The *Economist* reports that "Paul Bosland of the Chile Pepper Institute of New Mexico reckons [that] all chileheads are high on endorphins, painkillers released by the body to block the sting of the capsaicin" ("A Taste" 54). Either biological explanation may well account for how people are able to eat hot food, but neither can explain why people would want to start eating hot food in the first place. This desire has a cultural cause, not a physiological one. Modern-day Americans dining out cannot be said to crave chilies as a way of preserving food or disguising the taste of spoiled or low-quality ingredients, prime reasons for treasuring spices in past centuries. In addition, this physiological approach does not account for why American men in particular seem to find eating chili peppers so meaningful.

Searching for the answer to the chili conundrum, we might easily find ourselves back in New Orleans. Louisiana has been hailed the world's hot sauce capital, producing at least two hundred brands of hot sauces that are available in the United States (Plotnikoff D1). The classic Tabasco sauce, made from Tabasco peppers, is probably the most famous. The strength and heat of Louisiana hot sauces make them the most powerful type of tourists' food souvenirs—people can feel that they have eaten something potent. Bottles of hot sauce are popular items in the local tourist trade, and hot sauce marketing ranges from coasters designed to look like Tabasco sauce labels to posters of dozens of different brands. Stores offer counters where careful shoppers can sample dozens of varieties and get advice on selection. In one store, I counted thirty different brands of hot pepper sauces. None of these depicted the African American figures of the earlier hot sauce ads and labels selected by the postcard manufacturers; there were, however, depictions of animated peppers. I want to focus on just a few of these labels. Four used the theme of hell as a way of illustrating their heat: Jamaica Hell Fire, Gibb's Bottled Hell, Caribbean Choice Hell Fire, and Trappey's Red Devil Louisiana Hot Sauce. Two of these are decorated with a solitary devil, while the other two depict sufferers in hell. You might suppose that the sufferers are the people who purchase the hot sauce; instead, the peppers are the ones being tormented by the flames. On one label a devil is menacing the peppers with a pitchfork.

A novice hot sauce aficionado is going to suffer when trying these concoctions. In fact, most of the people I saw sampling the sauces *wanted* to suffer and were evaluating the sauces using pain as the main criterion. The two labels featuring devils with no peppers seem to be threatening the purchaser, albeit playfully, with damnation, the Christian interpretation of a punishing, permanent loss of self. The labels with animated peppers have a very different implication. They transpose the scary menace of hell onto the peppers, and the hot sauce purchaser is no longer intimidated but invited to sample a painfully real cultural experience, without danger. Since, in fact, the chili peppers hurt their consumers, one might expect to see images of tiny tourists being tortured by the peppers. Instead, the peppers are suffering.

The tourist with the burning mouth is not suffering meaningless pain; instead, he is getting firsthand knowledge of the pain of the peppers. This pain has a cultural history, attributed symbolically to the peppers on behalf of the peoples associated with chili peppers. The tourist's throbbing lips are evidence that he is enjoying an authoritative cultural experience. Consuming hot sauce distills the value of ethnic dining to its most potent expression. It offers proof that the cultural experience we crave has really been delivered. We can physically, palpably feel ourselves ingest this foreign essence, and we therefore know that it is real. The peppers are permanently damned, and now we can empathize. We literally feel bad for them and for the people they represent. Having suffered for them through an authentic dining experience and politely contributed to the coffers of the New Orleans tourist industry, we need do no more. We can play around with feeling like someone on the bottom rung of the social ladder, but it is safe because we won't be staying. In fact, we won't ever really arrive in the first place.

Experience without danger is precisely what most of the New Orleans tourist souvenirs promise. They encourage the tourist to flirt with danger, buy a kit to make a mojo hand or a voodoo doll, watch a striptease, tour former plantations, walk through swamps, visit crumbling mausoleums and think about Ann Rice's vampire novels (she has fan clubs that meet for group tours there), and consume hot and dirty things. To be a tourist means to be a consumer who becomes infused with New Orleans culture through consuming, both by spending and by eating. There's nothing to feel guilty about here. After all, New Orleans solicits this consumption, it wants tourists to devour it—so badly that it will even cook itself for us. A friend's husband visited a different conference in New Orleans several years later. He attended a gala evening featuring an enormous buffet of local cuisine. There were holes in the serving tables through which protruded the heads of people decorated to look like food. Each head hawked its particular food, encouraging people to come eat it.

Douglas Adams describes a similar scene in *The Restaurant at the End of the Universe*:

A large dairy animal approached Zaphod Beeblebox's table . . . with large watery eyes, small horns and what might almost have been an ingratiating smile on its lips.

"Good evening," it lowed . . . "I am the main Dish of the Day. May
I interest you in parts of my body?"

. . . "I think I'll just have a green salad . . ." [Arthur] muttered.

"May I urge you to consider my liver?" asked the animal, "it must
be very rich and tender by now, I've been force-feeding myself for
months." (119–20).

It seems unlikely that the buffet's creators were trying to do a clever spin on
comic British science fiction. Something else is being targeted here: a
predatory urge. We tend to think of predation in terms of eating meat, but
in speech we mean something more precise. Someone who brings home
roadkill would be considered a scavenger, not a predator. Predators, in our
mind, are those who prey on live, active things. Sexual predators prey on
living humans; we might call someone who had sex with a corpse a pervert,
but not a predator. Let's think of it this way: if we eat things that are dead,
or immobile, we are gatherers; if we eat things that are alive and active, we
are hunters. We like to think of ourselves as hunters, and we like to think
of *hunter* as a synonym for *predator*. A cow or a couch potato can eat something that's not moving, but it takes a real man to track down anthropomorphized food. Obviously this is not true, but we often act as though we
believe it, just as we believe (even if we disapprove) that someone who has
sex with a prostitute is more daring and on the edge than someone who
has sex with a long-term companion. No matter that the prostitute would
have sex with anyone who could pay, just as vendors will sell us oysters on
the half-shell whether we are tough and dashing or feeble and cowardly.

If we again strip the implications of predatory, daring dining or sex to
material concerns, there is something to the feeling of bravado. We picture
foreign countries and backwoods regions as teeming with various diseases,
any of which we might unwittingly take home after ingesting some local
flesh. We really want to experience some kind of psychological or spiritual
aftermath to these encounters, not to suffer from base side effects such as
discharges and diarrhea. Therefore, pursuing such prey is dangerous, even
when the prey cooperates. In fact, the easier the prey, the greater the per-
ceived risk of danger. Perhaps this is why encounters with prostitutes do not
lower a man's status with his male friends or make them consider him less

virile; similarly, a man who eats hot sauce on rare beef is considered quite manly, even if he would probably blanch in horror if required to kill the cow himself. He has shown himself sufficiently tough merely by daring inflamed lips, high cholesterol, and mad cow disease. Hot sauce has replaced hunting as the venue for performing masculinity in this country; being a predator now only requires audacious eating.

If you are a woman, you are more likely to think of yourself as the "prey" than as the predator, especially if you have ever had the misfortune of living in the neighborhood where a rapist has been active or have attracted a stalker. In fact, I sometimes feel as though we are actively encouraged to be fearful. The "sexual predator" lurking to get us is always a man, but he's not always considered a monster. Some women read bodice-rippers and shiver pleasurably at the description of a sultry, sulking hero who "devours" the heroine with his eyes. This lucky lass will soon be "consumed by his passion," and by her own passion, too. Her body will be described as ripe fruit, her genitalia as honey.

Some of my work has focused on hunters living in the past two centuries. Men such as José Ortega y Gasset (author of *Meditations on Hunting* [1943]) and Paul Shepard (*The Tender Carnivore* [1973]) write about predators and prey in ways that articulate our culture's general conception of these categories. Predators (pumas and other big cats, for example) are stronger, smarter, and more powerful than their prey; they are at the top of the food chain. Prey (buffalo and deer, for example) is weaker, less intelligent, passive, and sometimes even longing for death at the hands (or paws) of the predator. Predators are in control. Predators have a healthy appetite, and prey animals satisfy this appetite with their bodies. They are biology's yin and yang.

The qualities hunters attribute to predators and prey are not remarkably insightful or on target, at least not in a zoological sense. The natural world does not fit this binarism in a meaningful way. Elephants and gorillas, for example, have many of the qualities that supposedly describe predators. Predatory fish, regularly eaten by larger predatory fish, cannot be said to occupy one side of the dichotomy. Sometimes the predator is larger and stronger than the prey, but sometimes tiny microbes fell us. Even animals that seem archetypally like predators or prey are not *saturated* in these categories, perpetually rending flesh or being rent apart: lions and gazelles alike nap in the sun, play with their infants, and fall victim to sportsmen. The vision of nature offered by the typical nature show—the runt carried off by hyenas, the aging alpha wolf attacked by younger males, the sickly wildebeest picked off by jackals— is persuasive not because it offers the only realistic picture of the natural world. It doesn't. This predatory vision of nature is persuasive because it matches our culture.

We can see a clearer example of what our culture means by *predator* when we examine a midseason pilot series from a few years ago. "We've just been bumped a step down the food chain," proclaimed the promotional advertising touting the short-lived ABC series *Prey*. The opening episode features serial murderer Jack Lynch, who has a taste for remorselessly killing men and raping women. Genetic testing soon reveals that Jack is not human; he is a member of a more evolved species—smarter, meaner, and stronger. Therefore, according to the show's inner logic, all of his activities are preordained: no two species can occupy the same biological niche, so evolution compels Lynch to kill the males of competing species. While the series title ominously implies that humans are fodder for the more evolved species, *prey* instead apparently refers to the bottom rung of the social hierarchy. Jack looks just like an ordinary American guy, and his behavior is no different from that of some criminally aggressive American white guys. Since when is rape a result of superior evolution? This inane show does spell out our culture's symbolic understanding of the connection between predator and prey, which has more to do with power relationships than eating habits. It further demonstrates the pervasive tendency to cast women always and only as prey. In fact, though this new species does include women, they rarely make an appearance, and on one occasion it confirms that even superior evolution cannot keep a woman from becoming prey: on one episode, one of the superior men has to prove his willingness to kill indiscriminately by slaying his own mother.

Our culture likes to see itself as a mirror of the natural world. This makes our economic and social system look inevitable and above criticism: we cannot change human nature. The natural world also is used to validate our gender roles. The supposed attributes of predators and prey, not coincidentally, are also the attributes that experts of the past century attributed to men and women. Masculinity goes hand in hand with control, power, intelligence, and appetite, or so they say; femininity complements passivity, weakness, a willingness to be led, and a lack of appetite so severe that well-socialized young women have starved themselves to death. Men are supposed to like red meat and need it more than women; women on dates with men stereotypically toy with green salads. This latter belief has diminished somewhat over the last half century, from the days in my mother's childhood when my grandmother, strapped for cash, would allocate the small pot roast among her sons and find other food for her daughters. Nevertheless, the prevalence of eating disorders in our country suggests that appetite is still a trait considered somewhat taboo for a woman. In contrast, she's welcome to look "good enough to eat." So associated with prey are women that Bambi could be the name of the stag protagonist of the Disney classic or a woman named by people who wanted to emphasize that she was pretty and vulnerable.

As they are in our most extreme ideals of masculine and feminine attributes, fantasies about predatory behavior are at work in anthropomorphized food imagery in New Orleans. The locals catch the catfish, crawdads, and oysters that we will eat when we visit. When they offer this food for sale, the pervasive animated food images merge the catch with the people who catch it, and we get food cooking itself and offering itself for sale. The local people are erased because the things we want from them are unspeakable; the food's seeming importance escalates excessively, but we cannot explain it because we have displaced our desire onto substitute objects.

Disney's film *The Little Mermaid* complements the peculiar racial animation of the New Orleans tourist industry. Ariel, the heroine, lives in a world of black Caribbean fish friends who warn her against aspiring to live on land: "When the boss gets hungry," they warn her ominously, "guess who's going to be on the plate?" (Ashman and Menken). In her quest for personal development, she ignores them and heads for land, accompanied by Sebastian, a small crustacean buddy. This mermaid is no predator; we never see her crunching lustily into a whole lobster as does her counterpart in *Splash*. In fact, Ariel is such a noneater that she persists in using her fork as a comb and hair ornament. Sebastian also is no predator. He barely avoids being killed by the French chef, who chases him around the kitchen with sharp implements while singing about his love of fish—his love of cutting them up and cooking them. This scene is intended to be funny, though I can imagine that it might give some children nightmares. Sebastian escapes the chef only by disguising himself as food, and he fortuitously ends up on Ariel's plate. She laughs to see him there, and he scampers to safety. By implication, though, Ariel's prince might very well be eating Sebastian's relatives. Ariel herself might have. One of the costs of moving a step up in the food chain is the willingness to eat one's former friends.

Perhaps we are not directly hurting anyone if we go to New Orleans and indulge ourselves in its high and low culture. However, if we consider ourselves feminists, we need to beware of buying into the pleasures of predatory consumption. Because predatory behavior is associated with masculine power, it might seem liberating to imagine ourselves as wolves, or sexual predators, or even as prey. These pleasurable fantasies of power may seem freeing as well as free, but they come at the cost of encouraging us to see the world in a way that perpetuates exactly the sort of inequitable power relationships that we deplore. It makes the choices involved in our social hierarchies invisible.

NOTE

[1] These caricatures may originally have fulfilled a fantasy of privilege for the white purchaser, someone who probably never had servants. As historical replicas, however, they cease to have the same connotation they had in the 1930s. I suspect that they are appealing because they represent an imaginary past when race relations were less "troublesome," that is, when blatantly racist images could be purchased without guilt.

WORKS CITED

Adams, Douglas. *The Restaurant at the End of the Universe.* New York. Pocket–Simon and Schuster, 1980.

Ashman, Howard, and Alan Menken. "Under the Sea." *The Little Mermaid.* Burbank, Calif., 1988.

Barber, Cathy. "Hot & Bothered: When That Heat Hits, Don't Reach for Water; Try Milk and Mind the Chile Doctors." *San Jose Mercury News,* 3 Mar. 1993: D1.

hooks, bell. "Eating the Other." *Black Looks: Race and Representation.* Boston. South End, 1992. 21–39.

Plotnikoff, David. "Hot Sauces: The Wickedest Products on the Market Make Tabasco Seem Wimpy." *San Jose Mercury News,* 3 March 1993: D1.

Potpourri, 10 Nov. 1993: 18.

"A Taste of Adventure." *Economist,* 19 Dec. 1998: 51–55.

CONTRIBUTORS

MEREDITH E. ABARCA is a Ph.D. candidate in comparative literature at the University of California, Davis. Her research interests include nineteenth- and twentieth-century literature of the Americas. Her special focus is on minority literature, particularly on Mexican/American (Chicana/o) literature. Her research on the language of everyday cooking practices addresses her fundamental academic quest: bridging the distance between academic and nonacademic constructions of women's knowledge, subjectivity, and assertions of agency. Her essay "The Ambiguity of Three Mexican Archetypes: *La Malinche, La Virgen de Guadalupe,* and *La Llorona,*" in *Genre, The Interpretation of Culture: Images and Ideologies,* explores such concerns.

ARLENE VOSKI AVAKIAN is associate professor of women's studies at the University of Massachusetts Amherst. She is the author of *Lion Woman's Legacy: An Armenian American Memoir* (1992), in which food is a major character. Nourished by the food images in the memoir, she edited *Through the Kitchen Window: Women Writers Explore the Intimate Meanings of Food and Cooking* (1997, 1998). She also coedited *African American Women and the Vote, 1837–1965* (1997). She is currently investigating the relationship between food and the development of ethnic and gender identity. She is also researching white supremacist activism among twentieth-century women.

LINDA MURRAY BERZOK received her master's degree in food and food management from New York University in 2000. As part of her program, she completed a project on food prehistory at the Bronze Age archaeological site Noen U-Loke in Phimai, Thailand. She is also a professional writer, has taught food writing at New York University, and is currently working on a novel with a culinary setting. She is a member of the International Association of Culinary Professionals (IACP) and is publicity chair of the Connecticut Women's Culinary Alliance (CWCA).

BENAY BLEND received her Ph.D. in American studies from the University of New Mexico, Albuquerque, in 1988. She has published articles on topics ranging from women's issues to Native American studies in a variety of books and journals, including *Louisiana Literature, Southern Quarterly, Journal of the Southwest, American Indian Quarterly,* and *Red River Valley Historical Review.* She is an instructor in the English and History departments of the Louisiana School, a state-supported residential school for gifted students.

LYNN Z. BLOOM is Board of Trustees Distinguished Professor and Aetna Chair of Writing at the University of Connecticut, Storrs. In the past decade she has been writing creative nonfiction, embodied in practice and process in her most recent book, *Composition Studies as a Creative Art: Teaching, Writing, Scholarship, Administration* (1998), and in her textbook *Fact and Artifact: Writing Nonfiction* (1994). She has been cooking for years but rejects the notion of running a catering business in her spare time for two reasons: no spare time, and, she says, "I'd have to cook what other people want instead of what strikes my fancy."

PAUL CHRISTENSEN is professor of modern literature and writing at Texas A&M University and is a member of the Texas Institute of Letters. He is a poet and essayist and the author of eleven books, among them studies of the poets Charles Olson and Clayton Eshleman, an edition of the letters of Charles Olson and Edward Dahlberg, and a memoir, *West of the American Dream: An Encounter with Texas.* In addition, he has published five collections of poems. In 1991 he received an NEA grant for poetry.

CATHIE ENGLISH is a secondary English teacher in Aurora, Nebraska, and has been a teacher consultant with the Nebraska Writing Project for the past two years. She has also served as coordinator of the Young Authors Forum, an online Internet writing workshop for rural students in Nebraska. Her writing has been published in the *Nebraska Language Arts Bulletin* and the *Nebraska English Journal,* among other journals. She has also published a report on her students' oral history work with nursing home residents in the *National Writing Project's Quarterly.* She is pursuing a Master's degree in English at the University of Nebraska–Lincoln.

DORIS FRIEDENSOHN is professor emerita of women's studies at New Jersey City University, Jersey City. Her research interests include immigration, autobiography, and eating in contemporary America. She has lectured on these issues in Israel, Ireland, Tunisia, Spain, Portugal, Turkey, Mozambique, Japan, Belgium, and numerous other countries. She has published broadly on these issues, including in *Women's Studies Quarterly, American Quarterly,* and the *Radcliffe Culinary Times.*

LISA HELDKE is associate professor of philosophy at Gustavus Adolphus College, Saint Peter, Minnesota, where she writes and teaches as a pragmatist feminist philosopher. Her primary research interests are objectivity and the philosophy of food. She is the coeditor of *Cooking, Eating, Thinking: Transformative Philosophies of Food* (1992). Currently she is working on a book about cultural food colonialism.

SHERRIE A. INNESS is associate professor of English at Miami University, Ohio. Her research interests include gender and cooking culture, girls' literature and culture, popular culture, and gender studies. She has published nine books: *Intimate Communities: Representation and Social Transformation in Women's College Fiction, 1895–1910* (1995), *The Lesbian Menace: Ideology, Identity, and the Representation of Lesbian Life* (1997), *Tough Girls: Women Warriors and Wonder Women in Popular Culture* (1999), *Nancy Drew and Company: Culture, Gender, and Girls' Series* (editor, 1997), *Breaking Boundaries: New Perspectives on Regional Writing* (coeditor, 1997), *Delinquents and Debutantes: Twentieth-Century American Girls' Cultures* (editor, 1998), *Millennium Girls: Today's Girls around the World* (editor, 1998), *Running for Their Lives: Girls, Cultural Identity, and Stories of Survival* (editor, 2000); and *Kitchen Culture: Popular Representations in America of Food, Gender, and Race* (editor, 2000).

HEATHER SCHELL received her Ph.D. from the Program in Modern Thought and Literature at Stanford University. Her dissertation is titled, "The Victorian Book-of-Man-Eaters: On the Evolution of Cannibals, Seductresses, and Tigers." Currently she is a visiting assistant professor at Miami University. Her published articles focus on the social meaning ascribed to eating and being eaten.

LEANNE TRAPEDO SIMS is a Ph.D. candidate in the Department of Performance Studies at New York University. Her interests include Jews, freakery, dance, and food—and their incongruities. She has taught writing at New York University, literature at Touro College, New York, and The College of New Rochelle, New York, and a course in the culture of the grotesque at The New School, New York. She is currently working on a travel/family memoir.

Germany, 38, 114, 212
Gibb's Bottled Hell, 214
Gift, The (Mauss), 97
Goldman, Anne, 125, 155, 157, 161
Gone With the Wind (Mitchell), 204
Good Food Book (Brody), 75
Gourmet, 95
Great Depression, 18, 86, 91
Greece, ancient, 26, 28
Griffin, Stuart, 182–83
Guanajuato, Mexico, 172

Haber, Barbara, 10, 85
"Haciendo Tamales" (Candelaria), 132, 133
Hahnsville, Louisiana, 23
Halberstam, David, 91, 93
Haley, Alex, 145
Hall, Stuart, 118, 131–32
Hardy-Fanta, Carol, 134
Harrison, Mary, 97
Hawaii, 97
Hebrew, 56–57
Heldke, Lisa, 147
Hernandez, Gabriela, 174
Higham, John, 23
Hmong cuisine, 175–76
Hogan, Linda, 150–51, 155–56
House of Houses (Mora), 149, 154–55
Hua people (New Guinea), 96–97
Hucke, Julie, ix
Hungarians, 57, 63, 66
Hungary, 51
Hunger's Table (Randall), 149

If This Is Tuesday, It Must Be Belgium, 179
I Hate to Cook Book (Bracken), 73
Imperial Eyes (Pratt), 184

India, 28, 183, 211
Indonesian food, 176, 179, 181
Instituto Dinamico, 172
International Cook Revue, 64
Invitation to Indian Cooking, An (Jaffrey), 178
Iny, Meir, 60
Iron, Angel, 155–56
Israel, 55–56, 59, 62, 65–66
Israelites, 28
Italy, 26, 210
Italian food, 95, 103–4, 208
Italian identity, 19–21, 23–24, 28, 31, 37

Jaffrey, Madhur, 178
Jalisco, Mexico, 174
Jamaica Hell Fire, 214
Jane Eyre (Brontë), 202
Japan, 93, 182–83, 194n. 5, 208, 210
Japanese Food and Cooking (Brennan), 182
Jerusalem, 50, 59, 62, 65
Jell-O, 90, 92–94, 96–97, 190, 212
Joy of Cooking, The, 73, 75, 78
Joys of Jell-O, The, 72
Judaism, 33, 50–51, 53, 55–56, 157, 161, 185

Kadi, Joanna, 178
Kalcik, Susan, 87, 94, 95
Katmandu, 167
Kerouac, Jack, 186
Kirshenblatt-Gimblett, Barbara, 50
Kirbyville, Texas, 98
"Kitchens" (Morales), 157
knowledge of culture through food, 209, 210
Korean food, 95
Kyoto, 167